Lecture Notes in Computer Science

Edited by G. Goos, J. Hartmanis and J. van Leeuwen

Advisory Board: W. Brauer   D. Gries   J. Stoer

Springer
Berlin
Heidelberg
New York
Barcelona
Budapest
Hong Kong
London
Milan
Paris
Santa Clara
Singapore
Tokyo

Heinrich Hußmann

Formal Foundations for Software Engineering Methods

Springer

Series Editors

Gerhard Goos, Karlsruhe University, Germany

Juris Hartmanis, Cornell University, NY, USA

Jan van Leeuwen, Utrecht University, The Netherlands

Author

Heinrich Hußmann
Siemens AG, Public Communication Networks, Advanced Development
Hofmannstraße 51, D-81359 Munich, Germany
E-mail: hussmannh@acm.org

Cataloging-in-Publication data applied for

Die Deutsche Bibliothek - CIP-Einheitsaufnahme

Hußmann, Heinrich:
Formal foundations for software engineering methods / Heinrich
Hußmann. - Berlin ; Heidelberg ; New York ; Barcelona ; Budapest ;
Hong Kong ; London ; Milan ; Paris ; Santa Clara ; Singapore ;
Tokyo : Springer, 1997
   (Lecture notes in computer science ; 1322)
   ISBN 3-540-63613-7

CR Subject Classification (1991): D.2

ISSN 0302-9743
ISBN 3-540-63613-7 Springer-Verlag Berlin Heidelberg New York

© Springer-Verlag Berlin Heidelberg 1997
Printed in Germany

Typesetting: Camera-ready by author
SPIN 10545751   06/3142 – 5 4 3 2 1 0   Printed on acid-free paper

Foreword

Formal methods in computer science aim at a scientific foundation on which methods and tools for practical system construction can be based. Practice requires methods for the specification of software systems, tools for checking specifications for syntactic consistency, and support for generation of code from specifications, as well as tools for proving the correctness of manually produced code with respect to the specification. Unfortunately, the practical relevance of many publications on formal methods is limited.

On the other hand, many methods and tools used in practice nowadays do not make use of the current status in computer science research. They are lacking clear concepts, not to speak of a precise definition based on formal techniques.

Therefore, there is a need for research aiming at methods that are usable in practice and theoretically founded, in order to provide a basis for powerful tools in software engineering.

In this book Hussmann builds a bridge between the "pragmatic" methods for design of information systems and the formal mathematical background, by giving a formal definition for the method SSADM within the algebraic specification language SPECTRUM. SSADM, a British standard method belonging to the so-called structured methods, serves here as an example. Although SSADM has its methodical deficiencies, the example is well chosen since it is practically relevant. Moreover, it is well suited to demonstrate the power of formal techniques since it is sufficiently complex.

The book gives a complete formal definition for SSADM. This shows that such an approach is not only a theoretical possibility but is also feasible for methods of practical relevance. This is made possible by the usage of clear structuring concepts to build up the formal definition.

The formal foundation of SSADM is more than an example. It is presented in a way that can be seen as a general pattern according to which other software engineering methods also can be defined, in particular the modern object-oriented methods.

Our wish for this book is that it encourages other scientists to apply theoretical foundations of computer science to practical problems of software development in a similarly thorough way. Thus the importance of this book goes beyond SSADM and SPECTRUM.

Munich, November 1996 Ernst Denert
Manfred Broy

Preface

Research in software engineering proceeds in two almost unrelated streams of results. The *formal* stream is an offspring of mathematical logic and relies completely on the usage of a symbolic language. The *pragmatic* stream is derived from decades of practical development of large systems and applies informal (or only weakly formal) notations, like diagrams, tables and natural language.

This book contributes to bridging the gap between the formal and the pragmatic approaches to the systematic construction and description of software. The central claim of this book is that a thorough integration of formal and pragmatic methods is possible, and also fruitful, since it leads to significant improvements for both areas.

Formal and pragmatic methods are to some extent complementary, so it is possible to compensate the deficiencies of one approach with the other. This is particularly valid for the early phases of software development where requirements are developed and specified. Therefore, this book concentrates on the area of requirements engineering. Moreover, the focus is on methods for the development of business information systems. As a representative for a practically relevant method for the definition of requirements for information systems, the British standard method SSADM is chosen. A formal semantics for the key concepts of SSADM is given, using the formal specification language SPECTRUM.

This work presents results of three different kinds. First, the principal feasibility of an integration between formal and pragmatic methods is demonstrated. Second, the formalisation is used as a thorough semantic analysis of the concepts in SSADM. Third, a way is shown to obtain a hybrid formal-pragmatic specification using a mixture of SSADM notations and formal (SPECTRUM) specifications.

This book is based on a Habilitation Thesis which was accepted by the Technical University of Munich in spring of 1995. I would like to thank Professor Manfred Broy for his intensive support and encouragement for this work. I am grateful for the opportunities to exchange opinions with people of different background, including experienced practicians like Professor Ernst Denert as well as many highly motivated students. I gratefully acknowledge the excellent atmosphere among my collegues at the Technische Universität München. In particular I would like to thank Bernhard Rumpe and Cornel Klein for reading draft versions of this thesis, and Herbert Ehler, Rudolf Hettler and Friederike Nickl for important suggestions.

Last but not least I would like to thank my wife Gabi, with excuses for having spoiled so many weekends and evenings with work.

Tutzing, January 1997 — Heinrich Hussmann

Notice

This work is based on the software development method SSADM, version 4. The rights for SSADM are held by the British CCTA. This work does not claim to be compliant with the original SSADM method, and any statements made about SSADM are the personal opinion of the author.

This work has been partially supported by the Bayerische Forschungsstiftung through a cooperation of the Technische Universität München with FAST e.V. (Forschungsinstitut für angewandte Software-Technologie).

Table of Contents

Chapter 1
Introduction

Twenty-five years ago, the term *Software Engineering* was coined, which means research into the systematic construction of well-structured and problem-adequate software. In the meantime, Software Engineering has achieved significant progress. However, the new insights are distributed over various specialized and only loosely coupled sub-areas, containing such heterogeneous topics as systems analysis, programming languages and concepts, program verification, or testing theory. This monograph does not provide new results for any specific sub-area of Software Engineering. Instead, it tries to establish a close link between two fields of Software Engineering, which are so loosely coupled that we prefer here to call them different worlds.

The distinct worlds under consideration here are the world of mathematically well-founded program specification and development, and the pragmatic world of requirements definition for large business application systems. Both worlds use their own terms and have their own tradition. Most people belonging to one of these worlds view the other world with some reservation.

This introductory chapter explains in more detail the characteristics of these two worlds and focuses on the term of formality, which is central for the distinction between both worlds. Afterwards, the scope and the aim of this book are stated precisely, and a short overview of the technical contents of the following chapters is given.

1.1 Two Worlds of Software Engineering

This monograph tries to build a bridge between two different worlds which contribute to the science of Software Engineering. We will call these almost separate worlds the *formal* and the *pragmatic* world. In this introductory chapter, we give only a sketchy characterization of these worlds, more elaborate definitions are found in the second chapter.

1.1.1 The Formal World

The formal world of software engineering is closely connected to mathematics, in particular to mathematical logic and algebra. It tries to build up a mathematical theory and a calculus to deal with programs and requirements specifications in the style of a mathematical derivation. Several famous textbooks have prepared the ground for formal software development, among them [BW82], [Dij76], [Gri81], [Jon86].

In the formal world, any document has to obey a precisely defined syntax, and also the semantics of documents is defined with mathematical precision. This is possible if the syntax has a semantics in terms of another mathematical formalism, or if a calculus of deduction rules has been defined for the language under consideration, or both.

Programming languages fit well into the formal world since they have completely formal syntax and semantics in order to be executed on a computer. For the early phases of a software project, however, the intended behaviour of a program has to be specified in an abstract way, using some kind of specification language. Various formal specification languages have been developed, which can be used successfully for non-trivial pieces of software, like Z [Spi92] and LARCH [GH93]. These formal specification languages force the specifier to express him- or herself in terms of mathematical logic.

This point causes one of the main problems for a practical application of the purely formal approach. During the first steps towards a new or improved system, the specification of the intended system is developed gradually. In early stages, many terms are used which come from the application area and carry with themselves a large amount of implicit interpretation. It is impossible to encode all these details formally, so the formal specification will start already at an abstraction from the application domain. And since most specialists in the application domain (and even most software engineers) are unable to understand the formal specification, it is difficult to check whether the formal abstraction is adequate for the real requirements appearing in the application domain. So there is a severe danger to start at a wrong specification. On the other hand, once a formal specification is given, the formal world provides techniques which ensure that a resulting program precisely meets its specification.

Research in the formal world has proceeded up to the point where industrial application is envisaged, primarily for safety-critical systems. Computer-support is available in form of powerful theorem provers. However, due to the inherent problem with the adequacy of specifications, practical application concentrates on complex algorithms for well-defined problems, mainly from the area of systems programming. Only few experimental steps have been made towards programming of large application systems.

1.1.2 The Pragmatic World

The pragmatic world of software engineering did not arise from mathematics, but from experiences with the design of large application systems, in particular information systems and process control systems. It is much influenced by economical and managerial considerations. For this reason, this branch of software engineering has put serious effort into the engineering of the requirements for an intended system.

The pragmatic software engineering methods emphasize the rather early involvement of users of the intended system. In this world, precise syntax rules are less important than a notation which easily allows the analyst to capture any information about the requirements for the intended system.

In order to support this process of capturing information from the application domain, a number of graphical notations have been developed which are said to be understandable even for non-specialists in programming. Famous examples for such notations are data flow diagrams [DeM79], Entity-Relationship diagrams [Che76] or several variants of state transition diagrams [Har87, SM92]. These diagrams cannot be called formal, since they rely in some aspects on an appropriate interpretation of identifiers and textual phrases taken from the problem domain. However, these notations again can be distinguished into less formal and more formal variants. For instance, Entity-Relationship diagrams or State Charts [Har87] can be seen as relatively rigid concepts.

It has turned out that none of the graphical notations did suffice for a specification of all aspects of an intended system (which are usually classified in static, dynamic and functional aspects). Therefore, combined methods have been developed, which employ various graphical notations. The current state of the art has led to complex methods which comprise graphical and textual notations as well as recommendations how to develop systematically a sensible set of documents formulated in these notations. The British quasi-standard method SSADM (Structured Systems Analysis and Desgin Method, [DCC92]), which will be studied in detail below, is a typical example for a method combined from various techniques. Also most of the recently introduced object-oriented analysis and design methods (like Object-Oriented Analysis and Design [CY91], or the Object Modeling Method OMT [RBP91]) are built in this way, and combine various traditional notations.

1.1.3 Theory vs. Practice?

At a first glance, the distinction between the two worlds seems to be a new instance of the old controversy between theorists and practicians. One could be tempted to visualize the situation as shown in figure 1.1. Here a continuum between theoretical and practical approaches is depicted, which is meant as a universe containing both worlds. The theoretical as well as the practical approaches occupy some range of the continuum, but leave an open gap between them.

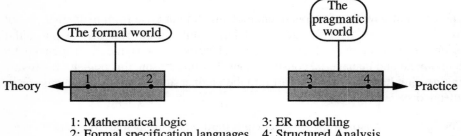

1: Mathematical logic   3: ER modelling
2: Formal specification languages 4: Structured Analysis

Fig. 1.1

However, at a closer look, it turns out that the situation is more difficult.

For a software specification and development method, its degree of formality and its degree of adaptation to practical needs are mostly independent properties. The pragmatic world contains methods which differ in their formality; and similarly the formal world contains methods which differ in their adaptation to practical applications. For instance, the most frequently used pragmatic notation (Entity-Relationship modelling) is one which is relatively close to the formal world. A recent study of 29 typical commercial software development projects in Germany [BHS92] has shown that only Entity-Relationship (ER) diagrams were used frequently (in 24 projects). All other methods or even notations were used only to a small extent. For instance, the oldest and most widely known method of Structured Analysis was used only in 9 out of these 29 projects. One of the reasons for this seems to be that ER modelling is well supported by tools (in particular by code generators), and therefore gives a clear contribution to the final product.

So the question of adaptation to practical needs is obviously independent of the degree of formality. On the "theory" side as well, figure 1.1 gives a wrong picture. It is not true that formal specification languages like Z are less formal than "pure" mathematical logic. They keep the degree of formality, but constitute a progress towards practical applicability.

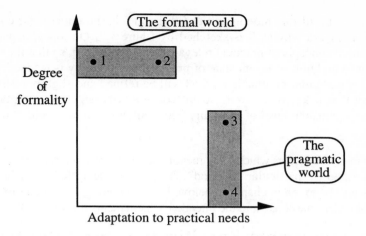

1: Mathematical logic   3: ER modelling
2: Formal specification languages   4: Structured Analysis

Fig. 1.2

Figure 1.2 shows the two properties as orthogonal dimensions of a universe and tries to locate the two worlds within it. The formal world and the pragmatic world show up here as one-dimensional parts of the scheme. The gap between both worlds is wide open also in this visualization: The formal world has not yet reached the degree of adaption to practical applications which is held by the pragmatic approaches. Similarly, the pragmatic world has not yet reached the degree of formality which is substantial for a method to belong to the formal world. The observations reported in [BHS92] and other studies support the claim that a notation usable in practice is likely to be found in the upper right corner of the diagram.

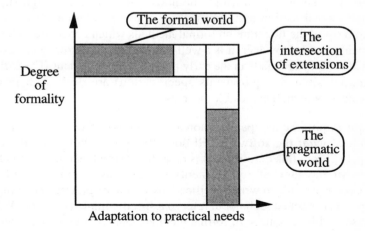

Fig. 1.3

It is the basic aim of this monograph to fill the gap in the upper right corner of figure 1.2 in such a way as it is sketched by figure 1.3. On top of a particular formal method, concepts of practical relevance will be defined, so that the level of formality is kept, but the current state of practical applicability is reached. On the other hand, a particular pragmatic method will be refined and slightly reshaped in such a way that it keeps its fundamental concepts (its degree of adaptation to practice), but gains the level of formality which allows it to meet with the formal world.

Obviously many key terms which were mentioned in the introduction above are not yet well defined (in particular "method", "technique", and "formality"). etailed definitions will be given in chapter 2 below. Before entering a detailed discussion, we will make clear the scope and the intended achievements for this work.

1.2 Requirements Specification for Information Systems

The whole field of software development is far too complex to be covered by a single book like this. Therefore, we restrict the scope of this work in two ways. We intend to treat only rather early phases of software development, and we cover merely a special but important kind of application systems.

1.2.1 Requirements Analysis and Specification

Several stages of software development can be distinguished. Without entering the discussion of various models of the development process, we can state that basically any piece of software goes through the stages of problem analysis, requirements specification, system design and system implementation. In this book, we will show that formal methods can contribute significantly to requirements specification and, indirectly, even to problem analysis. This is in contrast to most of the literature on formal methods which concentrates on the later development phases. However, it is a well-known fact that errors and mistakes are more constly if they are made in the early phases of development. The early phases (problem analysis and requirements specification) are dealt with in detail in pragmatic development methods for this reason.

A software requirements specification is "a document containing a complete description of *what* the software will do without describing *how* it will do it." [Dav90, p.17] From this definition, it is clear that formal techniques can basically contribute to the task of requirements engineering. Using a mathematical foundation, it is possible to write specifications which are precise and complete, but which remain abstract enough not to refer to a specific implementation. We will try to make use of this advantage of formal methods, but without losing contact to the body of practical experience which is available in form of pragmatic development methods.

Therefore, our plan is to choose a typical and widely used software development method and to analyse the concepts it provides for developing a requirements specification with the help of a formal method.

1.2.2 Information Systems

There are various kinds of software systems, which can be distinguished by their application areas. As a consequence of this specialization, also the internal structure and the development process for these kinds of software differs significantly. A simple classification of software systems is given in [Pre87]:

- System software

- Real-time software

- Business software

- Engineering and scientific software

- Embedded software

- Personal computer software

- Artificial intelligence software.

From the point of view of requirements engineering, among these categories the business software and the embedded software (which in most cases is also real-time software) are of particular interest. These two categories differ from the others in the aspect that the software products are developed in close cooperation with a single customer organisation, whose requirements are unknown to the development team and to some extent even unclear in general. This situation is particularly critical, since it leads to the problem of proper communication between the development team and application specialists. Pragmatic requirements engineering mostly tries to solve this communication problem. Following this argument, it is logical to concentrate on either business software or embedded/real-time software or both.

For the purposes of this book, the scope is restricted to business software, just for the reason to avoid some of the specific difficulties which are present in the design of embedded/real-time systems. This decision does not at all mean that the general approach described in this book cannot be applied to embedded/real-time systems.

Basically, the same ideas can be applied also to a pragmatic method which deals with the particularities of real-time systems, like SA/RT [HP87].

The class of software which is studied here also carries the name *(business) information systems*, since their central component is a large database, and their main purpose is to store and retrieve information.

1.3 Synergy between the Pragmatic and the Formal World

As it was already indicated in figure 1.3 above, the central aim of this thesis is to bridge the gap between the pragmatic and the formal world of requirements engineering, under the restriction to information systems. For this purpose, we will express the concepts of an existing pragmatic method (SSADM) within an existing formal method (SPECTRUM). A detailed introduction into these two representatives of the two worlds follows in chapters 3 and 4 below.

The motivation for this experiment is to combine the strengths of formal and pragmatic approaches and to avoid the weaknesses of both worlds. This introduction sketches the reasons why the two worlds can in fact be seen as complementary; the mutual compensation will be analysed in more detail in chapter 5 below.

1.3.1 Compensating the Deficiencies of the Pragmatic World

The pragmatic approaches provide concepts which have turned out to be useful for the practical development of software systems. A realistic method of this kind, like SSADM, provides an overwhelming amount of different notations.

Lack of Semantic System Model

What is clearly missing in most pragmatic methods, is an *integrating semantic system model* which defines the meaning of the various terms and notations, and which also helps to understand the relationships between the different notations. Due to the lack of such a semantic basis, it is quite difficult to find out precisely in which way some piece of specification entails a constraint for the system finally developed. It has been claimed that the advent of the so-called CASE tools will improve this situation, but also the tool support for most of the terms rarely exceeds editing, syntax check and storage facilities. In particular, the interconnections between documents in different notations are not well supported. Usually, a so-called "meta-model" is used as a common representation for all documents in a project, which gives only a semantic integration without any semantic foundation. We claim here that a thorough tool support is prohibited by the semantic weaknesses of pragmatic methods. Within this thesis, a detailed semantic model will be provided for a variant of the SSADM method.

Lack of Precision in Natural Language

At many places, the pragmatic approaches rely on textual explanations, which are added to more formal notations. A typical example is the so-called mini-specification which is added to the bottom-most processes in a data flow diagram in Structured Analysis. Unfortunately, such textual explanations are not organized as a complete and readable document in natural language, where they might be a serious help to developers and customers. Instead, they are pure attachments to a document or diagram which is otherwise written in an artifical language (for instance as a data flow diagram). This mixture of natural and artificial syntax again prohibits thorough tool support.

Compensation by Formal Foundation

The two problems which were mentioned above, and a number of others, have in common the problem of *missing semantic precision* for the pragmatic world. Fortunately, semantic precision is one of the strengths of the formal world. Moreover, formal notations are so general that they can be used as a common underlying basis for all notations occurring in a method. So the first aim is here to use formal notation to provide a precise semantic basis for pragmatic concepts. On such a basis, it is also possible to replace unprecise textual explanations by formal text, where this is adequate.

1.3.2 Compensating the Deficiencies of the Formal World

Formal specifications are semantically precise, but there are many obstacles for using them naïvely in the specification of an information system. Anthony Hall [Hal90] lists a number of objections against formal methods and calls them "myths". We agree basically with this position, but we think that for practical use in specification of information systems, a number of concepts should be built on top of formal notations.

Restricted Readership

A formal specification is only comprehensible for people with some background knowledge of mathematical logic. Therefore it is not understandable by experts in the application domain, and so it cannot fulfil its role as a "contract" between the customer and the developer.

The Scaling-Up Problem

The cumulative effect of many formal statements (axioms, definitions) is quite difficult to judge even by an expert. So, a formal specification of a really large system can be very difficult to handle even for specialists.

Compensation by Addition of Pragmatic Concepts

These two problems can be solved by introducing an additional *language layer* on top of the pure formal notation. Such an extension may give any concept from any pragmatic method into the hands of the specifier, as soon as this concept has been expressed formally in terms of the semantic system model. This way, the same level of customer and user involvement can be reached as in pragmatic methods. Moreover, a large specification becomes more manageable, since the additonal language layer encodes once and for all a number of technical concepts, which means that a significant part of the specification is no longer application-specific but generic. The specification of a particular application uses formal notation only at those places where it deviates from or adds onto the standard concepts of the method.

1.3.3 The Whole is More Than its Parts: Synergy

Besides the mutual compensation of weaknesses, an approach integrating formal and pragmatic notations may enable possibilities which are beyond the reach of any of the single approaches.

In particular, the whole theory of module refinement becomes available for such an integrated method. Making use of the precise semantics, techniques can be used to establish a detailed relation between the specification of a system and its design, which exceeds the possibilities available in formal methods nowadays.

Moreover, program (and module) verification can be readily used for development in the integrated approach, which can be necessary in the development of safety-critical systems.

1.3.4 SSADM and SPECTRUM - and Beyond

In this book, the integration will be carried out for two particular representatives of the formal and the pragmatic world, SPECTRUM and SSADM. In chapter 3 more detailed reasons for this choice can be found. However, this is just a choice of examples. Basically, the same approach will work with many other formal frameworks; and any other pragmatic method can be treated in a similar fashion, as soon as there is enough information available on its semantics.

It is worth an explicit remark that the general approach is not restricted to the classical, so-called *structured* pragmatic methods. The same idea can be applied to the various *object-oriented* approaches. We have refrained here from using one of these more recent methods only because they still seem to be evolving rapidly.

A particularly interesting situation arises if two or more pragmatic methods can be successfully integrated with a formal method by using *a common semantic model*. In this case, a thorough semantic integration arises between the pragmatic methods involved. In this respect, the integration approach may help in building well-defined links between conceptually different methods. However, these ideas are beyond the scope of this thesis and will only be sketched in the final chapter 12.

1.4 Overview

The following chapter 2 clarifies some of the key terms used in this work, like "method" or "formality". In chapter 3 and 4, both the pragmatic method SSADM and the formal framework SPECTRUM are introduced. In order to provide a sound basis for further examples, a small but complete toy project is provided in SSADM notations. On this more concrete basis, also the strengths and weaknesses of both worlds are analysed in more detail in chapter 5, which continues by a discussion of alternative ways to achieve integration. Chapter 6 contains the basic concepts of a common semantic basis for the different notations of SSADM. Based on these concepts, chapters 7 and 8 provide detailed information on the formal modelling of some of the central notations of SSADM. Chapter 7 covers the static aspects of an information system (Logical Data Modelling), chapter 8 the description of system dynamics (Entity-Event Modelling). Based on the material from chapters 6 through 8, chapter 9 demonstrates how the formal foundations can be used to study the important question of consistency for a pragmatic specification. Chapters 10 and 11 complete the picture by investigating the borderline between the formally founded SSADM and both more formal and more informal notations. In chapter 10, a step towards a hybrid formal-pragmatic method is made by employing formal notation as a substitute to textual explanations in SSADM. Chapter 11 deals with the technique Data Flow Modelling in SSADM as an example for a relatively informal notation and studies its integration into the common semantic framework. Finally, chapter 12 gives a summary of the achievements and a short outlook how the integration approach can be used for the analysis of other methods than SSADM.

This work may appeal to readers with very different interests and also different background. In particular, practicians of Software Engineering might be interested in the feasability of such an approach, but not in technical details of the formalization. Therefore, the thesis has been laid out in such a way that about half of the material (chapter 1 to 5) does not require a deep understanding of formal techniques. The chapters 6 through 9 present the main technical body of the integration between SSADM and SPECTRUM. Therefore, parts of these chapters are quite formal and relatively difficult to read. However, this level of detail is necessary to give a complete and self-containing semantics to the core concepts of SSADM. Chapters 10 and 11 are again less technical, they concentrate on the main ideas rather than on technical detail.

All important definitions of terms, both from SSADM and SPECTRUM, are put together in a glossary (appendix A). Further appendices contain the main parts of an SSADM specification for a small toy project (appendix B), its axiomatic counterpart (appendix C), and a library of basic specifications (appendix D).

Chapter 2
Terminology

In a study of pragmatic and formal software development methods, there should be no ambiguity about such central terms like "development method" or "formality". Therefore, this chapter tries to clarify some basic terms before entering the main theme of this thesis.

2.1 Development Methods

Our definition of the term of a "method"[1] is based on a definition given by D. Bjørner and L. Druffel: "A method is a set of procedures, to be used by humans, for selecting and applying a number of techniques and tools in order, efficiently, to achieve the construction of efficient artifacts - here software." [BD90] From this definition we take the main components of a method: procedures, techniques, artifacts. But we extend the definition by stating explicitly that using a method always leads to other artifacts besides software, like specifications and documentation. Moreover, we state clearly that the method provides syntactical rules for these artifacts.

> *Definition: Method.* A (software development) *method* is a notational and procedural framework to be used by humans for producing computer software and related products. It consists of three parts:

---

[1] Some authors use the word "methodology" synonymously with our use of "method".

- A set of *notations*, which define the syntax of *artifacts*, which are to be produced when carrying out the method. Such notations may be text documents or program code, but also diagrams, tables, or forms.
- A set of *techniques*, which encapsulate a number of notations together with basic *technical steps* of analysis and transformation for artifacts which are written in these notations.
- A set of *procedural guidelines* which define an order for systematic applycation of the technical steps.

Shortly, a method defines *what* is to be produced (the notations), *how* it can be produced (the techniques), and *when* it is to be produced (the procedural guidelines).

The definition has been coined in so general a manner that it covers methods from the formal as well as from the pragmatic world.

> *Example.* In the formal method Z, a piece of notation is the so-called *schema*, a typical technique is *data refinement*, using technical steps like *definition of abstraction function*, and the procedural guidelines are high-level explanations in the textbooks about how to proceed. Interestingly, the literature on Z relies here on examples, mostly.
> In the pragmatic method SSADM, a piece of notation is a *data flow diagram*, a typical technique is *data flow modelling*, comprising the notation as well as technical steps like the so-called *logicalization* of a data flow diagram. The procedural guidelines are the "stages", "steps" and "tasks" contained in the SSADM handbooks, which prescribe among many other things that at a particular point during a requirements analysis, a current physical data flow diagram must be logicalized into a current logical data flow diagram.

It is typical for formal methods that they use quite elaborate notations and techniques, but do provide only sketchy, example-guided material on procedural guidelines. Pragmatic methods, in contrast, have less rigid notations and techniques, but detailed procedural guidelines. This is partly due to the fact that formal methods are more general and can be applied to any kind of software, while pragmatic methods are more specialized. More important seems to be the heavy influence of managerial considerations on pragmatic methods. They often express a dream of a complete control over the development process which is criticized also by practicians, for instance in an ironical remark by DeMarco and Lister: "The people who write the Methodology are smart. The people who carry it out can be dumb." [DL87, p. 114] It is obvious that software development is a creative process and therefore will not always follow detailed procedural guidelines. This is one of the reasons why in this work the integration of formal and pragmatic techniques will take place mainly on the level of notations and techniques, and less on the procedural level.

2.2 Formality

Most authors define a method to be formal if its notations and techniques have a mathematical semantics (eg. [BD90], [Win90]). However, it is a matter of fact that mathematicians often lead their deductions in a quite informal way, which was demonstrated convincingly for instance by Peter Naur in [Nau82]. So it seems insufficient or even contradictory to identify formalism simply with a mathematical style of proceeding. Instead, the term of formality has its roots in the history of mathematical logic, which is part of the history of philosophy.

Formality was invented as a means to avoid the ambiguity and impreciseness of natural language. In the 17th century, G. W. Leibniz formulated[2] the dream of a language which allows two disagreeing philosophers to settle their dispute by sitting down and just *calculating* the right propositions, like mathematical numbers. In the 20th century, this dream was brought to reality, as far as possible, by Frege, Russell, Gödel and other mathematicians. One of the basic ideas here was a clear distinction between a *symbol* and its *meaning*. Symbols (including words of a natural language) are pictures of the reality, not the reality itself. The way how a symbol depicts the reality is called its *interpretation*. It is impossible to ensure that two people have exactly the same interpretation of symbols. Therefore a realization of Leibniz's dream cannot rely on the meaning of a symbol, but only on its *form*, on its mere syntactical appearance. The term of formality refers to "form" in this philosophical sense.[3]

It is no wonder that the question of formality arises in software requirements analysis, since the purpose of a requirements specification is to produce a document which depicts the reality in a manner such that the interpretation of the document is not subject to disputes. Formal method try to attack this problem by prescribing precise notations, and then defining techniques which rely only on the syntactical form of the artifacts. So it is a good test for the formality of a method, whether it provides techniques which work sensibly *even if all identifiers used in the artifacts are renamed to new, "meaningless" symbols.*

This notion of formality clearly captures methods like axiomatic specifications. The semantics of an axiomatic specification of natural numbers, for instance, and all the further statements derived about it, are true also if the natural numbers happen to be called "Xyz" instead of "Nat".

---

[2] In his work *Logica Mathematica sive Mathesis universalis sive Logistica sive Logica Mathematicorum.*

[3] "Was das Bild mit der Wirklichkeit gemein haben muß, um sie auf seine Art und Weise – richtig oder falsch – abbilden zu können, ist seine Form der Abbildung." L. Wittgenstein, Tractatus logico-philosophicus, 2.17.

Pragmatic Software Engineering methods cannot be simply called informal. In fact, there are some techniques present in such methods which are quite formal, and some which are completely informal. For instance, the entity-relationship approach to data modelling provides precise rules how a conceptual data model (an ER diagram plus entity descriptions) can be transformed into a relational data base scheme, and these rules are completely independent of the names of the entities or attributes. However, the technique of transforming a data model into Boyce-Codd normal form relies on intuitive knowledge about the meaning of names for attributes. (Here questions must be answered like "Does the customer's name depend on the customer number?")

So formality is not an absolute judgement for a method, but there are *degrees of formality*, as it was already indicated in figures 1.2 and 1.3 in the introduction.

> *Definition: Formality.* A technique of a method is called *formal*, if it relies only on the syntactical form of the used artifacts, and not on the particular choice of identifiers. A method is called formal, if all its techniques are formal. The degree of formality for two methods can be compared by measuring the relative part of formal techniques. A method which contains formal as well as informal techniques is called *semi-formal*.

Following this definition, classical methods of Software Engineering like SSADM are classifed as semi-formal.

Formality of a method is just one criterion among others, it is not a good thing *per se*. Formal techniques are mechanical and therefore offer a natural basis for computer-support by mechanical manipulation of documents. However, being independent of any particular interpretation of identifiers, formality cannot provide help in finding the right form. The process of *formalization*, of depicting the reality in symbols of a formal system, remains an intuitive activity, as it is stated by Naur: "If the informal basis is not clear and consistent then there is no hope for the relevance or usefulness of the description, irrespective of whether it makes use exclusively of an informal mode or also makes use of formalizations." [Nau82, p. 448]

In this work, we trust to some degree in the intuitive experience which has crystallized into pragmatic methods like SSADM, for providing an adequate informal basis to formal methods. On the other hand, we believe that formalization is inevitable in software development, since the behaviour of computers depends on programs, which are clearly formal: "Programs, however, are formal objects, susceptible to formal manipulation (for example compilation and execution). Thus, programmers cannot escape from formal methods. The question is whether they work with informal requirements and formal programs, or whether they use additional formalism to assist them during requirements specification." [Win90, p. 10]

2.3 Pragmatism

The term of pragmatism comes from philosophy, too. Its dictionary definition[4] is the "view that the truth of any assertion is to be evaluated from its consequences and its bearing on human interests". The pragmatic approach is not opposed to theory in general, but it insists on evaluating any insight, including theoretical insights, from its practical consequences. Therefore, a method can be more or less pragmatic, independent of its degree of formality. For instance, the specification method of Z is clearly much more pragmatic than the mathematical set theory it relies on. This is due to the fact that Z has been explicitly designed towards the needs of practical software development, building on top of experience with many examples.

> **Definition: Pragmatism.** A method is called *pragmatic*, if its notations, techniques and procedural guidelines are derived from significant practical experience and if its usefulness in practical applications has been proven. Methods can be compared in their degree of pragmatism by comparing the body of practical applications for which they are evidently useful.

This work aims at a formal and pragmatic development method. Since pragmatism cannot be achieved by theoretical research but by practical experience, it relies on the body of practical experience lying behind a standardized, frequently used development method and incorporates formality. However, the pragmatism of the whole integrated approach will remain a question to be answered by further practical experience.

---

[4]   The New Shorter Oxford English Dictionary (1993)

Chapter 3
SSADM –
A Pragmatic Requirements
Engineering Method

For the investigation reported here, the Requirements Engineering parts of the British method SSADM have been chosen as a representative for the pragmatic world. In this chapter, the decision in favour of SSADM is briefly motivated, and a short introduction into SSADM is given. This introduction is superficial in the sense that we concentrate on the basic concepts more than on technical details.

3.1 Motivation for the Choice of SSADM

The criteria which have led to the selection of SSADM among the abundance of pragmatic Requirements Engineering methods were the following.

- The method should represent the state of the art in Requirements Engineering to a reasonable degree.

- The method should be applicable or even specialized to the area of business information systems.

- The method should be highly pragmatic, it should be frequently used in practice.

- The method should be well stabilized and documented in textbooks.

- The method should cover as many aspects of an information system as possible with a reasonable degree of integration among different views of a system.

Using this list of criteria as a guidance, a survey of pragmatic methods was carried out by the author before starting this research effort. For the purposes of this text, just a brief review of the most relevant approaches is given here. For a comprehensive survey of pragmatic Requirements Engineering methods, the reader is referred to [Dav90] and [Par91].

Data-Transformation Approaches: Probably the most famous notation in requirements definition are data flow diagrams, as they were introduced by DeMarco [DeM79]. Data flow diagrams (DFDs) can be used to depict graphically the main activities in an organization or computer system together with the way they cooperate to transform input data into output data. Around this simple but powerful notation a rather sophisticated method has been developed [MP84, War86, Woo88] which is commonly called "Structured Analysis" (SA). The current state of art of which is summarized in the textbook "Modern Structured Analysis" [You89]. Structured Analysis has been heavily criticized for this structural fracture between requirements specification and design, even by some of its main proponents [CY91].

Data-Modelling Approaches: Another very popular diagram notation has been developed independently of requirements engineering. The Entity-Relationship (ER) diagrams [Che76] were intended for the design of database schemes, but they turned out as quite valuable for showing the static structure of information in an organisation or computer system. Advanced variants of Structured Analysis [MP84] have tried to incorporate ER diagrams.

Process-Oriented Approaches: An organisation or a system can also be understood as a collection of communicating processes. Michael Jackson has pioneered this area rather early with his Jackson System Development (JSD) [Jac82, Sut88], which has become very popular in the United Kingdom.

State-Transition Approaches: There are a number of refinements for the classical concept of a finite state machine, which are suitable for system specification. A very popular notation with good tool support is the State Chart formalism by David Harel [Har87].

Object-Oriented Approaches: Oriented towards concepts from object-oriented programming, the so-called Object-oriented Analysis groups the functionality of the system around the basic classes of data objects (which are very similar to the entities of the ER approach) and uses a message-passing mechanism for describing the communication between objects. Popular variants of object-oriented analysis have been defined by Coad & Yourdon [CY91] and by Shlaer

& Mellor [SM88]. OMT by Rumbaugh et al. [RBP+91] is more a composition of several approaches than a pure object-oriented method.

Compound Methods: Since none of the approaches from above is sufficient to express all aspects of an information system, new methods have been created by combining several notations have been combined into a single method. Typical examples for such compound methods are:

- OMT [RBP91], which combines an object-oriented variant of ER diagrams, State Charts and Data Flow Diagrams. These three notations are to be understood as three different views or facets of a single system.

- SSADM (see section 3.2 below), which integrates Modern Structured Analysis, ER-based data modelling and some parts of JSD together into a complex methodical framework.

A severe problem of the compound methods is to ensure the consistency between documents taken from different traditions. In this respect, OMT still leaves open many questions. SSADM seems to be more advanced in this respect.

This brief overview of existing pragmatic approaches shows clearly that the most interesting challenge is in addressing one of the complex compound methods. Such a method also comprises most of the concepts used in the individual different approaches. So the main choice was between a more traditional "structured" compound method (like SSADM) and a more modern object-oriented compound method (like OMT). For the purposes of the research effort described in this book, SSADM was chosen because of its more stable state, its more detailed procedural guidelines and its more advanced integration of notations.

However, it is obvious that future research in formal foundations for pragmatic methods has to include object-oriented methods, maybe in a more mature version like the Unified Method and the Unified Modeling Language (UML) [BRJ96]. However, it is the opinion of the author that many of the insights which are documented in this book can be transferred also to such a new approach to system modelling.

3.2 Modelling Techniques and Methodical Support in SSADM

"Structured Systems Analysis and Design Method (SSADM) is the UK government's standard method for carrying out the systems analysis and design stages of an information technology (IT) development project." [DCC92, Preface].

SSADM is a standard method, the responsibility for which is held by the Central Computing and Telecommunications Agency (CCTA), a governmental organisation of the United Kingdom. SSADM has a long development history, closely connected to the development of the LBMS (Learmonth and Burchett Management Systems) method. SSADM was launched in 1981, it is mandatory for UK governmental projects since 1983. Version 4 of SSADM on which this book is based has been released in 1990. All the details of SSADM are open to the public, it is freely available to the industrial and academic community. SSADM also plays an important role in the efforts to harmonize the standards for information system development in Europe (EUROMETHOD).

SSADM is well integrated into a framework of management and organisational guidelines, for instance the management method PRINCE and the risk assessment method CRAMM. For the purposes of this work, we concentrate on the pure information technology aspect. The reference on SSADM, version 4, is [CCT90]. A good introductory textbook is [AG90] which still presents version 3; more recent introductions are [DCC92] and [AS93]. The book [Eva92] covers the method in the style of a shortened manual. A comparison of SSADM with another industrial European method (GRAPES) is given in [DH92].

As it was already indicated above, SSADM uses three different elementary description techniques:

- Entity-Relationship Modelling (called Logical Data Modelling (LDM) in SSADM),

- Data Flow Modelling (DFM), similar to Structured Analysis,

- Entity-Event Modelling (EEM), similar to Jackson System Development (JSD).

These techniques are *not* simply used as a three-dimensional system of views of the required system. Instead, the three techniques are applied within those stages of requirements engineering, where they are particularly appropriate. A short overview of the structure of the development process according to SSADM is helpful for an explanation of this differentiated use.

SSADM proceeds in seven stages, from Feasibility Study to Physical Design, where the stages are grouped again into five so-called modules. For our purposes, we are interested only in the module "Requirements Specification (RS)", and in parts of the modules "Requirements Analysis (RA)" and "Logical System Specification (LS)". Figure 3.1 shows an overview of the modules and stages of SSADM, where the parts relevant for this work are highlighted. The module FS is subsumed by a treatment of RA and RS, since it just consists in a rapid walkthrough of some of the main steps of the other modules.

Module FS	Stage 0: Feasibility

| Module RA | Stage 1: Investigation of Current Environment |
| | Stage 2: Business System Options |

Module RS	Stage 3: Specification of Definition of Requirements

| Module LS | Stage 4: Technical System Options |
| | Stage 5: Logical Design |

Module PD	Stage 6: Physical Design

Fig. 3.1

The module "Requirements Analysis (RA)" deals with the "Investigation of Current Environment" (Stage 1) and "Business System Options" (Stage 2). Work in these stages concentrates on analysis of business activities. This work is independent of whether the current organisation already uses some computer support; it can even be seen as independent of the question whether finally a computerized system or some other solution will be introduced. The final goal of this module is the clear definition of the business area where the required system will be placed. In module RA, emphasis lies on a thorough, but not too detailed, understanding of business practices. Data Flow Modelling (DFM) can be used rather well for these purposes. For instance, the real flow of documents within an organization can be described as a data flow diagram. Therefore, SSADM mainly uses DFM in these stages. As a second supporting technique, also a sketchy form of Logical Data Modelling (LDM) is introduced, to capture such information as the structure of any documents flowing around within the current organization. Stage 2 is dedicated to the study of various options before defining the final version of the requirements; it does not introduce new technical concepts.

At the end of the Requirements Analysis module, the business area has been described in a way which abstracts from technical details, and it has been decided where the "system border" lies within this logicalized view of the business area. The following "Requirements Specification (RS)" module consists only of the Stage 3 "Specification of Definition of Requirements". Here the requirements for the chosen system are worked out in detail. For this delicate work, SSADM, in contrast to the classical "structured methods", judges DFM as no longer adequate. It is one of the key activities in Stage 3 (called Step 330 "Derive System Functions") to extract from the data flow model the basic building blocks for the functionality of the required system and the structure of "events" the system has to deal with. After this step, DFM more and more loses its importance and is replaced by Entity-Event Modelling (EEM). The logical data model is a basic part of EEM, so the LDM technique is not abandoned, but integrated even more into the detailed specification definition.

The EEM technique contains a notation for detailed operational descriptions based on the elements of the data model. In this respect, it is quite similar to the specification of "object life cycles" in most of the object-oriented approaches [RBP91, SM92]. The result of EEM is quite adequate to be directly reused for design purposes within the design work of stage 5. The intermediate stage 4 deals with the selection of an appropriate hardware/software environment; it is not concerned with functional requirements.

To summarize, the purposes of the three techniques in SSADM are:

- For DFM, to give an overview of business rules and practices without operational detail, mainly in the RA module.

- For LDM, to serve as a consolidating and integrating basis for all stages of development, including the RA, RS and LS module.

- For EEM, to specify operational detail abstractly, but ready for later use in design, mainly in the RS and LS module.

Figure 3.2 shows graphically the usage of the three techniques within the SSADM stages which are relevant for this work.

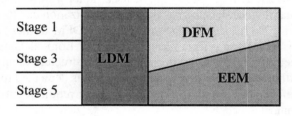

Fig. 3.2

A comparison to other development methods shows that SSADM tries to avoid the frequently criticized problems of the data flow approach by not going into detail for this technique. Data flow models tend to get unmanageable for a large project, if they are refined onto too detailed a level. Data flow models cannot be easily transformed into a good modular system design. But data flow models can be used effectively to find the "essential functions" of a required system during business analysis, as proposed in [MP84].

Compared to the object-oriented methods and JSD, SSADM contains a separate business-oriented system analysis phase with strong end-user interaction. The object-oriented methods more or less omit this phase and start directly with an execution- and design-oriented model of the required system. An important difference to OMT is that OMT claims state models (similar to EEM) and data flow modelling to be complementary views of a system. In SSADM however, the DFM technique (data flow modelling) is mainly used for preparing the transition to EEM.

3.3 Hotel Agency: A Toy Project in SSADM

Throughout this work, a common example will be used. This small example is intended as a toy project for demonstrating the translation of a requirements definition in SSADM style into axiomatic specifications. The example is so small that it can be treated entirely. Despite of its size, it does contain a few features which are not completely trivial.

We give only an informal summary of the example here, in order to prepare the ground for various smaller examples in the next chapters which are taken from the toy project. A complete listing of the most important SSADM documents for the toy project can be found in appendix B.

> *Informal Description: Hotel Agency.* A booking agency for hotel rooms is to be supported by a computerized information system.
>
> The agency maintains a list of customers; it does business only with customers from this list. A new customer is added to the list, if the agency has received a written application which includes a valid credit card number. To every customer on the list, a unique customer number is assigned. If a customer does not use the agency services (not even by a request) for a whole year, the customer is removed from the list.
>
> The agency has a fixed catalogue of hotel rooms on offer. In order to keep the example simple, the catalogue is restricted to single rooms. Every customer has a copy of the catalogue. If a customer wants to book a hotel room, he or she gives a request to the agency, by phone or by letter, which contains the following information: the customer number, the hotel, the period of time, and the number of rooms to be booked.
>
> There are two different kinds of hotels in the catalogue: For some of them the agency has pre-booked some quota of rooms. For such hotels, the customer can be immediately informed whether the room is available. For the other hotels, and in cases where the quota kept by the agency is not sufficient for the request, the agency sends an inquiry to the hotel and asks for availability. If a customer request cannot be fulfilled even after asking the hotel, the agency makes an attempt to offer the customer comparable rooms in another hotel. In any case, the customer is informed by letter,

whether appropriate rooms are available. If rooms are offered in this letter, the customer holds a reservation for 10 days.

If the customer does acknowledge the reservation within this period, then a voucher is sent to the customer, and the credit card account is charged. Also the hotel is informed of the fixed booking. In case the customer does not acknowledge in time, the reservation gets invalid.

Chapter 4

SPECTRUM – A Formal Specification Framework

The language SPECTRUM has been chosen as the formal basis of the work reported here. In this chapter, a brief introduction to SPECTRUM is given and a number of examples of specifications are shown.

4.1 Characteristics of SPECTRUM

The language SPECTRUM is the result of a research project at the Technische Universität München which aimed at a flexible formal specification framework representing the state of the art in axiomatic specification. Detailed information on the language is contained in [BFG+93].

The essential requirements for the design of SPECTRUM were the following:

- SPECTRUM is a modern *axiomatic specification language* . It follows a purely *descriptive* approach in the sense that the semantics of a specification is a class of mathematical structures (models) rather than a single model. Typical examples for other languages of this type are CIP-L [BBB+85] and PLUSS [Gau86].

- SPECTRUM comprises a very general language of axioms, including the full language of first-order predicate logic. This is in contrast to other axiomatic languages like OBJ [FGJ+85] or LARCH [GH93] which admit only a very restricted syntactical form of axioms (conditional equations) and designate a particular algebraic structure (the so-called *initial algebra*) as *the* semantic model of a specification.

- SPECTRUM is designed as a *wide spectrum language* which supports also an executable (model-oriented) sublanguage. The main advantage of this design is that the transition between a purely descriptive and an executable specification can be made and verified within a single syntactial and semantical framework.

- SPECTRUM incorporates many constructs which have turned out as useful in *functional programming*. In particular, higher-order functions (functions as objects) and parametric polymorphism have been taken over from languages like ML [HMM86] or Haskell [HJW92]. From the latter language also the concept of sort classes is inherited by SPECTRUM. In the first place, program development in SPECTRUM aims at the development of state-less programs in these languages. However, as this study shows, this does not prohibit applications of the language for specification tasks from daily systems development practice.

- SPECTRUM has a semantics which is closely related to the logic of computable functions LCF [Pau87]. From this ancestor SPECTRUM inherits a powerful deduction calculus which also can be used to derive properties of recursively defined functions.

For the practical application in a case study like this, the advantages of SPECTRUM are its high flexibility and its orientation towards short and generic specifications. The price which has to be paid for this is abstractness. The language in its current status is effectively usable only by specialists with a good knowledge of mathematical logic and functional programming. In the following section, we try to give a quite application-oriented introduction to SPECTRUM.

4.2 Axiomatic Specifications in SPECTRUM

An axiomatic specification consists of two parts: a *signature* which introduces a number of symbols for data domains and functions, and *axioms* which define basic properties which have to hold for any interpretation of the symbols. Mathematically, the semantics of a SPECTRUM specification is a *class of algebras*. This comprises every mathematical structure which gives a reasonable interpretation to the symbols of the signature and fulfills the axioms.

In this section, the language is explained informally[1] using the simple example of (generic) lists. Several variants and extensions of the list example are introduced to show the most important features of the language.

4.2.1 Basic Components of a SPECTRUM Specification

A simple specification of lists is shown in figure 4.1.

```
LIST0 = {          − − Simple specification for lists
           enriches Naturals;
           sort List α;

           []:             List α;
           cons:           α × List α → List α;
           . ++ .:         List α × List α → List α;

           length:         List α → Nat;
           first:          List α → α;
           rest:           List α → List α;

           [], cons, .++., length strict total;     first, rest strict;

           List α freely generated by [], cons;

           axioms ∀ x: α, ∀ u, v: List α in
           [] ++ u = u;
           cons(x, u) ++ v = cons(x, u++v);

           length([]) = 0;
           length(cons(x, u)) = 1 + length(u);

           δ first(u) = (length(u) ≠ 0);        δ rest(u) = (length(u) ≠ 0);
           first(cons(x, u)) = x;               rest(cons(x, u)) = u;
           endaxioms; }
```
Fig. 4.1

We are going to discuss the main parts of this text line by line. The first line simply introduces the name of the specification unit for further reference in import statements.

      LIST0 = {   − − Simple specification for lists

---

[1] At some places, we omit technicalities of the language like the priority declarations for infix operations.

The body of the specification is enclosed in curly brackets. The text after the two dashes is a *comment* in SPECTRUM. It is terminated by the end of the line.

      enriches Naturals;

The **enriches**-line is the SPECTRUM way to formulate an import of other specification modules. In this case, a pre-defined standard specification for natural numbers becomes available.

      sort List α;

The keyword **sort** introduces the declaration of *sort symbols*. A sort symbol is an identifier which is to be interpreted in any model of the specification by a set of data values. Often a sort symbol is simply an identifier as in:

      sort Nat;

The sort declaration for List, however, is of a more complex kind and shows one of the main features of SPECTRUM. It is a *sort constructor*, that is a sort which takes another sort as a parameter. The sort parameter is indicated, by convention, by a greek letter (α). This means that List α is a sort name for any substitution of a sort name for the α. This *sort expression* then denotes the data values of lists with elements out of the interpretation of the argument sort. This also admits the construction of nested sort expressions like the following:

      List List Nat;   − − Lists of lists of natural numbers

The next three lines are declarations of *function symbols*.

      []:   List α;
      cons: $\alpha \times$ List $\alpha \rightarrow$ List α;
      . ++ .:   List $\alpha \times$ List $\alpha \rightarrow$ List α;

The first part of a function declaration is the function name, which often is a normal identifier (as in the case of cons). But also symbolic names (as []) and binary *infix operators* (like .++., where the dots are placeholders for arguments) are allowed in SPECTRUM. In the case of infix symbols, often the word *operation* is used synonymously with *function*. The function name is followed by a *sort expression* which gives a description of the argument and result data of the function. In the list example, the sort parameter (α) again appears here, and therefore the functions are defined generically for all lists with an arbitrary element sort (*parametric polymorphism*). The three lines state that the [] function returns a list, that cons takes a list and a value of the element sort for the list and gives a list, and that .++. computes a list out of two other lists.

These were the *signature* parts of the specification. The remaining text defines *axioms*. The first three axioms are not simple formulae, but schematic *abbreviations* for axioms.

[], cons, .++., length **strict total**;   first, rest **strict**;

This line deals with the phenomenon of undefinedness. SPECTRUM interprets function symbols in a way which is more oriented towards programming than standard mathematical functions. "Undefined values" appear naturally in computing, for instance in the case of nontermination of a computation. Such values are represented in SPECTRUM by the special symbol $\perp$ (pronounced "bottom"). The most interesting aspects of the treatment of undefined values in SPECTRUM are the following:

- The symbol $\perp$ can be used in axioms. Moreover, there is a symbol δ for testing whether a value is defined ("definedness predicate").

- A few standard axioms appear so frequently that there exist standard abbreviations for them using the special keywords **strict** and **total**. The meaning of such statements is as follows (for a unary function symbol f):

f **strict**	is equivalent to	$f(\perp) = \perp$
f **total**	is equivalent to[2]	$\delta x \Rightarrow \delta (f(x))$

Strictness means that a function does not convert undefined values into defined values. Most functions in specifications for sequential computer programs are strict; non-strictness can be useful in the formal specification of concurrent and communicating systems. Totality means that the function never adds undefinedness by its own, so its result is undefined only if its argument is undefined, too.

List α **freely generated by** [], cons;

This *generation* axiom serves for quite a different purpose. With lists in the sense of data structures, we usually mean finite lists. So it is an additional property for the intended model class that every list can be constructed out of the empty list by a finite number of applications of a cons operation. Functions like cons are called *constructors*. This is a very important constraint since it allows the specifier to use an *induction principle* in logical deductions for lists[3].

---

[2]   Please note that the variable x is supposed here to range over defined and undefined values. SPECTRUM contains several forms of quantifiers, to include or exclude the undefined values. For details see [BFG+93].

[3]   This is a *second order* axiom, therefore it is not possible to express this with ordinary SPECTRUM formulae.

The keyword **freely** in the generation axiom is optional. If it is present in a generation axiom, the constructors are implicitly required to deliver *pairwise different* results. This is often, but not always, useful in a generation axiom. For instance, the constructor operations for finite sets should produce the same value independent of the order in which elements are inserted into a set. So for sets, a generation axiom without the word **freely** is adequate.

Finally, a set of first-order axioms is added to the specification. This set of axioms starts with the line

> **axioms** $\forall$ x: α, $\forall$ u, v: List α **in**

which introduces a number of logical variables. These variables are placeholders for arbitrary values of the appropriate sort. To be more precise, a universal quantification over these identifiers applies to all axioms in the block below it. The standard universal and existential quantifiers in SPECTRUM do quantify *over defined values only*, in order to reduce the definedness expressions which are needed in the axioms.

> [] ++ u = u;
> cons(x, u) ++ v = cons(x, u++v);

Most axioms use the *equality predicate* which is available automatically for every declared sort. In this example, the two axioms together give a complete definition for the .++. operator in terms of cons and []; the meaning of .++. is fixed as a *concatenation operator* for lists. The other axioms define in a similar style a function length for the length of a list and functions to get the first element of a list and to remove the first element of a list. Please note the two definedness axioms for the first and rest functions.

> δ first(u) = (length(u) $\neq$ 0); δ rest(u) = (length(u) $\neq$ 0);

If a function symbol is not declared as **total**, it is advisable to specify the definedness condition explicitly by an axiom like these two examples. Such functions are often called *partial* (in contrast to total functions).

The specification of lists is such a basic one that the constructors for lists are built into the SPECTRUM language. So the specification from above usually has not to be written by a user of the language. In particular, SPECTRUM provides a convenient syntax for lists which avoids many brackets. A term of the form

> $[t_1, t_2, \ldots, t_n]$,

where the t_i are of the same sort, is an abbreviation[4] of the following term of a list sort:

$$cons(t_1, cons(t_2, \ldots cons(t_n, []) \ldots))$$

So for instance the following terms denote lists of natural numbers of increasing length:

$$[], [1], [1, 2], [1, 2, 3]$$

This very basic introduction to SPECTRUM should be sufficient for a first understanding of most of the specifications which are given for SSADM. So readers with low interest in the technical details of formalization may skip from here to the next chapter. The following subsections give an introduction to a few more advanced concepts of SPECTRUM which appear at several places in the formalization.

4.2.2 Descriptive Specification

Up to this point, the examples were written in an *equational* style: All axioms were simple equations or definedness axioms. In this subsection, we illustrate the possibility to use arbitrary first-order formulae as SPECTRUM axioms, which may for instance also contain existential quantifiers. Examples are given in figure 4.2, which extends the list specification by two Boolean infix operators. The .elem. operator tests whether an element appears in a list, and the .subList. operator checks whether some list is a part of another list. Each of these operators is defined by a single axiom which uses existential quantifiers.

Besides this more implicit way of description, the specification LIST1 also differs from the simple example LIST0 in its use of *sort classes*. The identifier EQ which appears in LIST1 denotes the class of all sorts for which the standard equality is decidable.

```
LIST1 = {        − − Extended specification of lists
         enriches LIST0;

         List :: (EQ)EQ;

         . elem .:      α :: EQ ⇒      α × List α → Bool;
         . subList .:   α :: EQ ⇒      List α × List α → Bool;

         .elem., .subList. strict total;
```

---

[4] This notation is sensible only because of the associativity of the .++. operator.

---
axioms $\forall$ α:: EQ $\Rightarrow$ x: α, $\forall$ u, v: List α **in**

x elem u $\Leftrightarrow$ ($\exists$ v1, v2. u = v1++[x]++v2);

u subList v $\Leftrightarrow$ ($\exists$ v1, v2. u = v1++v++v2);

endaxioms; }

Fig. 4.2

The use of the sort class EQ is motivated by the following facts: The expressive power of SPECTRUM, in particular the possibility to use functions in a similar manner as data values, has the consequence that the universal equality on some sorts is undecidable. This is the reason why SPECTRUM distinguishes between sorts for which the equality is decidable (essentially everything except functions) and other sorts. This becomes important if the equality is used for generic sorts based on a parameter sort (or for the parameter sort itself). The specification LIST1 defines a test whether an element is contained in a list and a test whether a list is sublist of another one. Both functions are well-defined only for such lists where the the equality of the underlying domains is decidable. In the SPECTRUM example, this fact is taken into account by the parts of the specification which contain a double colon (::).

> List :: (EQ)EQ;

This line states that the generic sort List α belongs to the sort class EQ (where equality is decidable) as soon as the parameter sort α belongs to EQ. This is obvious since a list can be tested elementwise for equality. In the function signatures and at the beginning of the axiom block, the sort parameter α is restricted to sorts out of the EQ class by the following phrase:

> α :: EQ $\Rightarrow$ ...

Besides this relatively technical feature, the example clearly demonstrates that the powerful formula language of SPECTRUM can be used to obtain short specifications which are abstract and descriptive. Descriptiveness means here that the specification describes "what" a function does without giving any hint about "how" it is done.

4.2.3 Higher-Order Functions

It was already mentioned several times that functions can be used as ordinary data objects in SPECTRUM. So the *functional sort* $\alpha \to \beta$ is like any other sort (except that it does not belong to the sort class EQ). In particular, function sorts can be arguments or results of functions, as it is shown in figure 4.3.

```
LIST2 = {          – – Further extended specification of lists
         enriches  LIST1;

         filter:                  List α × (α → Bool) → List α;
         noDuplicates:            List α → Bool;

         filter, noDuplicates total;

         axioms ∀ x: α, ∀ u, v: List α, p: (α → Bool) in
         filter([], p) = [];
         filter([x]++u, p) =
                  if p(x) then [x]++filter(u, p) else filter(u, p) endif;

         noDuplicates(u) = (∀ x. length(filter(u, λy. y = x)) ≤ 1);
         endaxioms; }
```
Fig. 4.3

The function filter which is defined here takes two arguments: A list and a predicate for elements of the list. It derives another list which contains only those elements of the given list for which the predicate is true. This is a standard example from functional programming [BW88]. The SPECTRUM syntax also resembles functional programming languages, including the use of a built-in **if-then-else**. Please note that the identifier p appears in parameter position, but also as a function which is applied to an argument.

The function noDuplicates defined in figure 4.3 tests whether a list is free of duplicate entries. It demonstrates how a function can be denoted by a closed expression using the so-called λ-*abstraction*. The term λx.E converts the expression E (in which the logical variable x is used) into a function of one parameter which has the sort of x. The specification also shows that the style of functional programming can be mixed with a descriptive style of specification[5].

Higher-order functions like filter from figure 4.3 are extremely useful for the extraction of generic parts from complex specifications and therefore for a modular and abstract description style. Appendix D contains a number of other higher-order functions for sequences which are frequently used in functional programming.

4.2.4 Data Declarations

Since SPECTRUM is a wide-spectrum language, data types can be defined in several styles. The examples above have shown a quite powerful descriptive way to introduce new data types. But in a more programming-oriented style, it is often necessary to define data types more explicitly. For this purpose, SEPCTRUM has

---

[5] We have simplified the SPECTRUM syntax here slightly. SPECTRUM requires the expression y == x to be written here instead of y = x.

inherited from functional programming a number of language constructs which are similar in power to the record and pointer constructs of conventional programming languages. The so-called **data** declaration is defined as an abbreviation for a relatively long descriptive specification.

As an example, the specification of lists can be rephrased using a data declaration. The following line is equivalent to a large part of the LIST0 specification from above.

> **data** List α = [] | cons(! first: α, ! rest: List α);

This definition comprises the following particles of the LIST0 specification: The sort declaration, the declaration of the constructor functions [] and cons (including argument and result sort information), the (free) generation principle, the declaration of the observation functions first and rest (also including sort information) and the axioms defining the semantics of first and rest. The two exclamation marks indicate that the cons constructor is strict in both arguments; omitting them allows the construction of data sorts like the so-called "lazy lists".

So the single line above replaces the specification LIST0 except of the declaration and definition of the .++. operator and the length function. The data declaration also declares two additional functions which are not contained in LIST0 and which are called *discriminator functions*. These functions can be used to test a list value for its topmost constructor, which means here a test whether the list is empty or not.

> is_[], is_cons: List α → Bool;   is_[], is_cons **strict total**;

The axiomatic definition of these functions is as follows:

> is_[]([]) = true;   is_[](cons(x, u)) = false;
> is_cons([]) = false,   is_cons(cons(x, u)) = true;

Besides this powerful way to construct data sorts, in SPECTRUM a new sort identifier can also be defined as a simple abbreviation or *synonym* for another sort, which may be given as a complex sort expression. For instance, if a special sort identifier for lists of natural numbers (NatList) is needed, this can be easily defined on top of the generic list specification by the following line:

> **sortsyn** NatList = List Nat;

For a practical specification application, as the definition of SSADM semantics, a library of basic specifications is necessary, which contains other data types besides the lists, for instance finite sets. Appendix D contains the library of specifications which is used throughout the remainder of this book.

Chapter 5

Alternative Ways to an Integration of SSADM and SPECTRUM

This chapter explores basic design decisions for a framework which integrates SSADM and SPECTRUM. Before presenting our own approach, we will give a short sketch of the requirements and the most important options for the method integration. The exposition of the requirements is guided by a study of the complementary features of SSADM and SPECTRUM and states the aims to be achieved by the rest of this book. The basic alternatives for integrating SSADM and SPECTRUM are listed, discussed and decided upon. The rather sparse literature on the combination of formal and informal methods contains some experiences with specific approaches, which are surveyed in this chapter, too.

5.1 Contributions of SSADM to an Integrated Approach

As it was already indicated in the introduction, the features of formal and pragmatic methods are to some extent complementary. In the following section, we list and illustrate the main strengths of SSADM and explain how these features can be used to overcome problems which appear during practical application of formal methods. The next section concentrates on the strengths of SPECTRUM and analogously shows how the features of a formal method can contribute to the improvement of a pragmatic method. At the end of each subsection, we will summarize briefly what the aim of an integrating approach is with respect to the features which were discussed in the respective subsection.

5.1.1 Structured Requirements Engineering Process

Alan Davis states that the main difficulty of systems analysis is "organizing all the information, relating different people's perspectives, surfacing and resolving conflicts, and avoiding the internal design of the software." [Dav90, p.54] SSADM, as a pragmatic approach, gives assistance for these difficult tasks. It provides detailed procedural guidelines which help to organize the analysis. In particular, SSADM provides a title and a place for any result of an analysis step in such a way that it contributes to the whole development. This is achieved by the detailed structure of a development process into modules, stages, steps and tasks. Even the resolution of different personal perspectives is partly organized by SSADM. The stages 2 and 4 of the method are explicitly dedicated to the discussion of different options for the ongoing development. The following citation from an introductory book on SSADM illustrates the degree of advice given in SSADM. On the topic of "Business System Options" (BSOs) which appears in stage 2, [DCC93] says on p. 140:

> "Depending upon the size and importance of the project, between two and six outline options should be prepared. The first should be based upon a minimum set of requirements, i.e. those which must be met by any system. Another should be a comprehensive ‚bells and whistles' solution, meeting all functional requirements and offering high performance on the non-functional requirements. It may prove worthwile to develop intermediate options if there is a great choice. [...] In expanding each option, it is described in more detail, using DFDs and LDSs. As appropriate, cost/benefit analysis and impact analysis are undertaken. [...]"

Such a strong guidance of the analyst is unknown in the formal world. A typical methodical framework of the formal kind defines general development steps like transformations or data refinements starting from a given specification. The following citation, taken from a reference book on Z [Spi92], serves as an illustration for the level on which the formal methods deal with the structure of the development process.

> "When a program is developed from a specification, two sorts of design decisions usually need to be taken: the operations described by predicates in the specification must be implemented by algorithms expressed in a programming language, and the data described by mathematical data types in the specification language must be implemented by data structures of the program.

> This section contains the rules for simple *operation refinement*. This allows us to show that one operation is a correct implementation of another operation with the same state space, when both operations are specified by schemas. This is the simplest kind of refinement of one operation by another, and it needs to be extended in two directions to make it generally useful in program development." [Spi 92, p. 135 f.]

There exists a methodical framework which is well adapted to SPECTRUM (the KORSO framework [PW95]), which has the same flavour of defining and classifying atomic steps of development as this text on Z.

When comparing the overall view on the development process which is expressed by the two citations from above, it is clear that the formal approach concentrates on finding a very general concept of a development step and mainly ignores the question which actual step is to be applied in an actual situation. Moreover, it presupposes the existence of a (formal) specification.

In fact, the two ways in which pragmatic and formal approaches describe the development process do not compete with each other. The pragmatic approach chosen in SSADM gives general advice on how to structure the process and its results, and how to proceed in specific situations. The formal methods provide a kind of basic technology for carrying out development steps. So it is desirable to build pragmatic guidance on top of a formal notion of a development step or, equivalently, to give a more solid underpinning for the development process described by pragmatic methods.

Aim for the integrated approach: It is necessary for an integrated approach to stay consistent with the procedural guidelines of SSADM since they constitute a condensation of practical experience. An ideal integrated approach will give a sound basis for the steps as they appear in the pragmatic method.

5.1.2 Standardized Diagrammatic Notations

SSADM aims at a high degree of user involvement during the development of a requirements specification. This is partially enabled by diagrammatical notations which are said to be comprehensible also for non-specialists in data processing. The most prominent role during the very first steps on a development with SSADM is played by Data Flow Diagrams (DFDs). As an example, figure 5.1 shows a DFD which is part of the Hotel Agency case study[1]. This diagram shows the activities which are necessary to handle the arrival of a customer's booking request. In many cases, a reservation can be generated according to the quotas file, which keeps the

---

[1]   It has been cut out of the Required Logical DFM.

rooms the agency can assign without further inquiries. Sometimes it is necessary to ask the hotel for availability (create hotel inquiry).

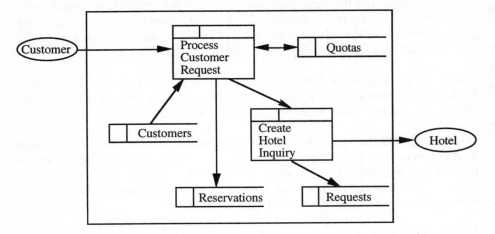

Fig. 5.1

It is questionable whether such diagrams are really easier to understand than, for instance, a well-written text. However, the wide-spread use of SSADM and other structured methods gradually leads to a situation where users have some, maybe superficial, experience with such graphical notations. In particular, during meetings like those invoked during stage 2 of SSADM, where a choice is made between the Business System Options, system analysts have to explain the notations and their meaning in a way which is adequate for application domain specialists.

In contrast to this situation, it is highly unlikely that users will get familiar with a formal notation like SPECTRUM. As an illustration, see below a sketchy attempt to encode some of the information in figure 5.1 in SPECTRUM. This small specification just gives the input/output interfaces for the two processes in the DFD (as a signature in SPECTRUM); the information on external entities and the link between both processes has been left out[2].

processCustomerRequest:
    CustRequest × Store Customer × Store Quota × Store Reservation
        → HotelInqData × Store Quota × Store Reservation;
createHotelInquiry:
    HotelInqData × Store Inquiry → HotelInquiry × Store Inquiry;

---

2   See chapter 11 for a more complete formal treatment of DFDs.

This kind of notation is definitely less comprehensible. For instance, to find out whether a data store is read, written or both, we have to look in the SPECTRUM text whether the sort of the store appears on one or both sides of the function arrow. In the diagram, this is very neatly shown by single- or double-headed arrows from and into the store symbols. However, this is a very simple kind of SPECTRUM specification. Understanding the text gets more difficult, if more powerful constructs, in particular logical axioms, are used. The prejudice against mathematics which is common among systems analysts and software developers makes such a notation unsuitable for practical use in requirements analysis.

Aim for the integrated approach: In order to keep the advantages of the pragmatic method, it is necessary to stay with the notations of SSADM within an integrated approach. Formal texts must be used in such a way that they are hidden for to the user. The diagrammatical information presented to the user may be transformed into a hidden formal specification, if this transformation is achieved by a completely automatic tool.

5.1.3 Large-Scale Orientation

The use of SSADM makes sense only for a project which is so large that the investments into the disciplined way of proceeding pays back by better overview and control. In particular, a typical SSADM project will involve a whole team working on the development. In order to keep the information for a large-scale project manageable, SSADM provides various views onto the system. A view is here a projection of the whole system into a single or a few dimensions of its complexity, in order to achieve a less complex representation. Typical views in SSADM are the static view of LDM and the dynamic view of EEM; but also EEM itself hosts various views (Event-Entity Matrix, Entity Life Histories, Effect-Correspondence Diagrams). All these views deal with the organisation of a large system built from many small pieces; only little attention is paid on the details for the smallest pieces (like attribute values or algorithms of data transformation). SSADM relies for such details on the use of sensible identifiers and textual explanations, which are intuitively understandable for the reader.

This is in sharp contrast to the formal world, where the question of "scaling up" from toy examples to large projects still is considered an unsolved (and only rarely attacked) problem. In figure 5.2, a very small part of the data model for the Hotel Agency case study is shown. The SSADM notation shows two rounded rectangles named "Customer" and "Reservation", which means that these are classes of data elements which have to be stored in the system. The connection between the nodes states that such data elements may be connected by a relationship called "holds".

The special form of the connecting line expresses particular constraints for such connections[3].

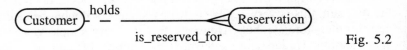

Fig. 5.2

Figur 5.3 below shows an attempt to encode the semantics of such a diagram in SPECTRUM.

```
CUSTOMER = {
        sort Customer, CustomerId;
        strict total;
        custId:                 Customer → CustomerId;        }

RESERVATION = {
        sort Reservation, ReservationId;
        strict total;
        resnId:                 Reservation → ReservationId;  }

CUST_holds_RESERVN = {
        enriches  CUSTOMER+RESERVATION+DEGREES;
        strict; exCustomer, exReservation, relHolds, ok total ;

        sort State;

        exCustomer:        State × CustomerId → Bool;
        exReservation :    State × ReservationId → Bool;
        getCustomer:       State × CustomerId → Customer;
        getReservation:    State × CustomerId → Reservation;
        relHolds:
               State → (CustomerId × ReservationId → Bool);
        ok:                State → Bool;

        axioms ∀ s: State, c: Customer, ci: CustomerId, r: Reservation,
               ri: ReservationId in
```

---

[3]   These constraints (degree, optionality) are igored here. See chapter 7 for a detailed treatment of ER diagrams.

```
δ getCustomer(s, ci) = exCustomer(s, ci);
δ getReservation(s, ri) = exCustomer(s, ri);
δ (relHolds(s) (ci, ri)) = exCustomer(s, ci) ∧ exReservation(s, ri);
getCustomer(s, ci) = c ⇒ custId(c) = ci;
getReservation(s, ri) = r ⇒ resnId(r) = ri;
ok(s) = IsOneMany(relHolds(s));
endaxioms;  }
```

Fig. 5.3

Like in the example above, the SPECTRUM text looks much more difficult than the SSADM diagram. It consists of four specifications (the specification unit DEGREES not being reproduced here). For each entity name, an entity sort and a sort of identifiers are introduced. For the system state, several observation functions are defined to test whether an occurrence for a given identifier exists, to get the actual occurrence for an identifier (if existing) and to get the information whether an instance of the "holds"-relationship exists between two occurrences. An "ok-predicate" is defined to test whether a given state obeys the restrictions for the relationship (which are given by the dashed line and the "crow's foot" in figure 5.2). The axiom defining this predicate uses pre-defined (higher-order) notions from the DEGREES specification to express such restrictions.

The technical details of transforming a Logical Data Model into a SPECTRUM specification are discussed in detail in chapter 7 below. At this point, a few superficial observations are sufficient. Generally, the formal specification is larger and more complex than the diagram. The formal specification in particular contains a mixture of application specific information (like the names "customer", "reservation", "holds") with technical information on the mechanism of a Logical Data Model in general (like the introduction of identifier sorts and the regular shape of the axioms). If the specification is changed, it is quite difficult to translate the changed specification back into a sensible diagrammatic form.

Obviously, the specification of a large data model is much easier to handle on a level of description like the diagram in figure 5.1 than by a plain SPECTRUM specification. So we aim at such a language level to be defined on top of the SPECTRUM language, for a more adequate treatment of large projects.

Aim for the integrated approach: An integrated approach must keep the large-scale orientation of SSADM. For this purpose, the integrated approach should enable a way of representing the concepts of SSADM. The specification of general concepts in SSADM has to be clearly separated from application-specific information.

5.2 Contributions of SPECTRUM to an Integrated Approach

5.2.1 Semantic Precision

Obviously, the main advantage of a formal approach is that it removes the inherent lack of precision in SSADM and replaces vague textual descriptions by mathematical formulae. This vagueness of description exists in SSADM on two levels: In the description of the semantics of the notations, and in the textual parts of a specification produced according to SSADM.

In the general description of SSADM, even carefully formulated definitions and explanations in natural language contain ambiguity and implicit information. For instance, when looking in the glossary of a user's guide to SSADM [Eva92], we find the following definition of an entity:

> "**Entity.** Something about which the system needs to hold information. There should be the potential for more than one occurrence of an entity, and each occurrence of that entity should be uniquely identifiable." [Eva92, p. 329]

This definition clearly addresses "entity" as a classification concept; only for a class of things it is useful to think whether there is a "potential for more than one occurrence". So an entity is more or less a name for a set of properties, and an occurrence is said to belong to the entity if it has all the required properties. On the same page the notion "effect" is defined as follows:

> "**Effect.** The change caused to a single entity as a result of an event. The change creates an occurrence of the entity, changes the value of one or more attributes, including state indicator, or deletes an occurrence of the entity." [Eva92, p. 329]

Now what does it mean to cause a change to an entity? It does not make sense to change the abstract notion, but only an actual set of occurrences of the entity. However, it is also not adequate to view an effect as an actual change to an actual set of occurrences. From the context, it becomes clear that an effect is a schematic description for a class of changes which can be applied to a set of occurrences of the entity. Such complicated sentences appall the reader and are avoided therefore in the literature on SSADM. However, also the more simple formulation may confuse a reader who does not have the necessary background knowledge and tries to understand the concepts. This is one of the reasons why Software Engineering methods are quite difficult to learn and to teach.

A similar effect appears also at those places where SSADM system specifications contain parts which are written in natural language. For instance, in the same user's guide, the "function definition" scheme of SSADM is illustrated by giving a small function definition for a function called "Cancel Delegate Bookings". (The case study is on a booking system for internal training courses of a company. The participants on such courses are called delegates, because they come from a particular branch of the company. The specified function removes a cancelled booking and tries to find a replacement for the vacancy from a waiting list.) The entry "function description" contains the following text:

> "The waiting list for that Course Title is examined for other Delegates from the same Branch for ease of billing. Either such a Delegate or else the one waiting longest will be offered a place as standby." [Eva92, p.147]

This specification does not explicitly state how to choose between several delegates from the same branch which are on the waiting list. Common sense is in favour of taking the one waiting longest also among the delegates from the same branch, but this does not coincide with the meaning of the word "else". It is easy to find such weaknesses in almost any textual specification, as it was convincingly demonstrated by B. Meyer [Mey85].

Aims for the integrated approach: The formal specification in SPECTRUM must provide clarity for the various notions which are defined and used in SSADM. It is important, however, to stay as close as possible to the available informal definitions. Ideally, the formalization of SSADM's notions could serve as a platform for discussing various peoples' opinions on semantic details of the notions. Besides that, for the textual explanations contained in SSADM specifications, a more formal replacement is needed, which can be provided by SPECTRUM.

5.2.2 Thorough Quality and Consistency Checks

Axiomatic specification languages like SPECTRUM have a very rigid notion of consistency. A set of axioms is inconsistent, if no mathematical structure (model) can be found which satisfies it. The proof of logical consistency is sometimes hard to achieve, but it is a very powerful validation facility for an axiomatic specification. This principle for the validation of small specifications is also used for showing that various independently developed specification parts fit well together.

The simple but powerful machinery of logical consistency is in strong contrast to the situation in pragmatic methods like SSADM. Aa an example for the kind of validation tests addressed in SSADM, see the following shortened excerpt from [Eva92]:

> **"Validation of DFD**
> [...]
> 1. Has each process a strong imperative verb and an object?
> 2. Are data flows in related to data flows out? Data should not be swallowed up by a process, only transformed in some way. [...]
> 3. Can the flows be reduced? [...] Six data flows in or out of a process should be sufficient.
> 4. Do all stores have flows both in and out? [...]
> [...]" [Eva92, p. 96 f.]

In this style, several quality check and validation rules are given for the documents to be produced, some such rules also cover cross-document consistency checks. However, an exhaustive set of conditions under which a whole specification is said to be consistent is not defined explicitly.

Current CASE tools obtain a serious amount of cross-document consistency tests by using a central repository (or encyclopedia) for storing all information on a project. This enforces for instance the consistent use of names for entities, events or other objects occurring in several documents. Such a repository is a database the structural scheme of which is usually called the *meta-model* of the tool. However, the meta-model is always derived from the method, and therefore meta-models for SSADM, for instance, have inherited many of the weak points in the terminology of the method.

A formal foundation can improve the situation here considerably. Every single axiom of an axiomatic specification can be understood as a statement expressing one single facet or view of the system which is specified. So the mathematical notion of consistency applies well to the question of integrating all these facets into a common picture. So the question must be studied under which conditions there exists a mathematical model for the set of axioms derived from a SSADM requirements specification. Since the axioms studied here will be generic or generated in a schematic way from semi-formal documents, also the consisteny proof should be carried out in a generic way, as far as possible.

Aims for the integrated approach: Following the formalization of SSADM concepts, the question of logical consistency of these specifications is to be studied. The aim is to find a set of conditions which ensures the consistency of all the documents within a SSADM specification. Ideally, this set of conditions will be formulated generically such that it can be easily applied to any actual SSADM specification.

5.2.3 Extensive Computer Support

Software tools for pragmatic methods (the famous CASE tools) usually are restricted to very basic services for the developer. The emphasis in current tools lies on graphical editors for diagrams and tables, combined with storage and retrieval functions on a multi-user repository. Only a few tools do offer the generation of executable code; and in these cases often the designer is required to enter fragments of code in some high-level programming language (called pseudo-code). It is also common practice to use the generated code just as a starting point for further manual revision and refinement.

Since formal methods rely on mechanical manipulation of their documents, they have a potential for a much higher degree of computer support. It is apparent also for the pragmatic methods that the extension of computer support grows with the degree of formality. For instance, there are practically usable database schema generators for ER diagrams or interactive simulators for State Charts. Rigorously formal methods often also offer interpreters or code generators, but they provide a new dimension of tool support by automatic or interactive theorem provers based on the manipulation rules of the method. In an approach integrating SPECTRUM and SSADM, mechanical theorem proving can be used on two levels:

- Generic activities concerning the formalization of SSADM concepts, like the proof of consistency from a set of conditions as mentioned above, can be supported mechanically.

- For actual projects, the development of critical algorithms can be supported mechanically without leaving the general framework of SSADM. This is of particular interest for safety-critical applications, if formal verification of the algorithms is required.

Aims for the integrated approach: Ideally, an integrated approach will make use of the available theorem proving facilities for proving the logical consistency in the above-mentioned sense. Moreover, it will be based on a conventional CASE tool for SSADM and will implement an integration of the theorem proving support into this tool, where adequate. These aims cannot be fulfilled within the scope of this work, but a basis will be provided for achieving them.

5.3 Options for the Integration

There are various ways to go for achieving an integration between the formal and the pragmatic world. In this section, we discuss the most important decisions which have been made for the approach presented here. The reasons for the actual decisions are based on the aims which were stated in the last section.

5.3.1 Complementarity vs. Foundation

Formal and pragmatic methods are complementary to each other; therefore it is sensible to combine them. For the user of an integrated approach, the crucial question is whether he or she will be actually exposed to the technicalities of a formal method. There are two options here which we call *complementarity* and *foundation*.

> *Option 1: Complementarity.* In a complementary approach to integration, two independent but closely related specifications are developed in the two frameworks (the formal and the pragamtic one). The pragmatic specification can be used as a guideline for drawing up the formal specification.

> *Option 2: Foundation.* In a foundation approach, the formal specification framework mainly serves as an underlying layer for the pragmatic framework. The formal language becomes a meta-language in which the semantics of the pragmatic notations are defined.

If option 1 is adopted, systems analysts with a good education in formal methods are needed. In option 2, however, the systems analysts do not have to use the formal machinery and therefore they do not need much education in formal methods. (However, they will benefit more from the integration if they have some basic knowledge of the formal background.) Figure 5.4 visualizes this aspect of the two options.

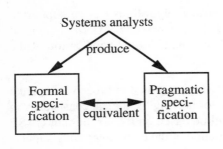

Complementarity

Foundation

Fig. 5.4

As the title of this book indicates, we have chosen the foundation approach. In the list of aims above, it was stated that the system analyst shall not be bothered with formal notations. In order to demonstrate the viability of the foundation approach, this work concentrates on clarifying the semantical background behind the pragmatic method of SSADM (shown as the task of the "method specialists" in figure 5.4).

As it is well known from programming languages, the definition of a semantic foundation for some notation always means a deep semantical analysis of the notation. In most cases, it is not possible or not advisable to define semantic foundations for the notation "as it is". Instead, the opportunity should be taken to clarify hidden semantic problems and to improve the notation itself. We see our approach to semantic foundation for SSADM along this line. For this reason, we would like to distinguish carefully between the original SSADM method and our variant of it, for which we are going to define semantic foundations and which is intended as a proposal for improvements of SSADM. We call our formal variant of SSADM notation in the sequel by the name *SSADM-F* (for "SSADM with formal foundations").

Besides the pure semantic foundation, this book also incorporates a short study of the possibilities to go beyond simple foundation towards a more thorough integration fo formal and pragmatic notation. In chapter 10, an interface will be defined which allows to use formal specification syntax at those places where SSADM relies on informal textual explanations.

For readers familiar with the "SSADM & Z" (SAZ) project, it may be interesting that one of the most significant differences of this work to SAZ is to use a foundation approach, whereas SAZ uses a complementary approach. For more information on SAZ, see section 5.4 below.

5.3.2 Extent of Method Foundation

A method like SSADM consists of notations, techniques and procedural guidelines. If formal foundations for a method are to be given, it must be decided which of these components is formalized.

> *Option 1: Notational Foundation.* The mostly diagrammatic notations of SSADM are expressed in SPECTRUM in such a way that a SSADM specification and also parts of it can be translated automatically into an axiomatic specification.

> *Option 2: Technical Foundation.* The SSADM techniques for deriving new documents out of existing ones are mapped onto a formal notion defined on the corresponding axiomatic specifications.

> *Option 3: Procedural Foundation.* The procedural guidelines of SSADM are specified axiomatically.

Obviously, notational foundation is inevitable. This work will give for the notations of SSADM foundations and it will concentrate on this topic.

Technical foundation is basically feasible on top of a foundation for the pragmatic notations. However, during the early stages of development the basis of a relatively stable specification is missing yet. So most of the steps in the early phases consist in intuitively guided revisions of documents where the semantics is changed instead of being preserved. The situation is different for the later steps of development where it must be shown that a design fulfils the requirements specification. These steps, however, are outside the scope of this investigation.

Procedural foundation is not studied altogether in this work. This is for the reason that SSADM itself gives a rather formal exposition of its procedural guidelines which seems to suffice in its clarity. An even more precise definition is useful only for the purpose of CASE tool support, and there exist tools which have succeeded in deriving a detailed procedural guidance from the definitions given in SSADM.

5.3.3 Syntactic vs. Semantic Reference

The foundation approach tries to explain the terms of one language (in this case SSADM notation) using terms of another language (in this case the formal specification language SPECTRUM). This means that the second language is used as a *reference* to capture the otherwise undefined denotation of the first language.

Even if the languages under consideration are fixed, there are various ways in which a reference can be constructed. In particular, for many purposes it may be sufficient to produce an axiomatic specification of the *syntax* of SSADM notations. Here, the word "syntax" is used with a general meaning; it also includes formal descriptions of the elements and formation rules of diagrams.

A more far-reaching approach is to capture the semantics of SSADM as well. In our view, the semantics of an SSADM requirements specification is a class of information systems which differ only in technical detail. Therefore a SPECTRUM specification for a given SSADM requirements specification should have the same kind of semantics, but within a precise mathematical framework.

The options are here:

> *Option 1: Syntactic reference.* The syntactical structure of the notations of SSADM (their allowed elements and their formation rules) are represented on a more abstract level, within a formal language.

> *Option 2: Semantic reference.* In addition to representing the syntax of SSADM, properties of the syntactical objects are described. For this purpose, the objects making up the semantics of SSADM are specified and related to the syntactical objects.

Obviously, we follow option 2 within this work.

As a simple illustrating example for the difference between syntactical and semantical reference, consider the well-known "diagram" shown in figure 5.5: An analog clock as it might appear for instance on a computer or TV screen.

Figure 5.5

A syntactic reference to this diagram extracts the essential information contained in it. The information is in this case a tuple which gives the positions of the two clockhands. We assume that the clock has 60 discrete positions for every clockhand (so it is a digital clock, in fact). In SPECTRUM, the information of the clockface then is represented as an abstract sort with a partial constructor function.

> **sort** Clock;
> mkClock: Nat × Nat → Clock;
> hour, minute: Clock → Nat;   hour, minute **total**;
> Clock **generated by** mkClock;

This specification contains only syntactical functions for constructing a value of sort Clock (mkClock) and for observing the syntactical information contained in such a representation (hour, minute). A few axioms are needed which also express only syntactical information:

> δ mkClock(h, m) = (0 ≤ h) ∧ (h ≤ 59) ∧ (0 ≤ m) ∧ (m ≤ 59) ∧ (h mod 5 = m div 12);
> c = mkClock(h, m) ⇒ hour(c) = h;
> c = mkClock(h, m) ⇒ minute(c) = m;

This specification defines which abstract values are admitted to represent clockfaces (using SPECTRUM's definedness predicate δ). The restriction h mod 5 = m div 12 captures the fact that the relative position of the small clockhand within the sector of one hour corresponds to the minute within the actual hour, as shown by the large clockhand. Such a syntactic reference may be useful for some purposes; for instance it is sufficient for translating the information into another representation. However, the description form above does not answer the question what the meaning of some actual clock picture is.

For a semantic reference, the objects and concepts must be introduced by which the meaning of the syntax under consideration is to be expressed. In the small example, the meaning of a clock picture can be seen as a point in time between noon and midnight (or between midnight and noon, respectively). In order to deal with such a semantic concept formally, we have to give a specification for it. In the example, the semantic concept can be simply modelled by a number between 0 and 720, which indicates the minutes passed after noon (or midnight, respectively). This leads to the following specification of a function passedMins:

passedMins: Clock $\rightarrow$ Nat;   passedMins **total**;

c = mkClock(h, m) $\Rightarrow$ passedMins(c) = 60 * (h div 5) + m;

The approach of a semantic reference adds a second level of objects to the formalization of the syntax under consideration, together with a translation of the syntactical objects into this second level. In a puristic view, also the second "semantical" level is of a syntactical (formal) nature, so in fact we give a mapping between two representations. However, the second representation usually has a closer connection to the intuitive understanding of the original syntax. Whether the specification of the semantic level and the translation are "correct" cannot be proven but only judged on the basis of informal explanations.

For SSADM, we introduce in chapter 6 a semantic level in form of a very simple specification of the essentials of an information system. For most of the notations in SSADM, we give a formal syntax and a specification of the semantics with reference to the generic specification of an information system. So the formal semantics of an SSADM specification is a class of algebras in the SPECTRUM semantics, each of which represents an information system adequate for the SSADM specification.

5.3.4 Meta-Language vs. Mathematical Framework

We have made clear above that we use SPECTRUM for defining the semantics of SSADM. However, also this decision is one out of several options. One could think of other frameworks which may be more adequate for our purposes. A very general decision is here whether to use any pre-defined language at all or whether to stay within the general framework of mathematics.

Option 1: Using a mathematical framework. The flexibility of the general language of mathematics can be useful in describing the features of a rich and powerful specification formalism like SSADM. In particular, for each of the concepts in SSADM, the most adequate mathematical formalism could be used (for instance, set theory for Logical Data Models and temporal logic for Entity Life Histories).

Option 2: Using a pre-defined specification framework. In contrast, a specification language like SPECTRUM can be used which has its own fixed formal syntax and a semantics which is again based on mathematical concepts. This gives a more homogeneous semantics definition.

There are good arguments in favour of each of these options. The main advantage of the first option is that it gives a definition of semantics which builds on the notational background developed in mathematics and therefore can help in classifying the ingredients of a method like SSADM. It may be more helpful to know that entity life histories are a kind of temporal restriction than to have a large set of axioms which encodes the same information within a particular logical language.

However, if various mathematical formalisms are combined, we have to struggle with the question whether the combination still is sensible and consistent. The combination of logical theories can easily lead to a situation which has no sensible semantics at all. In contrast, a pre-defined specification language comes with its own notion of consistency, and therefore a clear criterion exists whether the actual semantics still is sensible. Moreover, a framework like SPECTRUM is oriented towards programming and features a notion of implementation between specifications and executable programs. So the investigation of executable prototypes for a pragmatic specification can be dealt with appropriately. And finally, if the pure definition of semantics is to be extended to a hybrid specification method (combined from pragmatic and formal notations), it is advantageous to have a translation of the pragmatic notations into a formal specification language, which can easily be extended by additional formal text.

We have decided to use the pre-defined specification language SPECTRUM as our framework. In order to profit from the advantages of this decision, we concentrate in our semantical investigation on the question how to check the consistency of an SSADM specification and on the creation of correct prototype programs. We also try to explain the mathematical concepts behind each SSADM notation on the basis of our formal semantics. However, a general conceptual framework for analysing pragmatic methods and relating them to known mathematical concepts is beyond the scope of this study.

Options among the pre-defined specification frameworks: Also among the pre-defined specification languages, there is a whole range of languages which can be seen as alternatives to SPECTRUM. The main advantage some languages have over SPECTRUM is that they provide "built-in" support for specifying the structure and updates of a system state, which is a central concept for an information system. A typical example of a relatively pragmatic alternative of this kind is the mathematically founded requirements modelling language RML [GBM86]. But also several algebraic languages contain a concept of dynamically evolving algebras which can be used to represent a system state, for instance the COLD family of languages [FJ92]. Obviously, these object-oriented languages are good candidates for a meta-language for SSADM-F. However, the absence of any state concept in SPECTRUM can also be seen as an advantage. Since SPECTRUM is relatively close to plain predicate logic, it is a very general integration platform which can accommodate virtually every specification formalism besides SSADM-F. This is the reason why Zave and Jackson [ZJ93] also use predicate logic as the basis for multi-paradigm specifications. Moreover, the explicit treatment of a state also leads to an explicit dicussion of difficult topics in object-oriented modelling languages, like identification of objects.

5.3.5 One-Level vs. Two-Level Translations

The semantic foundation of SSADM obviously leads to the definition of a translation mechanism which takes the diagrammatic notations of SSADM as input and produces parts of algebraic specifications as output. An example for such a translation has already been given above in section 5.1.3, where an ER diagram (figure 5.2) was translated into a SPECTRUM specification of functions working on a system state. As it was mentioned there, this translation has a number of disadvantages:

- The translation from the diagram into the specification is rather complex and must be described outside the formal framework. A more direct representation of the diagrams would be preferrable.

- The specification does not separate project-specific and method-specific concerns. In particular, if the generated algebraic specification is changed, it is difficult to translate these modifications back to the pragmatic notation.

- The specification does not resemble the idea of semantic reference. For this purpose, it should distinguish between an abstract syntax for SSADM documents and a general semantic reference specification for SSADM.

Formulated as options, the question is whether the specifications obtained from the diagrams will be internally structured into a meta-level and an object-level or not.

> ***Option 1: One-level translation.*** The notations of SSADM-F are translated directly into a monolithic SPECTRUM specification, as it was done above for figure 5.2. The resulting specification does not refer explicitly to the notions of SSADM (like "entity" or "event"), but defines project-specific instances for them. Figure 5.6 gives a visualization of a one-level translation.

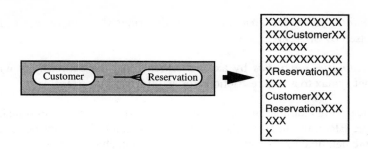

Fig. 5.6

Option 2: Two-level translation. In this option, the formal specification obtained from an SSADM-F specification is structured into two levels. The first level defines the concepts of SSADM (like "entity" or "event") in a formal specification which is independent of any specific project. We will refer to this level below as *method level*. The method level provides a SPECTRUM representation for all notational elements of SSADM-F.

On the second level, which we will call *project level*, actual SSADM-F documents taken from a specific project are represented within SPECTRUM, using the framework provided by the method level specification. Figure 5.7 gives a visualization of such a two-level translation.

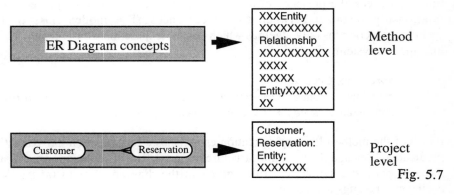

Fig. 5.7

Please note that the two-level translation explicitly provides identifiers for the concepts of the method (like "entity") within the formal specification. Such identifiers do not exist in a one-level translation.

We follow here the paradigms of two-level translation and semantic reference. In our approach, a method level specification for SSADM-F contains the following parts:

1 An *abstract syntax* for the documents (including diagrams) of SSADM.

2   A *semantic reference structure* which describes the general kind of system addressed by SSADM.

3   An *axiomatic semantics* by axioms which links the expressions within the abstract syntax to actual restrictions for an information system.

As an illustrating example, we show here some parts of a two-level translation for the sample ER diagram from above. Only the general idea is introduced here, a much more detailed discussion of the topic is given in chapters 6 and 7.

The *method level* specification, part 1, gives an abstract syntax for ER diagrams. It contains two sorts Entity and Relationship and a predicate relates. The predicate relates is a representation of the lines in the diagram (each of which connects two entities and carries a name). We ignore for this example the additional information about a second name and the variants of the line (dashed line, crow's foot).

> **sort** Entity, Rel;
> related: Rel → Entity × Entity;   related **total**;

In part 2, the simple reference concept of a system state is defined. A system state is structured into smaller parts which are called *occurrences*. Two observation functions check the presence of an occurence in the state and the presence of a relationship instance between two occurrences. The model class of this specification contains only algebras which resemble these most basic features of an information system.

> **sort** State, Occurrence;
> contained: State × Occurrence → Bool;   contained **total**;
> connected: State × Rel × Occurrence × Occurrence → Bool;

Part 3 of the method level specification establishes a link between the syntactical predicate relates and the semantic structure of part 2. The observations on any state have to obey the syntactical rules given in the diagram. For instance, every occurrence belongs to an entity.

> entity: Occurrence → Entity ;   entity **total**;

Here "occurrence" is a semantic notion and "entity" a syntactical one. Similarly, every relationship instance has to obey the syntactical rules about the involved entities.

> (*)   connected(s, r, o1, o2) ∧ related(r) = (e1, e2) ⇒
>   entity(o1) = e1 ∧ entity(o2) = e2 ;

On the *project level*, the information given in figure 5.2 is translated in a one-to-one fashion into the abstract syntax for ER diagrams. The translation illustrates the fact that Entity and Rel are just syntactical sorts: The project level specification just names the constants belonging to the syntactical sorts and states their (syntactical) interconnections.

```
customer, reservation: Entity;
        Entity freely generated by customer, reservation;
holds: Rel;
        Rel generated by holds;
related(holds) = (customer, reservation);
```

If the method level and the project level specifications are composed, the abstract axiom from above leads to actual restrictions on the sort State. The model class of the composed specification now contains only algebras which resemble the basic features of an information system and which coincide with the given ER diagram. For instance, the following situation is forbidden, where the "holds"-relationship connects two "Customer" occurrences:

```
connected(s, holds, o1, o2);  entity(o1) = customer;  entity(o2) = customer;
```

If these axioms are added to the axioms from above, a contradiction can be deduced. The semantic axiom (*) entails that entity(o2) = reservation, however from the "free" generation of the Entity sort follows that customer ≠ reservation. So these axioms together cannot be valid for any model of the formal specification.

Two-level translations are more complex than one-level translations. However, they are more adequate for our purposes, due to the following reasons:

- There is a trivial two-way translation from the pragmatic representation into formal expressions (the project level specification) and backwards. Therefore also changes to the generated specification do not prohibit a reverse translation into a diagram.

- Various interesting considerations do only involve the notions of the method and are independent of any project-specific information. The most important example is the proof that some set of conditions ensures the consistency of the whole specification for any project-level instantiation[4]. In a two-level translation, such a schematic proof can be carried out within the SPECTRUM framework. In the one-level variant, the translation process itself had to be included into the arguments, which is described outside the SPECTRUM language.

---

4   See chapter 9 for a detailed discussion of the topic of consistency.

5.4 Comparison with Other Approaches

There is relatively few literature on the integration of pragmatic and formal methods; a partial overview is given in [SFD92]. In this section, a representative selection of related work will be briefly surveyed. The alternative options which were discussed in the last section are used as a classification scheme here.

5.4.1 The SAZ Project

The project "SSADM and Z (SAZ)" at the University of York [PWK93, SAZ94] is very close to this work in the general topic, but differs in its aims. The SAZ project aims at a compound method integrating the formal specification language Z [Spi92] with the SSADM method.

In SAZ, two alternative uses of Z are proposed:

- Z can be used for an independent development, which is only loosely coupled to the SSADM development and serves for purposes of quality control.

- Z can be used as an additional notation to replace some of the textual parts in SSADM documents.

Using the terminology of section 5.3 above, SAZ clearly follows the complementarity paradigma, so it does not try to provide a formal foundation of SSADM. Instead, the methodical framework of SSADM is extended in such a way that a complete Z specification of the system of interest can be obtained without leaving the terminology and the procedural guidelines of SSADM. For this purpose, new steps and tasks are added to the procedural prescriptions of SSADM, which cover the transition from pragmatic to formal notation. Only for a few basic SSADM notations (mainly the Logical Data Model), schematic translation rules into Z are given. Interestingly, for these translations a prototype tool has been developed which is based on the CASE tool *System Engineer* (by LBMS).

The SAZ method can be seen in various ways as complementary to the work presented in this book. SAZ pays careful attention to the procedural integration of formal methods into the SSADM framework, whereas this work leaves the procedural aspects of original SSADM. SAZ does assume members of the development team to be educated in formal methods, whereas this work aims at a solution which can also be applied without any knowledge of formal methods. SAZ leaves the semantics of the original SSADM notation as informal as it is, whereas this work tends towards the development of a refined and "semantically clean" variant of the SSADM notations.

To summarize, the SAZ method is a solution which is ready for experimental application combining the current state of the art in pragmatic and formal methods, whereas this work is a first step towards a deeper integration of the semantic background of pragmatic and formal methods.

5.4.2 Semantic Foundation by One-Level Translations

Structured Analysis

Most of the existing literature on formal foundations for pragmatic notations addresses mainly Structured Analysis, that is DeMarco-style data flow diagrams. In SSADM, data flow diagrams have a less prominent role than in classical Structured Analysis, therefore only a small part of this book (chapter 11) is devoted to data flow diagrams. Most work published on the formalization of data flow diagrams follows the foundation (and not the complementarity) paradigm, but uses one-level translations.

France and Docker [FD89] present an axiomatic semantic reference specification for data flow diagrams. They distinguish between an abstract syntax ("picture level") and the semantic translation ("specification level"). However, the relation between the abstract syntax and the semantic specification is not made explicit; the translation still is described in a one-level style. The techniques used in [FD89] are oriented towards data flow diagrams with control flow extensions, as defined in [War86]. In [Fra92], a formal semantics for these control-extended data flow diagrams is worked out in more detail, using the formal state transition systems of SMoLCS [AR87] to represent the dynamics of a data flow graph.

A translation from classical Structured Analysis to VDM [Jon90] is described in [FKV91]. Here the result of the translation is intended as the starting point of a further development; the developer is expected to refine the result of a translation manually into a good formal model.

In [PvKP91], two variants for a (one-level) translation of classical data flow diagrams into VDM are presented, pointing out the decisions to be taken in giving such a foundation. One of these approaches is discussed in more detail in [LPT94] for purely sequential systems. This is one of the few papers which uses the specification language also for the description of the transformation itself; and in this sense is close to a two-level semantics as described above.

A Petri net semantics is assigned to data flow diagrams in [TP89]. Again, the semantics is only adequate for a slightly extended form of data flow diagrams (on the logical disjunction or conjunction of data flows), which provides more information than the naïve and informal way data flow diagrams are used in SSADM. Under similar assumptions, a stream-oriented semantics for data flow diagrams is proposed in [NW93].

In [PHP+94], an impressive demonstration of ambiguities and weaknesses of semi-formal notations in Real-Time-extended Structured Analysis is given; and it is shown how a formal semantics can help to clarify these situations. For this purpose, a purely mathematical semantics is employed instead of a particular specification language.

To summarize, the investigation of semantic foundations for data flow diagrams is relatively well developed, but most approaches concentrate on some kind of extension of the basic notation towards control flow and concurrency.

Data Modelling

Also for the technique of Data Modelling by Entity-Relationship Diagrams, which itself has good theoretical foundations, several approaches can be found in the literature for an integration with formal specifications. For instance, a model-theoretic semantics (in the style of algebraic specifications) is given to extended ER schemas in [Gog89]. This approach uses pure mathematics to formulate the semantics. One-level translation schemes from ER diagrams into a formal specification language (Z) are studied in [Gin92] and partially also in SAZ [PWK93]. A (one-level) translation of ER diagrams to SPECTRUM is given in [Het93].

5.4.3 Syntactic Approaches

The work of [Tse91] is relatively close to our work in its subject. It studies Structured Analysis (Data Flow Diagrams), Structured Design (Structure Charts) and Jackson Structures within an algebraic framework. Using the terminology from above, [Tse91] gives a purely syntactic reference for the various methods studied there. It contains interesting results about the mutual transformation of syntaxes used in software engineering methods, in particular on the detection of structured parts (in the sense of Structured Programming) within data flow diagrams. However, the semantic coincidence of the notations is not discussed there; it remains a matter of intuitive interpretation.

In this context, a whole research area should be mentioned which tries to establish a single syntactic framework (meta-model) to represent the information contained in commonly used diagrams and tables. This work aims mainly at the construction of a syntax which can represent different notations from different methods and on translation of the notations into this reference syntax; it follows option 2.2 from above. Examples are the "methodology engineering" approach [HÖ92] or the attempts to integrate different CASE tools, for instance in IBM's AD/Cycle Repository Manager. These syntactic references may *use* notations like "entity" or "event" within the reference syntax, but they do not *define* them further. Syntactic reference relies on an implicit and informal understanding of the meaning of the representations it uses.

Chapter 6

A Semantic Reference Specification for SSADM

This chapter shows how the axiomatic foundation for SSADM will be structured based on the decisions and ideas from the last chapter. A first section discusses the general organization of the SPECTRUM specification providing a formal foundation for SSADM. The subsequent sections define in detail the abstract specification of an information system which is used as a "semantic reference" throughout the rest of this book.

This and several other chapters (in particular 7, 8 and 11) will give a more detailed explanation of the actual syntax of SSADM documents and their semantics. Each of these chapters is based on the framework set in this chapter, but is dedicated to one of the main techniques of SSADM and its notations.

6.1 Architecture of the Formal Basis for SSADM

In this and other chapters below small pieces of SPECTRUM code are spread over the text, which can be assembled to a large but well-structured specification. In this section the overall organization of this specification is introduced.

The axiomatic semantics definition is structured following the approach which was motivated in the last chapter. So the basic parts of a two-level semantic foundation are:

1 A *method level specification* which exists once for a method – it is independent of any particular project instance carried out in the method.

   The method level specification consists of:

   1.1 A *semantic reference specification* which abstractly describes the most important features of the kind of systems which are addressed by the method. In the case of SSADM, this is an abstract specification of information systems.

   1.2 A specification of an *abstract syntax* which closely resembles the notations of the method. In the case of SSADM, the abstract syntax comprises notations like ER diagrams or Entity Life Histories. Since the method level specification is independent of any project instance, this specification just describes the syntactical possibilities, and not the way how they are actually used in a project.

   1.3 An *axiomatic semantics* for the notations referring to both the abstract syntax and the semantic reference specification. The purpose of these axioms is to specialize the class of specified systems to a specific project. In order to be still project-independent, these axioms refer to the abstract syntax; a specialized specification effect is achieved as soon as the method level specification is combined with a specific project level specification.

2 A *project level specification* which follows the abstract syntax defined in (1.2) and which represents in a simple one-to-one fashion the pragmatic notations of a specific project (like the Hotel Agency project).

Figure 6.1 tries to visualize the main specification parts involved in such an approach. In this figure, REF symbolizes the semantic reference specification (1.1), SYN the abstract syntax specification (1.2), SEM the axiomatic semantics (1.3) and PRO the project level specification (2).

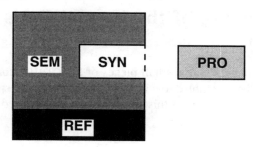

Fig. 6.1

As indicated graphically in figure 6.1, the method level specification depends on a project level instantiation, in order to actually describe a class of information systems. Two "stand-alone" specifications can be found in this setting:

- The semantic reference specification (REF) alone specifies (in the SSADM case) the class of all information systems, from an abstract viewpoint.

- The instantiated specification of REF, SEM and PRO together, where PRO follows the guidelines of SYN, specifies the class of information systems which are adequate for a particular SSADM requirements specification (like the Hotel Agency). (See figure 6.2.)

The abstract syntax specification (SYN) therefore serves as a *formal parameter* which defines constraints for instantiations such that the whole instantiated specification has a clear semantics. In SPECTRUM notation, this can be written as:

REF = { *semantic reference specification (1.1)* }

SYN = { *abstract syntax specification (1.2)* }

SEM =   **param** X = SYN
           body {
           enriches X+REF;
           axiomatic semantics (1.3)
           }

PRO = { *project level specification (2)* }

ReqSpec = SEM(PRO)

During the rest of this text, we do not apply this rather complex syntax, but we will always mark clearly which part of the whole system is currently addressed.

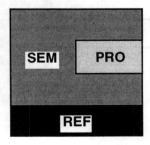

Fig. 6.2

A complex specification and development method like SSADM comprises an abundance of different textual and graphical notations. They are organized in

SSADM into three groups, corresponding to the main techniques present in SSADM. As it was already mentioned in chapter 3, the three techniques are:

- Data Flow Modelling (DFM), for early sketches of the functionality of the system and its environment. The central notation in this technique is the Data Flow Diagram (DFD).

- Logical Data Modelling (LDM), to describe the static structure of the data held by the system and to provide an integration basis for the other techniques. The central notation is here the ER diagram, accompanied by entity descriptions.

- Entity-Event Modelling (EEM), for a detailed description of the dynamic behaviour of the system. Central notations are here the Event-Entity Matrix, the Entity Life Histories (ELHs), and the Effect Correspondence Diagrams (ECDs).

In order to achieve an acceptable balance between formal definitions and general discussion in this book, only two of these techniques will be formally defined in full detail. We have chosen the notations of LDM and EEM for a full-scale presentation. This part of SSADM is sufficient for a complete specification of an information system, whereas DFM serves for early sketches during the process of requirements analysis. For LDM and EEM, in the chapters 7 and 8 all specifications will be given which are indicated in figure 6.1. DFM will also be covered formally (in chapter 11), but in a style which concentrates on the central ideas and leaves out some technical details.

For the central part of the foundation (LDM and EEM), the architecture of the whole system of specifications is as shown in figure 6.3.

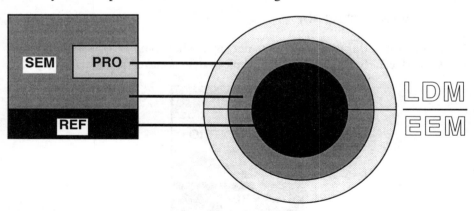

Fig. 6.3

The whole method level specification is depicted as a round area in figure 6.3, which is structured into concentric rings for different layers of the specification.

These layered rings represent the parts of the method level specification which have been identified above. In order to simplify the picture, we do no longer show the "plug-in" role of the abstract syntax specification (SYN). Instead, we have placed the abstract syntax specification (SYN/PRO) ast the top layer, where it forms the surface which is offered to specifiers working within the pragmatic notations. Between this outer ring and the semantic reference specification the "axiomatic semantics of notation" is placed, which links the syntactic layer with the reference specification.

Orthogonally to this ring structure, the specification is structured into sectors corresponding to various notations of SSADM. Obviously, two different parts of the specification are concerned with LDM and EEM; in the text these are the chapters 7 and 8. The LDM and EEM specifications (and the respective chapters) are again subdivided according to different notations, as shown in figure 6.4. Also within the reference specification different parts can be identified. The most central part of it is called the "core" reference specification. This core is extended by several abstract additions which are oriented towards a specific class of notations. In the case of SSADM, there are core extensions for LDM and EEM.

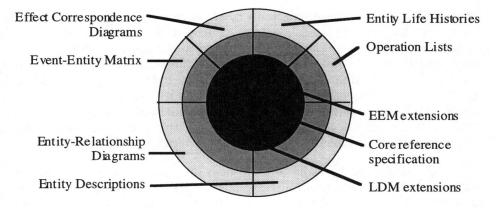

Fig. 6.4

The discussion above has been kept quite general, in order to encourage a reuse of the same structuring principles for the formal foundation also of other methods than SSADM. The next sections present the reference specification (core and extensions) which is specific for SSADM.

6.2 Core Reference Specification

This section defines the core part of the reference structure. The icon at the right margin of this paragraph indicates which area in figure 6.4 corresponds to this part of the specification. Icons of this style will be used throughout the chapters 6 to 8 as an orientation aid.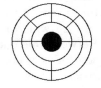

SSADM aims at the development of business information systems. A typical system to be developed with SSADM consists of a large database, which may be physically distributed over several locations, and many terminals which are used for input and output of data into or from the database. Physical distribution of the data base and the management of communication between the database and the terminals are design-oriented questions and are therefore completely ignored during the requirements specification stages. In practice, for many of these questions there exist ready-made solutions, so they even may not be subject of the software design, but are contained in the implementation platform.

This idea has been formulated very clearly by McMenamin and Palmer in their book "Essential Systems Analysis" [MP84], where it is recommended that a requirements specification should define a system model under the assumption of *perfect technology*. They have coined the term of "functional essence" for those functional elements which are still necessary under perfect technology. For finding the functional essence of the system under development, we should first assume that it will be sufficiently fast, stores sufficient amount of data and deals with physical distribution sufficiently well. This leads to a simple notion of a system and helps to manage the complexity of functional requirements.

The SSADM method basically follows these ideas. It proposes to introduce technical design decisions relatively late, and it contains a step which resembles the derivation of the functional essence: Step 150, which is called a "logicalization" activity in SSADM. Since SSADM uses such a logicalized view of the functionality, we feel encouraged to use a very simple semantic reference specification for SSADM which is indicated by figure 6.5.

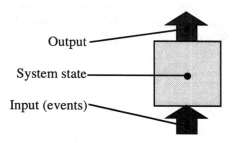

Fig. 6.5

As this figure shows, the most essential properties of an information system are that there is a (single) internal system state, that the system accepts some input and that it produces some output.

In SPECTRUM, this simple concept of a sequential system can be loosely specified as follows. There are three sorts corresponding to system state, input events and output.

> **sort** State, InpEv, Output;

We did not choose analogous sort names for input and output, since input events have another quality than output events. An input event, in addition to carrying data, marks a point in time when the input occurs and requires a reaction by the system. This aspect is not stressed for output, since we do not specify the reaction of the outer world in SSADM.

The system does not always accept any input event. Depending on the system state, a particular input event may be accepted or not. This is modelled by an "acceptance" (acc) predicate, which characterizes the situations (state plus input event) where the event is accepted. The output function out is partial (not every input event leads to some output), but if the output is defined, the event must have been accepted.

> acc: State × InpEv → Bool;   acc **total**;
> out: State × InpEv → Output;

The only axiom which is relevant for these two functions is the definedness condition for the acceptance predicate.

{C-1[1]} δ out(s, ie) $\Rightarrow$ acc(s, ie);

For all the axioms which belong to the full-deteil specification of SSADM (LDM and EEM parts) we use names as in this first example. Axiom names are written in SPECTRUM within curly brackets in front of the formula.

On the arrival of an accepted input event, the system state is transformed (see figure 6.6). The state transformation produces a new state out of an old one. In reality, this is closely connected to the progress of time, so figure 6.4 shown this as a dimension orthogonal to state structure and input/ output.

---

[1] As a convention for axiom names, the first letter indicates the chapter: C = Chapter 6 (Core), D = Chapter 7 (Data Modelling), E = Chapter 8 (Event Modelling).

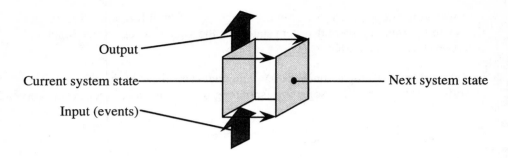

Output

Current system state —————————————— Next system state

Input (events)

Fig. 6.6

Formally, the function next derives from a state and an input event the successor state. The next state is defined if and only if the event is accepted.

next: State × InpEv → State;

{C-2}   δ next(s, ie) = acc(s, ie);

The triggering of state transformations by input events and their sequence in time are the aspects of a system which are most difficult to describe. Therefore many axioms are generated out of a SSADM specification for the purpose of further describing the core functions next and acc.

The overall behaviour of the system during a part of its functional life can be seen as a chain of state transformation steps. Each input event leads to another state which accepts the next input event. Moreover, some output may be produced on acceptance of an input event. In reality, the chaining of system states takes place within time. However we do ignore the dimensions of time here, as SSADM does. The case that two different events may happen exactly at the same time is simply excluded, we assume that one of them must be the first one. So we just study sequences of input events and their consequences on the system (see figure 6.7).

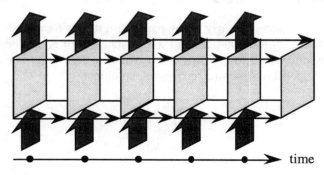

time   Fig. 6.7

Please note that this treatment of time does still admit the description of simple timing conditions. The completion of an hour (or a day or any other time unit) can be seen as an input event to the system which updates a data structure keeping the time and which may optionally cause other updates triggered by the actual time.

Formally, the chaining of system states can be seen as a simple derived function which works on a list of input events and a start state. The following function next* extends the state transition function next to lists of events.

next*: State × List InpEv → Bool;

{C-3a} next*(s, []) = s;
{C-3b} next*(s, [ie] ++ ui) = next*(next(s, ie), ui);

This completes the core specification for SSADM. An algebraic structure is included in the model class semantics of the core reference specification if it can be seen as a (very abstract) representative of an information system. The core specification has been kept as simple as possible, in order to avoid any unnecessary complexity during the axiomatic definition of the SSADM semantics.

For the two SSADM techniques which are studied in full detail, in the next two sections the necessary extensions of the core reference specification are defined. These extensions are the "hooks" for integrating the more detailed specification of the techniques and their notations. Besides this technical purpose, the short overview on the next few pages can be seen as a description of the way how the LDM and EEM techniques are semantically integrated in SSADM.

6.3 Core Extensions for Logical Data Modelling

Logical data modelling (LDM) is the name used in SSADM for the well-known Entity-Relationship approach. Chapter 7 below gives a detailed treatment of this technique. In this section, the basic framework for this exposition is provided, based on the core semantic reference structure.

LDM gives a *static* view on the data of the system. So it concentrates only on properties of the sort State from above; the functions acc and next are irrelevant here. The concepts for data modelling in SSADM basically rely on *state localization*. Localization is a quite important idea which is common to most user-oriented specification methods.

One of the fundamental principles in human understanding of complex problems is projection onto a single aspect. Localization is just a special case of this general principle, other variants of projection used in SSADM are the consideration of a single point in time or the abstraction from detailed update specifications. Localization is used by SSADM and other requirements specification methods to manage the complex states and state transitions which can occur in an information system. In particular, an appropriate treatment of the dynamic behaviour of an information system is broken down into the study of local behaviour of parts of the state[2]. This local study of behaviour is only possible if the underlying state concept supports the idea of describing a local part of the state.

In SSADM, the name for a localized part of a state is *(entity) occurrence*[3]. At a first view, occurrences are simply smaller parts of a large system state (see figure 6.8).

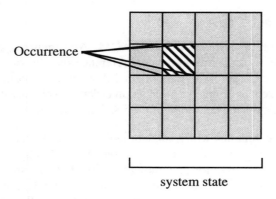

system state

Fig. 6.8

The purpose of occurrences is to localize and thereby ease the task of comparing complex states. Formally, occurrences are described by the SPECTRUM sort Occ.

     sort Occ;

For given system state, a test is needed whether a given occurrence is contained in the state. This can be modelled by a predicate on states and occurrences. We prefer here a higher-order function for the same purpose.

     contained: State → Occ → Bool;

{CD-1[4]} δ contained(s)(o);

---

2   See section 6.4 and chapter 8 for details.

3   We do not care about the more abstract notion of an entity for the moment (see chapter 7 for this).

4   As a convention for axiom names, the second letter, if present, indicates a special type of axiom. In the semantic reference specification, the two letters D and E are used for the core extensions to LDM and EEM.

Chapter 7 will give more details on state localization in SSADM; in particular the term of an occurrence will be related there with the concepts of ER modelling (entities and relationships), and the sort Occ will be refined to represent the internal record-like structure of occurrences in SSADM. At this later point, it will also become apparent what the advantages of the higher-order function are compared to a normal predicate.

An important semantic topic is whether the sort State for global system states is subject to later refinement. SSADM assumes the system state to be structured into occurrences and nothing else but occurrences. It is obvious that an information system must maintain various relationships between the occurrences in its system state. However, in SSADM all such inter-occurrence relationships are understood as local properties of the participating occurrences (technically spoken, as foreign keys). We can encode this principle of SSADM already at this early stage of formalization by the following simple axiom. The axiom says that two states are identical if and only if they contain the same occurrences. This can formulated compactly in SPECTRUM, where it is allowed to compare functions for equality.

{CD-2}   contained(s) = contained(s')   ⇔   s = s';

Axiom CD-2 does no longer admit models where relationships are additional parts of a system state, apart from the occurrences. However, a more execution-oriented implementation (for instance on a relational structure) is perfectly free to realize relationships as separate parts (for instance as tables), but it has to provide a level of abstraction where these implementation features are hidden.

It is an interesting observation that the axiomatic approach to semantic modelling provides quite simple and abstract means to define and discuss such properties of a specification method as the localization principle. Also other approaches, like the use of relationships as separate system components, could be specified in the same style; it is even possible to leave open the question of relationship representation to the implementation. We have decided here to be as specific as SSADM is.

6.4 Core Extensions for Entity-Event Modelling

Entity-event modelling (EEM) is a technique in SSADM which defines the dynamic aspects of a system. It describes the order in which events are allowed to occur and the parts of the system state which are affected by an event. Chapter 8 below gives a detailed treatment of this technique.

EEM specifies the *change* of states which are structured as specified by LDM. A state change takes place as the consequence of an input event, so EEM mainly deals with the relationships between a state, an input event and the next (changed) state of the system.

Also for the dynamic aspects, SSADM follows the idea of localization. Therefore, the changes of a system state are described on the level of the occurrences contained in the state.

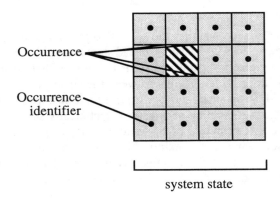

system state   Fig. 6.9

In particular, SSADM contains concepts to watch the progress made by a single occurrence over time. If the system state is changed and we want to observe what has happened to a particular occurrence, we need some mechanism which tells us which occurrence in the new state has evolved out of which occurrence in the old state. This is the reason why we postulate the existence of *occurrence identifiers*. In figure 6.9, the occurrence identifier of an occurrence is indicated by a dot which is meant as a "handle" for accessing the surrounding square.

Formally, we introduce a sort for occurrence identifiers and two functions, one for obtaining an occurrence by its identifier, and another one for testing whether the first function is defined, that is whether an occurrence identifer is bound in a state.

sort OccId;

get: State × OccId → Occ;
bound: State × OccId → Bool;   bound **total**;

{CE-1}   δ get(s, i) = bound(s, i);

There are different ways to partition a system state into smaller components where each component has an individual identifier. In SSADM, every occurrence contains a distinguished set of attributes which is called the *key value*. A key value is always unique within a global state, so for a given key value only a single occurrence with this key can be found. In object-oriented approaches (for instance [RBP+91]), special data sorts for identifiers are used which are independent of the contents of the occurrences (objects, in this case). For the general framework set by this chapter, we use an abstraction of both concepts. Chapter 7 below gives the specialization to the SSADM concept of key values. Both in SSADM and object-oriented approaches, each occurrence "knows about its identifier". We represent this general concept by a function which asks an occurrence for its identifier. Obviously, an occurrence can be retrieved from a state only under its own identifier.

$$\text{ident:} \qquad \text{Occ} \rightarrow \text{OccId}; \qquad\qquad \text{ident } \textbf{total};$$

{CE-2}   get(s, i) = o $\Rightarrow$ ident(o) = i;

The access to a system state via occurrence identifiers is a refinement of the more general concept of the contained predicate. The exact relationship is given by the following axiom.

{CE-3}   contained(s)(o) = ($\exists$ i. get(s, i) = o);

From the axioms CE-2 and CE-3 together, another definition of the contained predicate can be derived which avoids the use of an existential quantifier[5]:

$$\text{contained}(s)(o) = (\text{get}(s, \text{ident}(o)) = o)$$

If a system state changes into a new state, as indicated in figure 6.10, we can compare locally for every occurrence identifier whether the respective occurrence is updated.

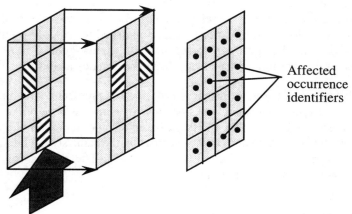

Affected
occurrence
identifiers

Fig. 6.10

---

[5]   This axiom uses the "strong equality" available in SPECTRUM. If ident(o) is not accessible, get(s, ident(o)) is undefined and therefore different to o.

There are several kinds of such updates: The occurrence identifier may be bound only in one of the two states (creation and deletion), or it may be bound in both, but the contents of the respective occurrences may differ. The updates in an information system will always be local to a relatively small set of occurrence identifiers. We call these identifiers the "affected" set of identifiers.

Formally, we use a predicate affects on an input event, a state and an occurrence identifier. For simplicity, we regard all the occurrence identifiers as unchanged which do not occur in both the current and the next state. Axiom CE-4 below states that every local state which is changed must be affected[6]. The inverse direction, however, should not be postulated, in order to conform with SSADM. It can be useful to call an occurrence identifier "affected" even if no actual change of the occurrence is observed. A typical situation illustrating this effect is that a user requests to change some data field, but then types in exactly the same value which was already stored in this field.

affects: State × InpEv × OccId → Bool;   affects **total**;

{CE-4}   (get(s, i) = get(next(s, ie), i)) ∨ affects(s, ie, i);

It is not sensible, however, to call an occurrence identifier "affected" by a state update, if it is accessible neither in the old nor the new state. This is expressed by the following axiom[7].

{CE-5}   affects(s, ie, i) ⇒ (bound(s, i) ∨ bound(next(s, ie), i));

There are several document types in SSADM by which a more precise specification can be given based on this general framework. The various cases of updates (creation, deletion, local modification) are distinguished in SSADM by the Event-Entity Matrix. The Effect Correspondence Diagrams give a more precise specification of the structure of the set of affected occurrence identifiers.

SSADM also has a notation to further specify the acc predicate, which defines in which cases an event is accepted by a system. This is the purpose of the so-called Entity Life Histories (ELHs). The ELHs are based on an observation of a local part of the system state over time and can be specified in the same style which was used above for defining the next* function (figure 6.7). The details for all these documents can be found in chapter 8.

---

[6] This is more obvious in the following logically equivalent formulation of CE-4: (get(s, i) ≠ get(next(s, ie), i)) ⇒ affects(s, ie, i).

[7] Formally, the axioms also admit it to call an occurrence identifier "affected", if it is accessible only in the current state and the next state is undefined. This turns out as useful in section 8.1.3 below.

Chapter 7
The SSADM Technique "Logical Data Modelling"

This chapter provides a formalization of the notations which are used in SSADM to describe the static data structure of an information system. Since SSADM uses a variant of the very common Entity-Relationship (ER) approach to data modelling, the material presented in this chapter can be easily adapted also to similar data modelling methods.

7.1 Entity-Relationship Diagrams

The Entity-Relationship (ER) approach to data modelling has been integrated very carefully into SSADM. This technique has its roots in the area of semantic database modelling. Due to its close connection with database design, it is nowadays used in practice frequently. Many different terminologies and notations have evolved from this practical use. In this book, the terminology and the graphical representation of SSADM (version 4) are used. However, most of the exposition can be carried over to other variants of the ER approach. In order to keep a slightly more general view of data modelling than pure SSADM, we discuss and adapt below some definitions from other literature on data modelling.

7.1.1 Entities

The literature on SSADM uses rather simple and vague definitions of the term of an entity. For instance:

> **Entity.** Something which is [of] interest to the organization, and which is described with stored data." [DCC92, p. 355]

A definition which is more fruitful for our purposes is given in a book on object-oriented analysis with the subtitle "Modelling the world in data" by Shlaer and Mellor [SM88]. If the word "object" is replaced in this definition by the word "entity", it reads as follows:

> "An entity is the abstraction of a set of real-world things such that:
> • all of the real-world things in the set – the occurrences – have the same characteristics
> • all occurrences are subject to and conform to the same rules."
>   (adapted from [SM88, p. 14])

This definition captures two different aspects which should be separated:

• From the *modelling* aspect, the definition says that an entity denotes a set of elements, which are called occurrences.

• From the *methodical* aspect, the definition gives some hints how entities can be used to model the real world by mathematical concepts.

For the purposes of this study, both aspects will be distinguished. For a formalization of the technique, only the first aspect (modelling) is of importance. The second (methodical) aspect is important in the sense that all heuristics and explanations which have been developed for the concept of an entity can be carried over easily to the more precise description of the concept within an axiomatic specification. But for the formal modelling, another aspect becomes important which is hidden in the above definition behind the word "abstraction". The question what an entity really *is*, is best answered by the simple reply: An entity is an identifier. This identifier is used as a symbol during the specification, and a particular interpretation (as a set of occurrences) is implicitly assumed for this symbol.

So for our purpose the following definition is appropriate:

> ***Definition: Entity.*** An *entity* is an identifier, which is to be interpreted as a set of elements which are called the *occurrences* of the entity.

The graphical notation in SSADM for an entity is a box with rounded corners which is labelled by the name of the entity, as shown in figure 7.1.

$$\boxed{\text{Customer}}$$

Fig. 7.1

7.1.2 Relationships

A definition of "relationship" in the spirit of [SM88] is (please note that SSADM does support only binary relationships):

> "A relationship is the abstraction of a set of associations that hold systematically between different kinds of things in the real world. A (binary) relationship is said to associate two entities."

Analoguously to the argumentation from above, the following more usable definition can be obtained out of this:

> **Definition: Relationship.** A *(binary) relationship* is an identifier. To each relationship two entities are associated. A relationship is to be interpreted as a (binary) relation between the occurrences contained in the interpretation of the involved entities.

A relationship is denoted in SSADM by a line connecting two entities, which are labelled by two names at both ends. The two names are synonyms; their only purpose is to ease and standardize descriptions in natural language. If a statement is made about the entity E in its relationship to entity F, the name close to E can be chosen to achieve readable formulations. For instance, on the basis of figure 7.2 the following two formulations ("link phrases") are equivalent:

"Customer X holds reservation R." and
"Reservation R is reserved for customer X."

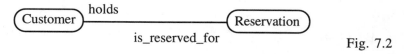

Fig. 7.2

In some other variants of the ER approach the notion of a relationship is generalized to n-ary relationships (relating n entities). The formalization given below can be easily adapted to such generalizations.

7.1.3 Relationship Qualifications

In SSADM, relationships can be further qualified in order to restrict the number of occurrences of an entity being associated by a particular relationship. If an entity E participates in a relationship to another entity F, the following cases are distinguished:

- If there is no restriction about the number of occurrences of entities E and F, the relationship is called "*many-to-many*" (n:m).

- If only one ocurrence of entity E can be associated with a given occurrence of entity F, but arbitrary many occurrences of entity F can be associated with a given occurrence of entity E, the relationship is called "*one-to-many*" (1:m). In this case, the entity E is called the *master* in the relationship, the entity F is called the *detail*.

- If, additionally, one and only one occurrence of the entity F can be associated with an occurrence of entity E, the relationship is called "*one-to-one*" (1:1).

The actual classification of a relationship according to this distinction is called the *degree* of the relationship in SSADM. The graphical representation of relationship degrees in SSADM uses the so-called "crow's foot" at the end of a (solid) line representing a relationship. If the crow's foot is present at the end pointing to entity E, many occurrences of entity E are allowed to participate in a relationship; otherwise only one. Figure 7.3 shows the three cases from above in this notation.

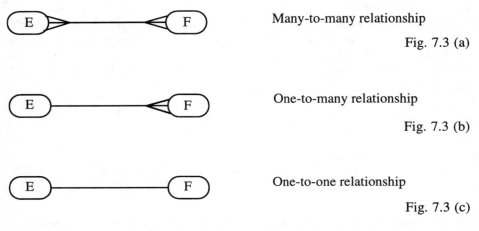

Many-to-many relationship

Fig. 7.3 (a)

One-to-many relationship

Fig. 7.3 (b)

One-to-one relationship

Fig. 7.3 (c)

SSADM does not encourage the use of many-to-many relationships. They are admitted only during early drafts of the logical data model. The formalization given below, however, will be sufficiently general to accommodate also many-to-many relationships without any problems. This is a first point where the formalized variant SSADM-F differs from SSADM.

In addition to its degree, a relationship is qualified in SSADM with respect to its *optionality*. If a relationship between entity E and F is *mandatory* for E, the existence of unrelated occurrences of E is forbidden. In this case, an occurrence of entity E has to be connected by the relationship to a F occurrence, as soon as it is created. The relationship can also be declared as *optional* for E. In this case, there may exist occurrences of entity F without an associated occurrence of entity E. Analoguously, the relationship can be declared as mandatory or optional also for the F entity. Figure 7.4 shows the graphical representation for optionality. If a relationship is optional for entity E, the part of the line pointing to E is shown as a dashed line.

Optional for E, mandatory for F

Fig. 7.4

The most common type of relationship is optional for its master, mandatory for its detail, and admits many details to participate, but only a single master. This is the only type of relationship which appears in the Required Logical Data Structure for the Hotel Agency example (see figure 7.6 below).

Finally, an additional restriction can be posed on two relationships, where relationship R1 associates entity E with entity F1 and relationship R2 associates entity E with entity F2. R1 and R2 are called *mutually exclusive* if for any occurrence of entity E either an occurrence of entity F1 is associated with it by R1 or an occurrence of entity F2 is associated with it by R2 (but never both). Figure 7.5 shows the graphical representation for mutually exclusive relationships by the so-called "exclusive arc".

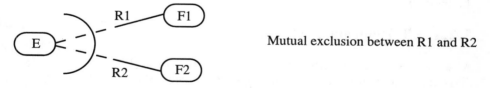

Mutual exclusion between R1 and R2

Fig. 7.5

Figure 7.6 below gives an example of a small ER diagram which is adequate for the Hotel Agency example. It obviously contains the entities "customer" and "hotel" to keep the data for the two main groups of correspondents of the agency. For each hotel, the agency keeps record of its quota of pre-booked rooms. The entity "reservation" obviously corresponds to a reservation for a specific hotel hold by a customer. The "request" entity is quite similar to a reservation, it corresponds to a customer request for which a reservation could not yet be given, and an enquiry was sent to the hotel. If a positive answer from the hotel arrives, the "request" occurrence is transformed into an occurrence of "reservation", otherwise it is removed.

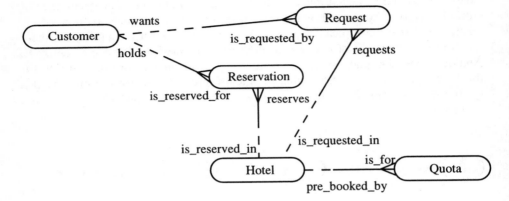

Fig. 7.6

7.2 Formalization of ER Diagrams

In this and the next section, we start to apply our formalization scheme to the notations of SSADM. We will give an abstract syntax for ER diagrams and we will relate these syntactical objects with the semantic reference specification from chapter 6. Since a complete treatment of all syntactical possibilities tends to get difficult to read, the abstract syntax is explained only by typical examples. A more complete translation scheme from the SSADM notations to SPECTRUM notation can be found in the last section of this chapter which contains a comprehensive reference to the formalization of LDM. The next chapter (on EEM) is organized in the same style.

7.2.1 ER Diagrams: Abstract Syntax

As a first step, we consider the graphical structure of an ER diagram. Following the ideas from chapter 6, we are going to embed the abstract information given by an ER diagram into a (method level) SPECTRUM specification. This means that we define a generic *parameter* specification which states requirements for the SPECTRUM representation of any actual diagram.

The syntactical structure is explained best by referring to an actual ER diagram. Figure 7.7 shows a part of the Logical Data Structure of the Hotel Agency which will be used as a running example here.

Fig. 7.7

Syntactically, the diagram contains the following information:

- It introduces a number of entity identifiers (customer, reservation, hotel).

- It introduces a number of relationship identifiers (holds, is_reserved_for, reserves, is_reserved_in).

- For each of the relationship identifers, the diagram defines two entity identifiers as participating in the relationship.

- For each entity identifier connected with a relationship, the diagram defines the degree of the connection (presence of a crow's foot) and the optionality of the connection (dashed line instead of solid line).

These syntactical items can be easily represented in SPECTRUM. For the entity identifiers, the project level specification representing the diagram is required to contain a sort Entity. The actual identifiers in the diagram can be defined as constants of this sort (by an enumeration type). For the generic parameter specification we are currently defining, it is sufficient to require that the sort exists and that there is a descidable equality predicate for it.

> **sort** Entity;   Entity:: EQ;

Analoguously, we require a sort Rel for the relationship identifiers. A function related captures the information which entities participate in a given relationship.

> **sort** Rel;   Rel:: EQ;
> related: Rel → Entity × Entity;   related **total**;

The totality of related is an example of an axiomatic requirement for the actual project level instantiation. Such a condition is quite similar to a "context condition" in classical programming languages. In this example, the totality requirement corresponds to the fact that every relationship must be connected at both ends in the diagram. Obviously, the semantics does make sense only for ER diagrams which fulfil this condition.

In the diagram, each line is labelled by two relationship names. The intended semantics for these pairs of identifiers is that they denote mutually inverse relationships. This information is captured by a function inv which delivers the inverse of a given relationship identifier.

inv: Rel → Rel;   inv **total**;

Obviously, the inv function has to obey a few simple conditions, and the related function must be defined consistently with the inv information.

{DS-1[1]}   inv(inv(r)) = r;
{DS-2}   inv(r) ≠ r;
{DS-3}   related(r) = (e1, e2) ⇔ related(inv(r)) = (e2, e1);

The information about degrees and optionality can be encoded quite simply, since each of the relationship names corresponds exactly to an "end" of a relationship line in the diagram. The presence of the crow's foot and the dashed line, respectively, are represented as Boolean attributes for these "ends" (where the presence of a crow's foot and the dashed line are indicated by a value of "true").

multiple, optional: Rel ↛ Bool;   multiple, optional **total**;

As an example, the entity information of the small ER diagram given in figure 7.7 can be represented by the SPECTRUM specification given in figure 7.8.

We have put this specification into a figure (and into a box) in order to distinguish it clearly from specification parts which were given above. The specification in figure 7.8 is no longer a generic parameter requirement, but an actual parameter instantiation fulfilling the requirements.

A more detailed definition of the translation mechanism from the diagram into such a representation can be found in section 7.5 at the end of this chapter. The example should be sufficient to convince the reader that such a translation is quite straightforward and easy to mechanize. A complete translation of figure 7.6 is given in appendix C (section C.1.1).

---

[1]   As a convention for axiom names, the second letter S indicates that the axiom is a syntactical requirement (context condition). The first letter D is used for all axioms in this chapter.

```
ER_Diag = {
          data Entity = customer I reservation I hotel;
          data Rel = holds I is_reserved_for I reserves I is_reserved_in;

          inv:                Rel → Rel;
          related:            Rel → Entity × Entity;
          multiple, optional: Rel → Bool;

          axioms
          inv(holds) = is_reserved_for;
          inv(is_reserved_for) = holds;
          inv(reserves) = is_reserved_in;
          inv(is_reserved_in) = reserves;
          related(holds) = (customer, reservation);
          related(is_reserved_for) = (reservation, customer);
          related(reserves) = (reservation, hotel);
          related( is_reserved_in) = (hotel, reservation);
          multiple(holds) = false;      multiple(is_reserved_for) = true;
          multiple(reserves) = true;    multiple(is_reserved_in) = false;
          optional(holds) = true;       optional(is_reserved_for) = false;
          optional(reserves) = false;   optional(is_reserved_in) = false;
          endaxioms; }
```

Fig. 7.8

To represent exclusive arcs, it is convenient to introduce an additional sort of *arc identifiers*. This convention is also recommended by textbooks on SSADM for more complex diagrams. The sort ExclArc provides arc identifiers and the function crossed gives for an arc the set of relationships crossed by it[2].

```
          sort ExclArc;        ExclArc:: EQ;
          crossed:             ExclArc → Set Rel;         crossed total;
```

There are a few conditions which have to be met by exclusive arcs. On one hand, all the relationships crossed by an arc must be connected to the same entity. On the other hand, it does not make sense to cross a mandatory connection with an arc. The semantics of a mandatory connection requires the relationship to be present, whereas the semantics of the exclusive arc admits it to be missing (if another variant is chosen). To avoid this contradiction, we require the crossed relationship ends to be optional. This is an example for a clarification of SSADM notation (into SSADM-F) which was triggered by the semantic analysis[3].

---

[2]   See appendix D for a SPECTRUM definition of polymorphic finite sets.

[3]   However, it would be also possible to formalize any other definition of the semantics for such a situation. We have chosen a definition which leads to simple semantic axioms.

{DS-4}   r1 ∈ crossed(c) ∧ r2 ∈ crossed(c)
            ∧ related(r1) = (e11, e12) ∧ related(r2) = (e21, e22)
            ⇒ e11 = e21;
{DS-5}   r ∈ crossed(c) ⇒ optional(r);

This completes the syntactic representation of Logical Data Models. We are now ready to discuss the definition of axiomatic semantics.

7.2.2 ER Diagrams: Axiomatic Semantics

Based on the abstract syntax, we can now define an abstract axiomatic semantics for ER diagrams. The specification given here is an enrichment of the reference specification for information systems from chapter 6. The new axioms use the semantic terms from chapter 6 as well as the SPECTRUM encoding of ER diagram syntax. They define the constraints to an information system which are expressed by an ER diagram.

The definition of an entity states that an entity name is to be interpreted as a set of occurrences. The definition leaves open subtle questions as whether such sets may overlap, that is whether a single occurrence may belong to two different entities. From the data modelling background of SSADM it is obvious that the sets of occurrences are meant to be pairwise disjoint.

Moreover, we have to merge this semantic idea with the basic concept of an information system which was defined in chapter 6. In particular, the sort Occ has been defined there. The interpretation of the sort Occ in any model of the specification is a set of occurrences. In this context, the interpretation of the syntactic concept of entities can be made simpler. A mathematical description for entities is now a (disjoint) classification of occurrences. For every occurrence (whether it is actually present in the system state or not), an entity (name) is defined to which the occurrence belongs. This is formally achieved by the function entity.

           entity: Occ → Entity;   entity **total**;

The totality requirement for entity is a first example for a semantic axiom. In every model which fulfils both the axioms of the semantic reference specification and this axiom, any occurrence is required to belong to a particular entity. Obviously, this condition is generic, since it can be tested effectively only if the actual entities are given, that is after instantiating the syntax parameter to a project level translation of an ER diagram.

Generally, there are two different but equivalent approaches to a formal modelling of the relationship concept in ER diagrams. Either the relationship instances are considered as separate parts of a system state, which are different from entities, or the participation in a relationship is seen as a property of an occurrence itself, similar to an attribute. As it was already indicated in chapter 6, the semantics of SSADM adapts the second one of these approaches. This fact has been already encoded in the axiom CD-2 (see section 6.3).

In addition to the general localization principle, we would like to view a relationship instance as some kind of system-global object, as well. For this purpose, another observation function on system states is defined, which is quite similar to the contained function. Similar to entity occurrences, a system state contains relationship instances. A relationship instance is a binary predicate on occurrences. This can be expressed by a functional sort in SPECTRUM:

$$Occ \times Occ \rightarrow Bool;$$

The predicate connected takes a system state and a relationship identifier and delivers the corresponding relationship instance as a binary predicate.

$$connected: \quad State \times Rel \rightarrow Occ \times Occ \rightarrow Bool; \quad connected\ \textbf{total};$$

A relationship instance is allowed to connect two occurrences only if they belong to the entities which are named in the ER diagram for the respective relationship identifier. This is expressed by the following axiom.

{D-1} δ (connected(s, r) (o1, o2)) $\Leftrightarrow$ (related(r) = (entity(o1), entity(o2));

The models we are interested in have to fulfil both the general axiom CD-2 on state localization and the axiom D-1. The localization axiom entails that an occurrence has to store locally the information to which relationship instances it belongs. If the participation in a relationship instance is released or established, this means an update of the occurrence itself. The axiom D-1 additionally claims the existence of a more global view onto relationship instances. See chapter 9 for an explicit model construction which proves the consistency of these requirements.

Under no circumstances, it should be allowed for an occurrence in the system state to be related with another ocuurrence which is not contained in the same system state. This important property is often called *referential integrity*. Referential integrity is easily formalized by the following axiom.

{D-2}   connected(s, r)(o1, o2) $\Rightarrow$ contained(s)(o1) $\wedge$ contained(s)(o2);

We have formulated the function signature (using the higher-order facilities of SPECTRUM) in such a way that we can easily incorporate standard definitions from relational algebra into our semantics. For instance, the meaning of the inverse relationship names can be defined by specifying and using the concept of an inverse relation.

{D-3}   connected(s, inv(r)) = INV(connected(s, r));

The INV function is a higher-order operation on general binary predicates, the
definition of which is mathematical standard.

INV: $(\alpha \times \beta \to Bool)$ **to** $(\beta \times \alpha \to Bool)$;
{DA-1[4]} $INV(R) (x, y) \Leftrightarrow R (y, x)$;

The keyword **to** in the signature of INV is essentially equivalent to the function
arrow $(\to)$. SPECTRUM carefully distinguishes between general mathematical
functions, which are not required to be realizable by computer programs, and
functions which are meant to be implemented. The function arrow $\to$ covers only
implementable (to be more precise: continuous) functions. The keyword **to**
indicates that all mathematical functions are admitted; therefore it is adequate for
general mathematical concepts. This distinction is not yet important for the INV
function symbol, but it is necessary for some analogous auxiliary functions which
are introduced below.

Also the semantics of relationship degrees and optionalities can be mapped onto
concepts of relational algebra. However, these semantic definitions are of a slightly
different kind. The axioms which were given up to this point have constrained the
sorts of the semantic reference specification, like State and Occ. This means that
any system state and *any* occurrence at any time has to fulfill these axioms. It is not
adequate to model the degree and optionality restrictions in the same style. Such a
way of modelling would have the consequence that all update operations on system
states had to deliver states obeying the degree and optionality conditions. This is
only possible if the update operations get a rather complex syntax. A typical
example is the deletion of a whole set of ocuurences which are cyclically related by
mandatory relationships. In such a case, we would need an update operation which
deletes all affected occurrences and all affected relationship instances within a single
step. Besides being complex, such a solution does not agree with the notion of an
elementary update operation as it is used in SSADM (see chapter 8). So we define
predicates (relDegreeOK, relOptionOK and relExclOK) which test a system state
whether it fulfils the three classes of integrity conditions expressed in the ER
diagram. For all update operations for the system state, these integrity predicates
should be preserved as invariants.

relDegreeOK, relOptionOK, relExclOK: State $\to$ Bool;
relDegreeOK, relOptionOK, relExclOK **total**;

---

4   As a convention for axiom names, the second letter A indicates that this is an auxiliary axiom
    for defining the semantics. The first letter D is used for all axioms in this chapter.

In terms of relational algebra, the degree restrictions deal with the so-called *uniqueness* of a relation. Following [BW82], we call a relation between sets A and B *left-unique* if "no element of B is related to different elements of A."[5] This can be easily defined as a higher-order operation on general predicates.

L-UNIQUE: $(\alpha \times \beta \to$ Bool) **to** Bool;   L-UNIQUE **strong**[6];
{DA-2} L-UNIQUE(R) $\Leftrightarrow \forall$ x1, x2, y. R(x1, y) $\wedge$ R(x2, y) $\Rightarrow$ (x1 = x2);

The connection to our semantic specification puts together the uniqueness requirement with the syntactical information whether the crow's foot is present for a relationship in the diagram. If the crow's foot is missing at a relationship, the corresponding instance is required to be left-unique. Again the higher-order formulation of the connected function leads to a compact axiom.

{D-4}   relDegreeOK(s) $\Leftrightarrow \forall$ r. multiple(r) $\vee$ L-UNIQUE(connected(s,r));

In a similar way, the optionality restrictions can be formalized. This restriction is called *totality* in relational algebra. A relation R between sets A and B is called *left-total*, if each element of A is related to an element of B[7]. Since a SPECTRUM sort is not well-suited to specify a set of values precisely, we use an additional predicate to be precise about the domain of a relation.

L-TOTAL: $(\alpha \to$ Bool) $\times (\alpha \times \beta \to$ Bool) **to** Bool;   L-TOTAL **strong**;
L-TOTAL(D, R) $\Leftrightarrow (\forall$ x. D(x) $\Rightarrow \exists$ y. R(x, y));

The semantic axiom for ER diagrams is similar to the case of degree restrictions. If the relationship end is shown as a solid line in the diagram, then any corresponding instance is required to be left-total. The only difference is that we use here the function contained to provide the domain predicate. The totality restriction applies only to occurrences which are actually contained in the system state.

{D-5}   relOptionOK(s) $\Leftrightarrow \forall$ r. optional(r) $\vee$ L-TOTAL(contained(s), connected(s));

Finally, the concept of exclusive arcs can be mapped onto the *disjointness of domains* for general relations. Analogously to above, we have the following axioms.

---

[5] [BW82], p. 495.

[6] The keyword **strong** means for the mathematical function which is the interpretation of the given function symbol that is always defined, regardless of the definedness of the arguments.

[7] [BW82], p. 495.

D-DISJOINT: $(\alpha \times \beta \rightarrow$ Bool$) \times (\alpha \times \beta \rightarrow$ Bool$)$ **to** Bool;

$\qquad\qquad\qquad\qquad\qquad\qquad\qquad\qquad\qquad\qquad\qquad$ D-DISJOINT **strong**;

{DA-4}   D-DISJOINT(R1, R2) $\Leftrightarrow$ $\forall$ x, y1, y2: $\neg$ (R1(x, y1) $\wedge$ R2(x, y2));

{D-6}   relExclOK(s) $\Leftrightarrow$

$\qquad\qquad$ $\forall$ r1, r2. ($\exists$ c. r1 $\in$ crossed(c) $\wedge$ r2 $\in$ crossed(c) $\wedge$ r1 $\neq$ r2)

$\qquad\qquad\qquad$ $\Rightarrow$ D-DISJOINT(connected(s, r1), connected(s, r2));

The few functions and axioms which were given above are sufficient for a characterization of ER data modelling in SSADM. The style of this formal definition is very loose. Generally, the axioms are oriented towards essential observations on states instead of explicit construction for states. This corresponds well to the static nature of LDM. However, it must be kept in mind that the axiomatic specification, in its current state, does admit quite trivial models. For instance, a model is admitted where the sort State is realized by a single value and where contained(s)(o) is false for any occurrence o. Such a model corresponds to a completely empty database and therefore it must be admitted. The concepts of entity-event modelling (which are covered by chapter 8 below) provide additional axioms which force particular system states to actually contain specific occurrences. This refinement will rule out the trivial models of the LDM specification.

7.3 Entity Descriptions and Attributes

A Logical Data Model does not only name the entities, it also prescribes a detailed common structure for the occurrences of an entity. This detailed description of entities is not denoted diagrammatically in SSADM, but it is given by text which has to be filled in by the specifier into a standard form. The filled form is called an *entity description*. For each entity, a requirements specification has to provide an entity description.

The recommended form for an entity description in SSADM contains various fields for entering organizational information and information on non-functional properties of an entity (like expected average volume). Other fields repeat information on the participation of the entity in relationships, which is defined already in the ER diagram. The most important part of this form is a table listing the *attributes* belonging to the entity. Figure 7.9 shows an example of an entity description as far as it has been adopted for the formally based variant SSADM-F.

```
┌─────────────────────────────────────────────────────────┐
│  SSADM-F Entity Description                               │
│  ┌─────────────────────────────────────────────────────┐ │
│  │ Entity name    Customer                             │ │
│  └─────────────────────────────────────────────────────┘ │
│  ┌──────────────────────────┬────────────┬────────────┐  │
│  │ Attribute name           │ Mandatory  │ Primary Key│  │
│  ├──────────────────────────┼────────────┼────────────┤  │
│  │ Customer number          │     √      │     √      │  │
│  │ Customer name            │     √      │            │  │
│  │ Customer address         │     √      │            │  │
│  │ Credit card information   │     √      │            │  │
│  │ Date last request        │            │            │  │
│  └──────────────────────────┴────────────┴────────────┘  │
└─────────────────────────────────────────────────────────┘
```

Fig. 7.9

An *attribute* models a single characteristic possessed by all the things (occurrences) that were chosen to be modelled by a single entity [SM88]. This single characteristic is expressed by an attribute identifier which is similar to a normal variable which can store data values. An appropriate definition for attributes is:

> **Definition: Attribute.** An *attribute* is an identifier which is associated with an entity. An attribute of an entity is to be interpreted as a function mapping occurrences of the entity onto values of some data domain.

Similar to a relationship, an attribute of an entity may be *mandatory* or *optional*. If an attribute A of entity E is declared as mandatory, each occurrence of E must have a defined value for the attribute A. If the attribute A is optional, the value of A for an occurrence of E may also be undefined.

A group of attributes E is called a *unique key* if the attribute can be used to identify uniquely an occurrence of E within a system state. Two different occurrences of E with the same values for these attributes cannot coexist within a system state.

For the purposes of this study, we cover just the definition of a single group of key attributes (the *primary key*), whereas full SSADM admits several groups of key attributes for the same entity. Moreover, we do not enclose so-called foreign keys in the sample attribute descriptions. A foreign key is an attribute whose purpose is to give a refernce to another occurrence. Its value is a key value of an entity. We assume here that all information about references to other entities is given in the ER diagram by relationships and that the link information for an occurrence is kept implicit and separate from attributes. See chapter 9 for a detailed discussion of the internal structure of an occurrence.

At the present point, we are not specific about the data domain from which attribute values are taken. This is quite adequate for the practical use of SSADM, since during early steps of analysis attributes are often defined without giving a precise definition of the allowed values. In a later section (7.4.3), we will come back to the question of how to state domain restrictions for attributes.

7.4 Formalization of Entity Descriptions

In a worked-out Logical Data Model, each entity appearing in an ER diagram is accompanied by an entity description. In this section we define an abstract syntax which contains the same information as entity descriptions in SSADM, and assign an axiomatic semantics to it.

7.4.1 Abstract Syntax

An entity description is given as a table (see figure 7.10 above for an example). In our adaptation of SSADM, it contains for each entity a list of attribute names and the information whether the attribute is mandatory and whether it belongs to a primary key. This information can be encoded in a quite straightforward way within SPECTRUM.

The syntactical sort of attribute names is called Attr. The additional information given in the entity description is encoded by functions which deliver a set of attribute names. It is admitted to use the same attribute name within different entities.

> **sort** Attr;   Attr:: EQ;
>
> attrs, mandatory, primaryKey: Entity → Set Attr;
> attrs, mandatory, primaryKey **total**;

There are a few restrictions for these syntactical predicates. It is only sensible to call an attribute mandatory for an entity if it belongs to this entity. A primary key for an entity must be a mandatory attribute of the entity. Each entity must have a primary key. These three conditions are formulated by three axioms.

{DS-6}   mandatory(e) ⊆ attrs(e);
{DS-7}   primaryKey(e) ⊆ mandatory(e);
{DS-8}   primaryKey(e) ≠ emptySet;

The translation of an entity description into a project level specification is obvious. As an example for a project level specification, figure 7.10 contains the translation of figure 7.9 from above (using slightly abbreviated attribute names). A readable syntax within SPECTRUM can be achieved by giving a list representation of the sets together with the function set which translates a list into the corresponding set.

```
Customer_Descr = { strict total;
        enriches ER_Diag + SET;
        data Attr =
                custNo | custName | custAddress
                | creditCardInfo | dateLastRequest;

        attrs, mandatory, primaryKey: Entity → Set Attr;

        axioms
        attrs(customer) =
                set [custNo, custName, custAddress,
                        creditCardInfo, dateLastRequest];
        mandatory(customer) =
                set [custNo, custName, custAddress, creditCardInfo];
        primaryKey(customer) = set [custNo];
        endaxioms; }
```
Fig. 7.10

7.4.2 Axiomatic Semantics

We now define a further refinement of the semantic system model using the abstract syntax of entity descriptions. Essentially, (entity) occurrences are refined by observation functions for attribute values, and the meaning of the mandatory attributes and the primary key are fixed axiomatically.

On the semantic level, attributes belong to entity occurrences. Each entity occurrence may contain a value for each attribute in its entity description. To model this, we define a sort of attribute values and a function which asks for the value of an attribute for an occurrence. Since at this point we don not yet distinguish between attribute domains, the sort AttrVal corresponds to the "universe" of all possible attribute values.

```
        sort AttrVal;
        . @ . :          Occ × Attr → AttrVal;
```

There are two possible reasons why a particular attribute value for a given occurrence may be undefined. Either the attribute does not belong to the entity description or the value of the attribute has not been set yet. The function def serves for distinguishing these cases. The def function is defined if and only if the attribute belongs to the respective entity. If def has a defined (Boolean) value, it tells us whether an attribute value is available for the attribute.

　　　　　　def:　　　　　Occ × Attr → AttrVal;

{D-7}　　δ (def(o, a)) = (a ∈ attrs(entity(o)));
{D-8}　　δ (o @ a) = δ (def(o, a)) ∧ def(o, a);[8]

The definition of a primary key is a further constraint to system states. Within a system state, two occurrences of a given entity are identical as soon as they coincide in their primary key attributes.

{D-9}　　contained(s)(o1) ∧ contained(s)(o2) ⇒
　　　　　　　((o1 = o2) ⇔ (entity(o1) = entity(o2)) ∧
　　　　　　　　　　　　　　(∀ a. a∈ primaryKey(entity(o1))) ⇒ o1@a = o2@a)));

By this axiom we have fixed that an occurrence can be uniquely identified within a state by the primary key attributes. However, this is also the purpose of occurrence identifiers. The following formula can be derived now:

　　　　get(s, i1) = o1 ∧ get(s, i2) = o2 ⇒
　　　　　　((i1 = i2) ⇔　　(entity(o1) = entity(o2)) ∧
　　　　　　　　　　　　　　(∀ a. a ∈ primaryKey(entity(o1))) ⇒ o1@a = o2@a)));

This means that the information given by an occurrence identifier must be equivalent to the values of the primary key attributes. In an implementation, an adequate solution is to use the composition of the primary key values as occurrence identifiers (see chapter 9).

The optionality of attributes is quite similar to the optionality of relationships. Therefore, the same way of encoding is used. The predicate attrOptionOK tests whether all mandatory attributes in an occurrence are set.

　　　　attrOptionOK:　　　Occ → Bool;　　　　attrOptionOK **total**;

{D-10}　　attrOptionOK(o) ⇔ (∀ a. a ∈ mandatory(entity(o)) ⇒ def(o, a));

The reason why we did not simply claim by an axiom that every occurrence must obey the optionality restrictions for its attributes is similar as it was for the other ok-predicates above. We would like to admit an occurrence to be in an "intermediate" state where it exists already but where not all mandatory attributes have been set yet. If these occurrences were forbidden, it would not make sense to speak of the action "to set the primary key attributes for a newly created occurrence". This,

---

[8]　A semantic particularity of SPECTRUM (three-valued propositional logic) requires the use of a sequential variant of the logical ∧-operator here. In order to keep the text readable, we ignore this subtle difference here and in several other axioms.

however, is a phrase which is commonly used in SSADM (in operation lists, see section 8.5).

A different situation arises if we consider the occurrences which are contained in a system state. It is obviously necessary that such occurrences have defined values for their primary key attributes (otherwise the identification mechanism would not work properly)[9]. Therefore, we require for all occurrences which are contained in a system state that the primary key attributes are defined.

{D-11}   contained(s)(o) ∧ a ∈ primaryKey(entity(o)) ⇒ def(o, a) ;

These few axioms give a sufficient semantical characterization for the Logical Data Modelling part of SSADM. The only topic in LDM which remains to be discussed is the definition of domain restrictions for attribute values.

7.4.3 Integrating SPECTRUM's Sort System into Entity Descriptions

We have separated the topic of domain restrictions from the general discussion, because it shows some significantly new aspects of the integration between formal and pragmatic notations. Typical domain restrictions for the values of an attribute are "natural number" or "natural number between 1 and 99" or "string of length 10".

In order to achieve a thorough integration between the specification formalisms of SPECTRUM and SSADM, it would be desirable to take advantage of the strong built-in sort system of SPECTRUM. Unfortunately, the specification above has already assigned a sort to any attribute value: the general sort AttrVal. The generic treatment of SSADM constructs has lead to a specification on a meta level. It is relatively difficult to combine this meta-level sorts with the sort system which is adequate on the project level.

This difficulty could be overcome by using a more powerful type system than the one used in SPECTRUM. Using so-called *dependent types*, it is possible to refine the general sort AttrVal into a sort which is dependent on the actual attribute and the entity name, and so provides the correct sort for each case. However, we would like to stay within the framework of SPECTRUM for this study and therefore we present an approach which uses SPECTRUM's concept of sort classes for an acceptable solution.

We assume that the SSADM-F entity descriptions are extended by another column which indicates the domain restriction. In contrast to the constructs which were

---

[9]   This requirement is often called *entity integrity* in the literature on database systems [Dat90].

studied above, we do not define a fixed syntactical vocabulary here. Instead, it is assumed that the new column contains a SPECTRUM expression for a predicate over attribute values. Using the following sort synonym, the entries in this column must be of sort Domain.

> **sortsyn** Domain = AttrVal → Bool;

A separate specification ATTRVAL defines the sort AttrVal together with the necessary domain predicates. For most projects it will be sufficient to use a predefined standard specification for ATTRVAL. Figure 7.11 below introduces some of the most popular domain types, which are sufficient for the running example. However, the specification ATTRVAL can be adapted to project-specific needs; in this sense the two-level paradigm is weakened here. An adaptation of the ATTRVAL specification gives access to the full power of SPECTRUM for data type specification. Possible applications of this mechanism range from the usage of problem-specific (and easily modifiable) data domain identifiers to an integration of complex abstract data types.

The specification ATTRVAL makes extensive use of the functions which are automatically introduced by a SPECTRUM data declaration. This mechanism was explained in section 4.3.4.

```
ATTRVAL = {
        strict total;
        enriches Naturals + String;

        data AttrVal =
                natural(!natval: Nat) I string(!strval: String)
                I boolean(!boolval: Bool);
        sortsyn Domain = AttrVal → Bool;

        nat, bool, str: Domain;
        nat_in:        Nat × Nat → Domain;
        str_in:        Nat → Domain;

        axioms ∀ n, n1, n2: Nat; v: AttrVal in
        nat(v) = is_natural(v);
        str(v) = is_string(v);
        bool(v) = is_boolean(v);
        nat_in(n1, n2) (v ) = is_natural(v) ∧ (n1 ≤ natval(v)) ∧ (natval(v) ≤ n2);
        str_in(n) (v) = is_string(v) ∧ (length(s) = n);
        endaxioms;  }
```

Fig. 7.11

This simple ATTRVAL specification offers three constructs for defining standard data types and two constructs for defining finite domains of numbers and strings.

For practical applications, several extensions, for instance to floating point numbers and to a project-specific terminology of domains, should be added. Appendix C contains a variant of the ATTRVAL specification which has been adapted to the full Hotel Agency example.

An example of an SSADM-F entity description using domain definitions is given in figure 7.12.

SSADM-F Extended Entity Description

| Entity name   Customer |

Attribute name	Mandatory	Prim. Key	SPECTRUM Domain
Customer number	√	√	nat_in(0, 9999)
Customer name	√		str_in(20)

Fig. 7.12

In order to integrate these extensions into the framework from above, the abstract syntax of entity descriptions is extended by a function which corresponds to the new column.

attrDom: Entity × Attr → Domain;

{DS-9} δ attrDom(e, a) = (a $\in$ attrs(e));

On the semantic level, a single axiom is added which just postulates that any defined value of an attribute has to fulfil the domain predicate which is given in the entity description. (Recall that Domain is a synonym for AttrVal → Bool.)

{D-12}   def(o, a) $\Rightarrow$ attrDom(entity(o), a) (o@a);

This concludes our treatment of Logical Data Modelling in SSADM. More information on the consistency and prototyping of data model specifications can be found in chapter 9.

7.5 LDM Project Level Translation Schemes

To conclude this section, the most important translation rules from SSADM–F notations to abstract syntax are shown in detail. We give here a short synopsis of the rules how the SSADM-F documents for the Logical Data Model of an actual project are translated into SPECTRUM specifications which can then be "plugged in" into the axiomatic semantics definition.

We use tables with two columns for representing the translation schemes. The left column contains a pattern out of the SSADM-F documents, the right column shows (in the same row) the corresponding SPECTRUM text. *Italic font* is used to designate "meta" variables for the translation schema itself.

Translation Schemes for the ER Diagram

ER Diagram: Entities	
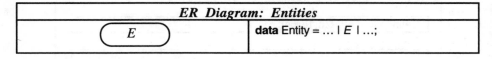	**data** Entity = ... I E I ...;

ER Diagram: Relationships	

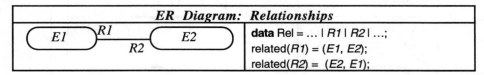	**data** Rel = ... I $R1$ I $R2$ I ...;
	related($R1$) = ($E1$, $E2$);
	related($R2$) = ($E2$, $E1$);

ER Diagram: Degrees	

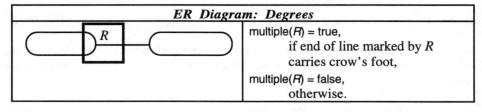	multiple(R) = true,
	    if end of line marked by R
	    carries crow's foot,
	multiple(R) = false,
	    otherwise.

ER Diagram: Optionalities	

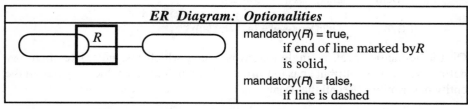	mandatory(R) = true,
	    if end of line marked by$R$
	    is solid,
	mandatory(R) = false,
	    if line is dashed

ER Diagram: Exclusive Arcs	

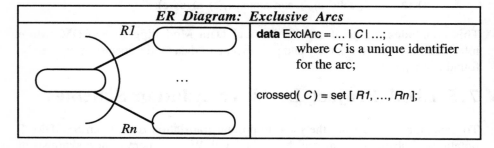	**data** ExclArc = ... I C I ...;
	    where C is a unique identifier
	    for the arc;
	
	crossed(C) = set [$R1$, ..., Rn];

Translation Schemes for Entity Descriptions

Entity Description: Attributes	

SSADM-F Entity Description
 	
 Entity name E
 	
 Attribute name / Mandatory / Primary Key
 $A1$ — $M1$ — $K1$
 ⋮ — ⋮ — ⋮
 An — Mn — Kn
	data Attr = … | $A1$ | … | An | …;
	
	 attrs(E) = set [$A1$, …, An];
	
	 mandatory(E) = set (m1++…++mn);
	     where for $1 \leq i \leq n$:
	 mi = [Ai], if Mi is ticked,
	 mi = [], if Mi is not ticked.
	
	 primaryKey(E) = set (k1++…++kn);
	     where for $1 \leq i \leq n$:
	 ki = [Ai], if Ki is ticked,
	 ki = [], if Ki is not ticked.

Entity Description: Domain Restrictions	
SSADM-F Entity Description Entity name E Attribute name / / SPECTRUM Domain A — — D	attrDom(E, A) = D;

Chapter 8

The SSADM Technique "Entity-Event Modelling"

This chapter gives a formalization of the notations which are used in SSADM to describe the dynamic change of system states. Entity-Event Modelling (EEM) is the most proprietary technique of SSADM. In some aspects, EEM has similarities to Jackson System Development (JSD).

8.1 EEM: Introduction and Terminology

As its name indicates, Entity-Event Modelling is closely related to the term of an Entity which was treated in chapter 7 above on Logical Data Modelling. Logical Data Modelling describes the static structure of a system state; EEM describes the way how such a system state evolves over the lifetime of the system. EEM uses the static structure of the system states as an aid to localize also the description of the dynamic behaviour of the system. Therefore, it combines the terms from the static system description (entities, relationships, attributes) with terms specialized to dynamic system change, in particular the term of an event.

In a system development using SSADM, the EEM techniques are used at a point where the basic informal requirements have been already agreed upon. EEM is used to fix the technical details of a system fulfilling these informal requirements and to check the requirements for consistency. During the process of finding the informal requirements, the Data Flow Modelling (DFM) technique is used in SSADM. We have decided for this presentation to postpone the treatment of DFM to chapter 11 and to introduce EEM first. The reason for this is that EEM is much more detailed and therefore better suited to formalize the characteristic properties of systems addressed by SSADM. Chapter 11 below will explain the more informal data flow techniques on the background of the relatively fine-grained semantic concepts introduced in this chapter.

The EEM technique contains an abundance of notation, so the formalization tends to get quite complex. In order to cope with this complexity, we will treat EEM in five separate steps. In this first section, the terminology of EEM (in particular the terms of event, option and role), are introduced and immediately related to the semantic reference specification. This part does not yet involve any SSADM documents. In the four subsequent sections, the four main notations in EEM (Event-Entity Matrix, Effect Correspondence Diagram, Entity Life History and Operation Lists) are introduced and semantically founded, step by step.

8.1.1 Events

The central term in EEM besides "entity" is the "event". An introductory book on SSADM gives the following definition:

> "**Event.** Something which impacts upon a system and causes it to be updated." [DCC92, p. 356]

It is typical for system analysis methods that updates of the system state are dealt with in more detail than simple inquiries of the actual contents of the system state. The central concepts of EEM are oriented towards events which cause system updates, so the same holds for our formalization.

As in the case of "entity", we have to distinguish carefully between the actual instances of events (some activity taking place in the real world which causes a system update) and the abstract denotation for it. An event is written in SSADM simply as an identifier, and therefore it denotes a whole class of actual event instances. Each of the actual instances leads to a transformation of a given system state. So an event identifier gives some classification of event instances in terms of the caused state transformations.

> *Definition: Event.* An *event* is an identifier which is interpreted as a property of transformations of the system state. The admitted state transformations are disjointly classified by the event identifiers.

Typical examples for state transformations in the Hotel Room Agency example which should be classified by an event identifier are the following:

- The arrival of a request from a customer.

- The arrival of the information that a customer converts a reservation into a fixed booking.

- The change of a customer's mail address.

For each event instance, the caused transformation of the system state can be described schematically. For instance, any event instance of the event "change of a customer's mail address" will modify only a single occurrence of the entity "customer", and in this occurrence it will change the single attribute "address". Some of the documents in EEM provide such a schematic description of the system update:

- The Event-Entity Matrix shows that the only entity involved in an "change of mail address" event is "customer".

- The Effect-Correspondence Diagram shows that there is only a single occurrence of "customer" updated.

- The Event-Entity-Matrix and the Operation Lists together show that only the attribute "address" is changed.

The documents mentioned in the list above are concerned only with the description of one single update caused by an event. The Entity-Life Histories add the information in which order such updates are admitted. All these descriptions are based on the classification of updates using event identifiers.

8.1.2 Roles and Options

The modifications an event causes for a system state are further classified using the terms of *role* and *option*.

The concept of a "role" is needed since a particular event instance does not always update all occurrences of an entity in the same way. In the Hotel Agency example, it can be the case that the agency has had to ask a hotel directly for availability of a room, and gets a negative response from the hotel to this question. The agency tries to fulfil the wishes of the customer in this situation by choosing another hotel which is comparable to the requested hotel. Here, the same event (negative response from the hotel) affects two occurrences (hotels). The two hotels involved are the one which was requested originally and the one which is offerred as an alternative. Both occurrences belong to the same entity "hotel", but structurally different updates are made to the two occurrences. So we refer to one occurrence as belonging to the entity "hotel" in "requested" role and to the second one as belonging to the entity "hotel" in "alternative" role.

> *Definition: Role.* A role is an identifier which is sensible only if connected with a specific entity and a specific event. It is used to partition the set of occurrences of the entity into subclasses which are updated differently by instances of the given event.

The "role" concept further refines the entity affected by an event. In a similar fashion, the event can be refined into several "options". The same event may have quite different effects, depending on some condition. In our example, the arrival of a negative reply from a hotel has different consequences, depending on whether an adequate alternative for the request can be found among the pre-booked quotas. Also the distinction whether the response from the hotel is positive or negative can be seen as a fine-grain structure of the class of "hotel reply" event instances. It is reasonable to use the same event identifier ("hotel reply") for all these cases, but to distinguish the description of the system updates by a sub-classification into options. In the example, three different state transformation schemas are specified for the "hotel reply" event, one for the option "positive response from the hotel", one for the option "negative response, but alternative found" and one for the case "negative response and no alternative found".

> *Definition: Option.* An option is an identifier which is used as an additional qualification for a specific event. The specification of an actual state transformation caused by an event instance is split into subcases by an option. The classification of an event instance by an option may depend on the actual state of the system.

8.1.3 Semantic Reference Concepts for EEM

The semantic reference specification from chapter 6 has been designed in such a way that events, options and roles can be easily mapped onto it. Before entering the detailed discussion of the various document types in SSADM, we describe here how the basic terms are expressed in terms of the reference specification.

Since events, options and roles are identifiers, for each of them a syntactical sort is defined.

     sort Event, Option, Role;   Event, Option, Role :: EQ;

In the semantic reference specification, the sort State represents the system state. The sort InpEv corresponds precisely to what was called an "event instance" above. An input event may lead to an update of the system state[1]. These input events are classified by the event identifiers in an analogous way as occurrences are classified

---

[1]   The function next: State $\times$ InpEv $\to$ State describes the update of the state.

by entity identifiers. So we introduce a function which determines the event identifier of an input event. Like the entity classification, this function is total.

event: InpEv $\rightarrow$ Event;   event **total**;

As it was explained above, option identifiers give an additional classification for input events, depending on the system state. This classification obviously must be given for any input event which is accepted by the actual system state[2]. So the classification function option takes the sort State as an additional parameter and is partially defined. It is admitted that an event is classified by an option even if it is not accepted (to allow for instance an acceptance test to be dependent on the actual option).

option: State $\times$ InpEv $\rightarrow$ Option;

{E-1}   acc(s, ie) $\Rightarrow$ δ option(s, ie);

Roles can be described in a similar style. A role always refers to a particular occurrence in a state. More precisely, it indicates that the part of the state observed through an occurrence identifier is updated in the transition from the current state to the next state (by creation, modification or deletion of an occurrence). So the role classification has an additional parameter of sort OccId. This classification function is partially defined, too, depending on whether the occurrence identifier is affected by the input event[3].

role: State $\times$ InpEv $\times$ OccId $\rightarrow$ Role;

{E-2} δ role(s, ie, i) = affects(s, ie, i);

The function affects has been specified as total, and the axioms which were given for it in chapter 6 (CE-4 and CE-5) do not imply acc(s, ie). So, the role classification is independent of the acceptance of the input event. This fact will be used below for deriving a formal test for acceptance from the documents which are prepared in Entity-Event Modelling (ECDs and ELHs).

In terms of the specification architecture from chapter 6 (reference specification, abstract syntax, axiomatic semantics), the sorts Event, Option and Role belong to the abstract syntax part of EEM and the axioms E-1 and E-2 to the axiomatic semantics. In order to stay precisely within the framework from chapter 6, these

---

[2]   The function acc: State $\times$ InpEv $\rightarrow$ Bool determines whether an input event is accepted by the state.

[3]   The function affects: State $\times$ InpEv $\times$ OccId $\rightarrow$ Bool determines whether an occurrence identifier is affected.

specification parts will be repeated in the following sections at their appropriate place.

The next section discusses how the project level details for the three classifications (events, options, roles) are defined in SSADM-F. The classification into events, options and roles sets the framework which is used by the documents of the EEM technique to further specify the dynamics of an information system. The axiomatic semantics for EEM gives axioms which use the constructions of event, option and role and entail constraints for the state transition function for the system state (that is, next and its definedness condition acc).

8.2 Event-Entity Matrix

In the rest of this chapter, the documents of the EEM technique in SSADM are studied in more detail. Section 8.2 deals with the Event-Entity Matrix, the subsequent sections address Effect Correspondence Diagrams, Entity Life Histories and Operation Lists, respectively. For each of the document types, we first give an informal introduction, then an abstract syntax and finally the axiomatic semantics.

8.2.1 Event-Entity Matrix: Introduction

The most basic document in EEM is the *Event-Entity Matrix*. As indicated by its name, this matrix provides information on pairs of an entity and an event. This two-dimensional matrix is indexed by the event and entity identifiers. Its entries roughly classify the kind of update which will caused by an event instance to an occurrence, using a letter code for several types of access:

• No change of any occurrence of the entity (no entry);

• Creation of occurrences of the entity (entry C);

• Deletion of occurrences of the entity (entry D);

• Modification of the contents of occurrences of the entity (entry M).

Figure 8.1 below shows a part of the SSADM Event-Entity Matrix for the Hotel Agency example. Please note that in this matrix an entity is shown as modified (M) not only if some of its attributes are modified but also if its participation in one or more relationship instances changes.

Event \ Entity	Customer	Request	Reservn
Customer Request	M	C	C
Hotel Reply	M	D	C
Fixed Booking	M		D

Fig. 8.1

The Event-Entity Matrix is used in SSADM mainly as a starting document for deriving a finer description (Entity Life Histories) and is not kept up to date with later refinements of the specification. In contrast to this, we assume for our variant SSADM-F that the Event-Entity Matrix is "taken seriously": We assign an axiomatic semantics to it and we require it to be consistent with the other EEM documents. This decision is supported mainly by two arguments. From the semantic point of view, it is quite useful to have a document which comprehensively lists and classifies the events. But also from the pragmatic point of view, the experience with several CASE tools has shown that overview matrices are among the most useful aids a computer-supported system can offer to the specifier of a complex system. Based on these decisions, we will propose now a slightly refined form of the matrix to be used in SSADM-F.

8.2.2 Semantic Analysis and Refinement of Notation

Unfortunately, the original SSADM form of an Event-Entity Matrix does not provide enough information to serve as an overview document for the more advanced concepts of EEM. In particular, it does not support options and roles. For instance, the matrix in figure 8.1 contains two "C" entries in the line for the event "Customer Request". These entries are motivated by the following fact: On receipt of a booking request from a customer, there are two options. In the case where the booking request can be satisfied by the pre-reserved quotas, a reservation occurrence will be created immediately. In the other case, an inquiry is sent to the hotel and a "request" occurrence is created and kept until the reply arrives[4]. However, it cannot happen that both a "request" and a "reservation" occurrence are created! So the "pure SSADM" form of the Event-Entity Matrix is slightly misleading. It is more convenient to split the "customer request" line in the matrix into two lines, corresponding to the two event options, as it is shown in figure 8.2.

---

4   The „request" entity represents the data of the user request which must be kept in the system until it can be decided whether a room reservation can be created for it.

Event \ Entity	Customer	Request	Reservn	Hotel [reqd.]	Hotel [altern.]	Quota
Customer Request						
immediately offered	M		C	M		M
inquired from hotel	M	C		M		R
Hotel Reply						
available as reqd.	M	D	C	M		M
alternative available	M	D	C	M	M	M
not available	M	D		M		
Fixed Booking	M		D	M		

Fig. 8.2

In figure 8.2, also the columns have been split in a similar style as a representation for entity roles. This is necessary only for a small part of the matrix, in the "hotel" column. Since the roles apply only locally to a specific event, the splitting of the column is even restricted to the part of the column which refers to this event.

Moreover, figure 8.2 uses a fourth access code represented by the letter "R". This code marks an entity some occurrences of which are read but left unchanged by the update caused by the respective event. An example is the event "customer request". Even if the option "inquired from hotel" is chosen, the presence of some quota occurrences may be necessary, in order to check whether the available quota is sufficient. Such a "read-only" access to occurrences is explicitly mentioned in the Effect Correspondence Diagrams in original SSADM; we propose here to show this form of access also in the Event-Entity Matrix.

For the formalized variant SSADM-F, we will assume the refined form of the Event-Entity Matrix as it is shown by figure 8.2. If a more compact overview is needed, this can be easily achieved by collapsing the subcases representing options and roles.

From a semantic viewpoint, the Event-Entity Matrix contains two different kinds of information.

• It lists all event, option and role identifiers and shows their admitted combinations. An event identifier can be combined only with the option identifiers listed below it. A role identifier makes sense only for the combination of event and entity indicated by its position(s) in the matrix.

- It gives a first schematic description of the type of access to entities by an input event, depending on its classification by event and option.

Correspondingly, the Event-Entity Matrix contributes to the formal specification in two different aspects. By the first aspect, it defines simple rules to be obeyed by the classification functions event, option and role. Secondly, it gives constraints for the state transition next. The next two sections give a more detailed explanation of this idea.

8.2.3 Event-Entity Matrix: Abstract Syntax

As for all abstract syntax specifications, this section defines the parameter requirements for the formalization of an actual project level matrix. The Event-Entity Matrix has two semantic purposes: It defines the basic vocabulary for events, options and roles; and it classifies system updates on the level of access types.

As it was already said above, the event, option and role identifers are represented by SPECTRUM sorts[5].

     sort Event, Option, Role;   Event, Option, Role :: EQ;

For an actual project, the list of event, option and role identifiers can be obtained easily from an Event-Entity Matrix as in figure 8.2. Each name which appears as a main entry in the first column is translated into a constant of sort Event; the sub-entries in the first column give the option identifiers (sort Option). It is admitted for the same option identifier to be used for several events. The identifiers which appear in square brackets within the matrix body are the role identifiers (sort Role). The three sorts can be defined in SPECTRUM as enumeration sorts (see figure 8.3).

```
EE_Matrix_Labels = {
        data Event = custReq I hotelReply I fixedBkg;
        data Option =
                stdOpt I immOff I inqFromH I availAsReqd I altAvail I notAvail;
        data Role = stdRole I reqd I altern;     }
```
Fig. 8.3

As in figure 8.3, we introduce in addition to the option and role identifiers from the diagram additional "standard" values for both sorts.

     stdOpt: Option;   stdRole: Role;

---

[5]   These sorts have been mentioned already in subsection 8.2.1.

The purpose of these "standard" values is to simplify the further formal treatment of EEM. For instance, the axiom E-1, which was already given above, claims that for every accepted input event a classification into event identifier and option identifier is available. So, an option classification is needed also for non-optional events like "Fixed Booking". For all non-optional events, we take stdOpt as the only admitted option. Similarly, the classification of affected occurrences by roles is easier if we use the "standard role" stdRole for those entities for which no role distinction is given.

The information which combinations of events and options are admitted is now captured a by set-valued function.

$$\text{admOpts:} \quad \text{Event} \to \text{Set Option;} \qquad \text{admOpts } \textbf{total};$$

Figure 8.4 shows the translation of the label information given by the Event-Entity matrix from figure 8.2[6].

```
EE_Matrix_Options = { strict total;
        enriches SET+EE_Matrix_Labels;
        admOpts: Event → Set Option;
        axioms
        admOpts(custReq) = set [immOff, inqFromH];
        admOpts(hotelReply) = set [availAsReqd, altAvail, notAvail];
        admOpts(fixedBkg) = set [stdOpt];
        endaxioms; }
```
Fig. 8.4

Obviously, the set admOpts(ev) contains exactly those options which are listed as sub-cases for the event ev. In the case where no options are given (as for fixedBkg), we insert the standard option as a single option. So we can require the result set of admOpts to be nonempty. Axiom ES-2 explicitly makes sure that the standard option is not mixed with other options.

{ES-1[7]}   admOpts(ev) ≠ emptySet;
{ES-2}   stdOpt ∈ admOpts(ev) ⇒ admOpts(ev) = set [stdOpt];

The admissibility of roles can be defined in a quite similar style. The only difference is that the function admRoles takes two arguments of sort Event and Entity to indicate the part of the matrix where the role distinction is valid.

$$\text{admRoles:} \quad \text{Event} \times \text{Entity} \to \text{Set Roles;} \qquad \text{admRoles } \textbf{total};$$

---

6   The translation rules are defined schematically in section 8.7.3 below.

7   As a convention for axiom names, the second letter S indicates that the axiom is a syntactic requirement (context condition). The first letter of E is used for all axioms in this chapter.

{ES-3}   admRoles(ev, e) ≠ emptySet;
{ES-4}   stdRol ∈ admRoles(ev, e) ⇒ admRoles(ev, e) = set [stdRole];

Figure 8.5 shows the definition of admRoles which is derived from the sample matrix. It contains an axiom for every combination of an event with an entity. Such a combination addresses a small sub-matrix which may contain several lines for different options of the event and several rows for different roles of the entity. For instance, in figure 8.2 a submatrix with three lines and two rows belongs to the event "hotel reply" and the entity "hotel". The result of admRoles is the set of role names which appear as sub-column headings in this submatrix. In the most frequent case, where the sub-matrix has only one row and no role headings are present, the value of admRoles is the singleton set which consists only of the standard role.

```
EE_Matrix_Roles = { strict total;
        enriches EE_Matrix_Labels + ER_Diagram;

        admRoles:  Event × Entity  → Set Role;

        axioms ∀ ev: Event in
        admRoles(ev, customer) = set [stdRole];
        admRoles(ev, request) = set [stdRole];
        admRoles(ev, reservation) = set [stdRole];
        admRoles(custReq, hotel) = set [stdRole];
        admRoles(hotelReply, hotel) = set [reqd, altern];
        admRoles(fixedBkg, hotel) = set [stdRole];
        admRoles(ev, quota) = set [stdRole];
        endaxioms; }
```

Fig. 8.5

In figure 8.5, an abbreviation is used for the frequent case where a whole entity column does not contain any role distinctions. In this case, a universally quantified variable for the events can be used to shorten the definition.

Now we are ready to define the entries of the matrix. For the syntactical representation of the letter code entries in the matrix, the letters are represented in SPECTRUM by an enumeration sort AccessType. For given event, option, entity and role, the matrix entry is given by the function EEX[8].

        data AccessType = C I D I M I R;

        EEX: Event × Option × Entity × Role → AccessType;

---

[8]   We use the name EEX instead of EEM to avoid confusion with the acronym for „Entity-Event Modelling".

It is an interesting question how the missing entries in the matrix are represented. A quite natural approach would be to use the special pseudo-value "undefined" of SPECTRUM for these cases. However, in contrast to logic programming languages, SPECTRUM does not contain a "closure principle" to declare all uncovered cases in a function definition as undefined. This has been excluded since a closure operator would lead into a non-monotonic logic (see also [BMR93]). If a missing entry in the matrix was identified with the undefinedness of EEX, then the undefinedness had to be specified explicitly by an axiom for each empty entry of the matrix. This is problematic for more complex projects, where the Event-Entity Matrix tends to be sparsely populated, since most events affect only a small subset of the available entities. So for a practically applicable representation it is important to use an abstract syntax which specifies only the "positive" cases where an entry is present. For this purpose, we introduce an additional function admTargets which can be used as a test whether for a given combination of event, option, entity and role there is a matrix entry. The function admTargets takes an event and an option as its arguments and delivers a finite set of pairs of entity and role as its result, which corresponds to the list of all entries in the respective matrix line. Obviously, the input and output of the function are only admitted combinations as defined above.

$$\text{admTargets:} \quad \text{Event} \times \text{Option} \rightarrow \text{Set (Entity} \times \text{Role);}$$

{ES-5}   opt $\in$ admOpts(ev) $\Rightarrow$ δ admTargets(ev, opt);
{ES-6}   (e, rol) $\in$ admTargets(ev, opt) $\Rightarrow$ rol $\in$ admRoles(ev, e);

As it can be seen from these definitions, pairs of an entity identifier and a role identifier appear frequently in EEM. We call such a pair a *target* and use a sort synonym Target for it. Targets are the main identification mechanism used in SSADM to classify updates on the level of occurrences. Readability of the abstract syntax is improved by the use of an abbreviation for the standard target where an entity appears in "standard role".

sortsyn Target = Entity $\times$ Role;

$:   Entity $\rightarrow$ Target; $ **total**;
{EA-1[9]} $ e = (e, stdRole);

Analoguously, we define a sort OptEvent for the frequent tuple consisting of an event and an option, and an abbreviation for an event in "standard option".

---

[9]   As a convention for axiom names, the second letter A indicates that this is an auxiliary axiom.

sortsyn OptEvent = Event × Option;

```
% :    Event → OptEvent;     % total;
{EA-2}   % ev = (ev, stdOpt);
```

Using these abbreviations, the signature of the admTargets-function can be simplified.

admTargets: OptEvent → Set Target;

Based on these abbreviations, figure 8.6 shows the admTargets-function which can be extracted from the matrix in figure 8.2.

```
EE_Matrix_Targets = { strict;
        enriches EE_Matrix_Options + EE_Aux_Defns;
        admTargets: OptEvent → Set Target;
        axioms
        admTargets (custReq, immOff) =
                set [$customer, $reservation, $hotel, $quota];
        admTargets (custReq, inqFromH) =
                set [$customer, $request, $hotel, $quota];
        admTargets (hotelReply, availAsReqd) =
                set [$customer, $request, $reservation,
                (hotel, reqd), $quota];
        admTargets (hotelReply, altAvail) =
                set [$customer, $request, $reservation,
                (hotel, reqd), (hotel, altern), $quota];
        admTargets (hotelReply, notAvail) =
                set [$customer, $request, (hotel, altern)];
        admTargets (%fixedBkg) = set  [$customer, $reservation, $hotel];
        endaxioms; }
```

Fig. 8.6

Also the signature of the EEX function can be simplified.

EEX: OptEvent × Target → AccessType;

The following axiom ensures that for each case described by the admTargets-function the matrix contains a defined entry.

{ES-7}   tg ∈ admTargets(oev) ⇒ δ EEX(oev, tg);

Now each entry in the Event-Entity Matrix can be translated into a single axiom for the function EEX. Figure 8.7 shows the result of the syntactical translation of the matrix in the example.

```
EE_Matrix_LetterCodes = { strict;
        enriches EE_Matrix_Roles;
        data AccessType = C | M | D | R;

        EEX: OptEvent × Target → AccessType;

        axioms
        EEX((custReq, immOff), $customer) = M;
        EEX((custReq, immOff), $reservation) = C;
        EEX((custReq, immOff), $hotel) = M;
        EEX((custReq, immOff), $reservation) = C;
        EEX((custReq, immOff), $quota) = M;
        EEX((custReq, inqFromH), $customer) = M;
        EEX((custReq, inqFromH), $request) = C;
        EEX((custReq, inqFromH), $hotel) = M;
        EEX((custReq, inqFromH), $quota) = R;
        EEX((hotelReply, availAsReqd), $customer) = M;
        EEX((hotelReply, availAsReqd), $request) = D;
        EEX((hotelReply, availAsReqd), $reservation) = C;
        EEX((hotelReply, availAsReqd), (hotel, reqd)) = M;
        EEX((hotelReply, availAsReqd), $quota) = M;
        EEX((hotelReply, altAvail), $customer) = M;
        EEX((hotelReply, altAvail), $request) = D;
        EEX((hotelReply, altAvail), $reservation) = C;
        EEX((hotelReply, altAvail), (hotel, reqd)) = M;
        EEX((hotelReply, altAvail), (hotel, altern)) = M;
        EEX((hotelReply, altAvail), $quota) = M;
        EEX((hotelReply, notAvail), $customer) = M;
        EEX((hotelReply, notAvail), $request) = D;
        EEX((hotelReply, notAvail), (hotel, reqd)) = M;
        EEX(%fixedBkg, $customer) = M;
        EEX(%fixedBkg, $reservation) = D;
        EEX(%fixedBkg, $hotel) = M;
        endaxioms; }
```

Fig. 8.7

Please note that the translation of the Event-Entity Matrix does specify only the "positive" cases where an entry is present. For other cases, including senseless combinations of arguments, the function is underspecified (and not necessarily undefined!). Other functions (admOpts, admRoles, admTargets) have been defined for the purpose to identify those cases for which the EEX function is sensibly applied. If applied appropriately, these functions have an equivalent effect to a "closure operator": They can be used to capture the "negative" cases which are not comprised by the translation of the matrix into EEX. This combination of a well-defined set-valued function with an underspecified function is a general scheme which is used also at several other places in this formalization.

8.2.4 Event-Entity Matrix: Axiomatic Semantics

Based on the abstract syntax, we give now a set of axioms which interprets the Event-Entity Matrix as a set of constraints to the semantic reference specification. These constraints are structured into general restrictions (according to the event, option and role vocabulary) and the interpretation of the access types in the Event-Entity Matrix.

First, the model class is restricted to those cases which behave as regularly as it is prescribed by the classification into events, options and roles. The basic idea for this has been explained already in section 8.1.3 above. The sort InpEv from the core reference structure plays here the role of the event instances. We state that for every event instance the actual event, option and role classification is defined. The option can be determined only if the event is accepted by the actual system state. The role is defined only for affected occurrence identifiers[10].

event:	InpEv → Event;	event **total**;
option:	State × InpEv → Option;	
role:	State × InpEv × Occld → Role;	

{E-1}   acc(s, ie) $\Rightarrow$ δ option(s, ie);

{E-2}   δ role(s, ie, i) = affects(s, ie, i);

Obviously, the option and role classifications must obey the rules for admitted combinations, as they can be found in the Event-Entity Matrix. For the options, this is stated by a simple axiom.

{E-3}   option(s, ie) = opt $\Rightarrow$ (opt $\in$ admOpts(event(ie)));

For the role classification we need an entity identifier in order to find the appropriate column of the matrix. By axiom CE-5, it is ensured that any affected identifier belongs to an occurrence in either the current state s or the next, updated state next(s, ie), or to both. We have to exclude explicitly the case that the identifier occurs in the two states with a different entity. This rather technical but obvious condition is expressed by the next axiom.

{E-4}   next(s, ie) = s' $\land$ bound(s, i) $\land$ bound(s', i) $\Rightarrow$ entity(get(s, i)) = entity(get(s', i));

---

10   These functions and axioms have been defined already in subsection 8.2.1.

Now we can define a function idEntity to obtain the entity for an affected occurrence identifier. The specification for this function covers also the case where an occurrence is affected, but the next state turns out as undefined (axiom E-5b). This is necessary, since we want to base the test for acceptance on the information in the Event-Entity Matrix.

idEntity: State × InpEv × OccId → Entity;

{E-5a} δ idEntity(s, ie, i) = affects(s, ie, i);
{E-5b}   get(s, i) = o $\Rightarrow$ idEntity(s, ie, i) = entity(o);
{E-5c}   next(s, ie) = s' $\wedge$ get(s', i) = o $\Rightarrow$ idEntity(s, ie, i) = entity(o);

For any affected occurrence identifier, now an entity (by idEntity) and a role (by role) are defined. Since for such a pair of an entity and a role the abbreviation Target was introduced above, we define also an abbreviating function for the combination of idEntity and role, which we call target.

target: State × InpEv × OccId → Target;

{E-6a}   target(s, ie, i) = (idEntity(s, ie, i), role(s, ie, i));

Throughout the further semantics, the target assignment forms the main source for describing the update of an occurrence.

Analoguously, an abbreviating function for the pair of an option and an event can be defined.

optEvent: State × InpEv → OptEvent;

{E-6b}   optEvent(s, ie) = (event(ie), option(s, ie));

With the help of the idEntity function and these abbreviations, two axioms now constrain the admitted target classification according to the contents of the Event-Entity Matrix. If a role is assigned to an occurrence identifier, it must occur in the part of the matrix identified by the event and the entity.

{E-7a}   role(s, ie, i) = rol $\Rightarrow$ rol $\in$ admRoles(event(ie), idEntity(s, ie, i));

Moreover, the assigned targets must obey the restriction expressed by admTargets.

{E-7b}   optEvent(s, ie) = oev $\Rightarrow$ target(s, ie, i) $\in$ admTargets(oev);

Together with axiom ES-7 for the Event-Entity Matrix, this last axiom requires that for every affected occurrence identifier there is a non-empty matrix entry. This is the place where empty matrix entries are interpreted: It is excluded that an affected identifier can get a classification which corresponds to an empty entry.

Altogether, these few axioms ensure that for all occurrence identifiers which are affected by a particular input event, a classification into event, option, role and entity is available which can be used to look up the Event-Entity Matrix or to interpret other EEM documents. Before proceeding further with the axiomatic semantics, it may be useful to recall what the consequences of the various axioms are for a given system update.

> *Example.* Let us assume that there is a system state s which is modified due to the acceptance of an input event ie into a new state s'. We are interested in the localized observation of this modification, so we additionally assume an occurrence identifier i as the subject of our observation.

The first axiom which must be taken into accout is CE-4[11], which entails:

$$\text{affects}(s, ie, i) \lor (\text{get}(s, i) = \text{get}(s', i))$$

So a not yet precisely specified source provides us with the information whether i is affected by the actual input event or not. If i is not affected, then due to this axiom both states contain the same occurrence for this identifier. So let us consider the more interesting case, where the occcurrence is affected. In this case, the axiom CE-5 gives us the fact that i must be bound in s or in s'.

$$\text{bound}(s, i) \lor \text{bound}(s', i)$$

We assume here that i occurs in the current state s and use e for the respective entity (e $=_{\text{def}}$ entity(get(s, i))). By axiom E-5b, the idEntity function for our case now gives this value e:

$$e = \text{idEntity}(s, ie, i)$$

Due to the axioms E-1 and E-2 from above, we have appropriate classifications into event, option and role. The axiom E-3 guarantees that the combination of event and option is admitted. By axiom E-7a, the role is admitted for this entity and event. By axiom E-7b, a non-empty entry of the Event-Entity Matrix exists, which specifies more detailed conditions for the affected occurrence identifier.

Please note that for any occurrence identifier, there are only two possibilities: Either nothing is changed by the update, or the whole

---

[11] CE-axioms belong to the core reference specification, where it is extended towards EEM.

classification scheme applies, and so the matrix contents can be used to specify the differences.

In this context, the access codes in the Event-Entity Matrix can be interpreted in a quite straightforward way. The observation functions on the state are used to connect the letter code in the matrix with an actual statement that an occurrence is created, deleted, modified or read[12].

{E-8}   next(s, ie) = s' $\land$ affects(s, ie, i) $\Rightarrow$
          let m = EEX(optEvent(s, ie), target(s, ie, i)) **in**
              (m = C $\Rightarrow$ $\lnot$ bound(s, i) $\land$ bound(s', i))
    $\land$ (m = D $\Rightarrow$ bound(s, i) $\land$ $\lnot$ bound(s', i))
    $\land$ (m = M $\Rightarrow$ bound(s, i) $\land$ bound(s', i))
    $\land$ (m = R $\Rightarrow$ bound(s, i) $\land$ bound(s', i) $\land$ get(s, i) = get(s', i));

Example: This axiom has (among others) the following consequence for a model of the Hotel Agency Specification: If an input event is accepted by the system which is classified as a "fixed booking" event, in standard option, and if moreover to some occurrence identifier i for entity "reservation", the "standard role" is assigned, then i has to be accessible in the current state and no longer accessible in the successor state. (See the last but second axiom in figure 8.7.)

Additional EEM documents define precisely under which circumstances an input event is accepted (Entity Life Histories), and which occurrence identifiers are affected and assigned to specific roles (Effect Correspondence Diagrams).

---

[12] The **let**-construction which is used in axiom E-10 introduces abbreviating identifiers. The semantics of the axiom remains the same if the **let-endlet** is removed and the identifier oev is expanded to optEvent(s, ie).

8.3 Effect Correspondence Diagrams

All introductory literature on SSADM starts the explanation of Entity-Event Modelling with the Event-Entity Matrix and then moves on to the Entity Life Histories. This is also the order in which the documents appear in the procedural guidelines of SSADM. We have decided here to present Effect Correspondence Diagrams before the Entity Life Histories. The reasons for this unconventional decision are as follows:

- An Effect Correspondence Diagram describes the basic structure of the response of the system to a single event. Due to this central role in the system specification, the Effect Correspondence Diagrams are helpful in getting an overview of the functionality of the system.

- Since an Effect Correspondence Diagram deals with a single event and therefore only with two system states (the current and the next state), it has a much more static flavour than Entity Life Histories. In some sense, the Effect Correspondence Diagrams form the bridge between the purely static Logical Data Model and the purely dynamic modelling of event sequences in Entity Life Histories.

- Effect Correspondence Diagrams seem to be postponed in the literature often only because they are relatively difficult to explain informally. Using a formal semantics, a precise definition can be given.

8.3.1 Effect Correspondence Diagrams: Introduction

In SSADM, for every event an Effect Correspondence Diagram (ECD) is drawn to specify which entity occurrences are affected by an event instance. An ECD can be seen as a more refined view of the block of lines in the Event-Entity Matrix which belongs to an event. In the ECD, all the entities which are contained in these lines are shown, together with a graphical representation of the mutual relationships which exist between them. Figure 8.8 gives an example of an ECD, in this case for the event "customer request" in the Hotel Agency example.

An ECD is a static description of the part of a system state which is updated by an event. In complex information systems, a single event may update several occurrences of several entities (maybe in different roles). It is not possible to specify the absolute number of affected occurrences, since this number may vary from one event instance to another. Therefore, the ECD specifies a condition which must be met by the set of affected occurrences for every event instance. This condition is formulated in graphical form, similar to an ER diagram. An ECD consists essentially of rounded boxes which are labelled by entity names (and possibly roles), together with binary relationships (correspondences) between the boxes. The correspondences often coincide with relationships of the data model.

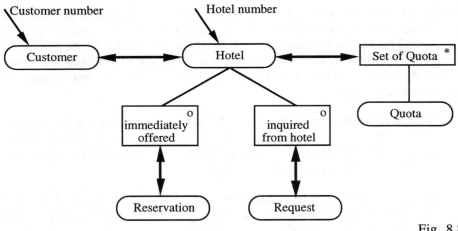

Fig. 8.8

In figure 8.8, the "Customer" and the "Hotel" entity are marked as so-called *entry points*, by a small arrow pointing towards the entity box. This resembles the fact that for these entities a single occurrence can be identified out of the data transmitted by the input event. If a customer sends a booking request to the agency (by letter or by phone), she names in this request the customer number and the number of a hotel from the catalogue of the agency. Since there is exactly one customer and exactly one hotel occurrence affected by the event, a one-to-one correspondence between the entities "Customer" and "Hotel" is shown in the diagram. The one-to-one correspondence is drawn as a so-called "correspondence arrow" (a two-headed arrow).

Depending on the selected hotel occurrence and on further input data, a set of quota informations (pools of pre-booked rooms) can be selected. This set is shown in the ECD as a separate "set of"-box, with the entity "quota" underneath it. This has the advantage that the one-to-one arrow can be used to show the correspondence. It is possible that the set of quota occurrences is empty (for instance if the agency does not hold any quota for the actual hotel).

The further structure of the affected part of the system state depends on the option of the event. There are two cases: Either the request can be immediately satisfied by pre-reserved quota hold by the agency; in this case a reservation can be made, which means the creation of a single "reservation" occurrence. Otherwise, the hotel must be asked by the agency for availability, in which case a single "request" entity is created. The ECD shows the distinction between these two cases using a tree-like case distinction where the branches (cases) are marked by small circles in the upper rigth corner of the box. Similarly, the box which represents the elements of a "set of"-construction is marked with a star in its corner. SSADM has inherited this notation from Jackson System Development (JSD). It is used at several places in SSADM, for instance also in the Entity Life Histories (see section 8.4). In the example, a selection construction is connected with the "hotel" entity, since the hotel occurrence has correspondences which depend on the option. More case distinctions could be inserted for other entities, if necessary.

Effect Correspondence Diagrams are a quite static and descriptive means of specification. They do not prescribe any particular order in which the occurrences are identified and the options are determined, depending on actual user input. This is worked out later in Dialogue Design and Logical Process Design. For understanding an ECD, one should abstract from these operational details. The input event determines for a given system state a specific option and a specific choice of occurrences for all the entities (and roles) listed in the Event-Entity Matrix. The ECD shows which of these occurrences are affected and how they are connected. The ECDs even do not distinguish between those occurrences and relationship instances which exist in the current state and those which are created by the update to the next state.

8.3.2 Semantic Analysis and Refinement of Notation

We are going to discuss now the basic semantic idea for the Effect Correspondence Diagrams, aiming at our semantic reference specification. As in the case of the Event-Entity Matrix, this will lead to an adapted and refined variant of the ECD syntax.

The basic building blocks of ECDs are nodes which are labelled with an entity and may be further qualified by a role. Obviously, a missing role is to be replaced by the "standard role" in our framework. So, we can assume all nodes to be labelled by an entity and a role or, using the terminology from the last section, by a *target*. In the semantic reference model, to any affected occurrence identifier a role and an entity are assigned by role and idEntity, so also in the semantics a classification into targets is available. The obvious purpose of the ECDs is to express constraints for the semantic classification of occurrences by targets.

The semantics of entry points and one-to-one correspondences are easy to understand. If a target is marked as an entry point, this means that exactly one affected occurrence identifier is assigned to this target. A one-to-one correspondence between target 1 and target 2 means that exactly the same number of occurrence identifiers is assigned to target 1 as it is to target 2. This semantics has the consequence that the two ECDs shown in figure 8.9 are equivalent. Both ECDs express the fact that exactly one occurrence identifier of customer and hotel (both in standard role) are affected by the event.

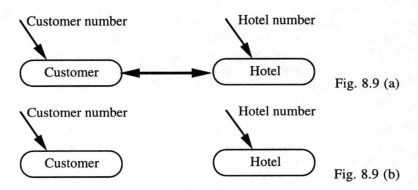

The correspondences are more difficult to understand if "set-of"-nodes are considered. For instance, consider the ECD of figure 8.10.

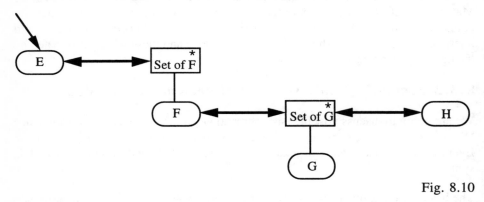

Fig. 8.10

The ECD states that there is exactly one E-target. The natural interpretation of the "Set of F"-correspondence is that this E-target corresponds to a finite (and possibly empty) set of F-targets. So there is no restriction on the number of F-targets. If we proceed with this interpretation, then we find that there is also no restriction for the number of G-targets. We may have more G-targets than F-targets (if every F-target corresponds to a non-empty set of G-targets), but also fewer G-targets than F-targets (if some of the F-targets correspond to empty sets and the others to singletons of G-targets). Generally, the interpretation based on the number of occurences does lead only to very weak constraints for the specified system.

But there is a stronger interpretation of ECDs which seems to be more adequate. Most of the correspondences in an ECD are constructed alongside relationships in the Logical Data Model. For instance, let us assume here the logical data model shown in figure 8.11.

Fig. 8.11

If we interpret the correspondences as restrictions for relationship instances, we can speak about *individual* correspondences of a single occurrence and therefore we get a much more precise view of the structure of the targets. Figure 8.12 (a) below shows a typical pattern of targets which is admitted by the ECD. The occurrences belonging to a target are symbolized here by lowercase letters, where the starting letter indicates the respective target. Please note that the set of occurrences assigned to target G {g1, g2, g3} is partitioned into two subsets, each of which corresponds to an occurrence with target assignment F.

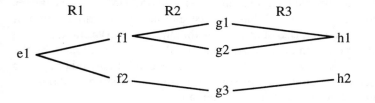

Fig. 8.12 (a)

Figure 8.12 (b) shows a very similar correspondence structure which is *not* admissible with respect to the given ECD. There is a one-to-one correspondence between F-occurrences and sets of G-occurrences and also a one-to-one correspondence between sets of G-occurrences and H-occurrences. However, these one-to-one correspondences do not transitively give a one-to-one correspondence between F- and H-occurrences, so they do not fit into the framework set by the ECD.

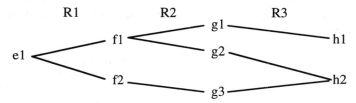

Fig. 8.12 (b)

The semantic analysis now has led us into a situation which is quite typical for the formalization of pragmatic methods. There are two alternatives for the formalization of ECDs.

• One possibility is to preserve the relatively free use of ECDs in SSADM. In this case, the semantics of ECDs cannot rely on individual correspondences for occurrences, and therefore will give only weak constraints for the specified system. This is unsatisfactory, since ECDs clearly have a potential for a quite precise specification mechanism, as it was shown above.

• The other alternative is to restrict correspondence arrows in ECDs to those cases where they are constructed alongside a relationship from the ER diagram. As a consequence, a more diciplined use of ECDs than in standard SSADM is required. The advantage of this approach is that the ECDs can be used as a powerful formal specification tool.

A similar choice between alternatives appeared already during the treatment of the Event-Entity Matrix. There we decided to include the fine-grain distinction into options and roles into the matrix, which is a generalization of the original SSADM syntax. Also for the ECDs we will choose the second alternative which allows us to build a powerful formal specification mechanism with an SSADM-like appearance. However, it should be kept in mind that the first alternative (a formalization of SSADM "as it is") could be carried out as well within the SPECTRUM framework; it would even give a simpler semantics than ours. Our decision is motivated by the general orientation of this work towards a synthesis between formal and pragmatic methods. In an attempt to comparison or standardization of existing methods, for instance, one might be forced to use the first alternative.

So we will use a refined syntax for ECDs which shows slight differences to original SSADM. The differences are as follows:

• In SSADM-F, the one-to-one correspondence arrows have to be labelled with a relationship identifier. SSADM-F does admit only such correspondences which depend on a relationship.

• Since SSADM-F does not support secondary keys, it is obvious that the entry points must be labelled with the primary key attributes. Therefore this redundant information is omitted.

Figure 8.13 shows a variant of the ECD from figure 8.8 which is adapted to SSADM-F notation.

The adaptation to SSADM-F often leads to a re-design of an ECD, as from figure 8.8 to figure 8.13. In this case, the unlabelled one-to-one relationship has been removed. (It was redundant, anyway, according to the discussion above.) Instead, two new correspondences are shown on the ECD, which relate the "customer" target with the "reservation" and "request" target and are based on the data model. Only one of these correspondences is present, depending on the actual option. This variant of the ECD shows clearly that the "customer" occurrence involved in a "customer request" always gains either a link to a "reservation" or to a "request" occurrence. So figure 8.13 can be seen as an improvement over figure 8.8. This improvement of the pragmatic notation was triggered by the formal semantic analysis.

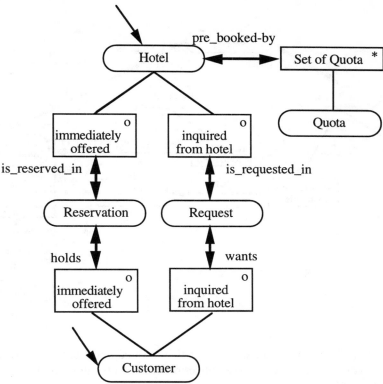

Fig. 8.13

As a second example, figure 8.14 below gives the ECD for the event "hotel reply".
This ECD is structured into a part which applies for all options (request, customer,
requested hotel) and a part which distinguishes two "tracks" for the two options in
which a reservation can be created. It is quite typical that the unconditional part of
the diagram refers to relationships which exist in the current system state when the
event arrives (is_requested_by, requests). In contrast to this, the conditional part
mainly shows relationships which are established in the new state (is_reserved_for,
is_reserved_in). In this example, the hotel entity appears in two different roles.
SSADM proposes to draw the boxes for a single entity closely together and to
surround them by a separate "entity border", as it can be seen in figure 8.14.
However, for the semantics, the labelling of the node with a role name is sufficient,
the additional box is just a redundant graphical convention.

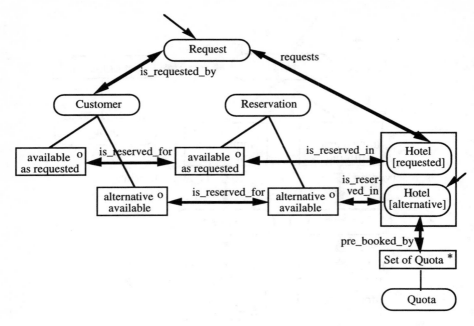

Fig. 8.14

The ECDs of figures 8.13 and 8.14 are the two most complex ones appearing in the Hotel Agency example. The whole collection of ECDs for this small example can be found in appendix B.

8.3.3 Effect Correspondence Diagrams: Abstract Syntax

Our approach to the ECD syntax relies on the basic vocabulary for events, options and roles which is set up by the Event-Entity Matrix. The main information contained in an ECD is the *correspondence relation* it describes and the set of *entry points* it defines. This structure is closely resembled by the abstract syntax of an ECD.

An effect correspondence diagram shows a set of nodes and defines, using these nodes, a set of entry points and a correspondence relation. We study the information given by the nodes first. Three types of nodes have already been mentioned above: simple target nodes, optional nodes and "set of"-nodes. Figure 8.15 (a)-(c) recalls these three types of nodes.

Target   Single target without options

Fig. 8.15 (a)

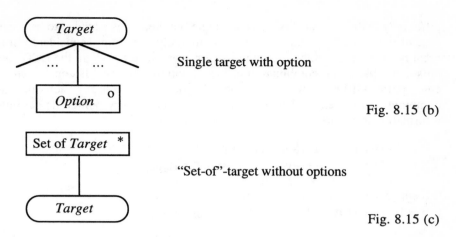

Single target with option

Fig. 8.15 (b)

"Set-of"-target without options

Fig. 8.15 (c)

For reasons of orthogonality, one should also think of "set-of"-targets with specified option. Although this case does not appear frequently in practice, we cover also this possibility, see figure 8.15 (d).

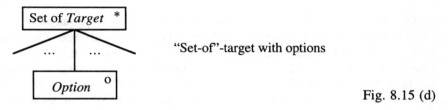

"Set-of"-target with options

Fig. 8.15 (d)

So a node in the ECD can be represented by a small extension of the concepts which are already available for Entity-Event Modelling. A node is a *target* (that is a pair of an entity and a role) which is enhanced by *optionality* and *cardinality* information. The *optionality* information tells whether an explicit option has been specified or not. The *cardinality* information tells whether the node is a single or a "set-of" node.

Obviously, the cardinality information is a new concept which is proprietary to ECDs, so we introduce a data sort for the two possible cardinality values.

    data CardType = single I setOf;

We do *not* introduce a new sort for the ECD-nodes themselves here, since a node in the ECD does not have its own identity. The reasons for this decision will become clearer if we turn now to the two main contents of an ECD: The entry points and the correspondence relation. Let us concentrate on the entry points first.

An entry point is an arrow which points to an ECD node, that is to a target, option, cardinality combination. It is obviously useless to have two entry points which differ only in their cardinality, since a "single" cardinality is intended to be a special case of the "set of" cardinality. This – admittedly semantic – consideration is of great help in simplifying the syntax. An entry arrow to a node in the ECD simply tells that a particular combination of event, option and target is considered as an entry point. Formally, we can define a set of entry points for each admissible combination of event and option. For each of these entry points, its cardinality information is given[13].

$$\text{entries:} \qquad \text{OptEvent} \to \text{Set Target};$$
$$\text{eType:} \qquad \text{OptEvent} \to \text{Target} \nrightarrow \text{CardType};$$

{ES-8a}   entries(oev) $\subseteq$ admTargets(oev);
{ES-8b}   tg $\in$ entries(oev) $\Rightarrow$ δ (eType(oev) (tg));

This representation of entry points is simple and elegant. But the translation from the diagram to the abstract syntax is slightly more complex as it was for other documents studied above. In particular, the composition of the OptEvent argument to the entries and eType functions needs careful attention.

An OptEvent is an event plus an option. Obviously, the event for an entry point is taken from the event to which the whole ECD belongs. In the case of an optional node, also the option argument is given explicitly. However, in the case of a non-optional node in the ECD, the intended semantic meaning is *not* the standard option, but a coverage of *all* admissible options for this event. This can be seen from the example in figure 8.13, which has two non-optional nodes marked as entry points (hotel and customer). For the respective event (customer request) only the options "immediately offered" and "inquired from hotel" are admissible, not the "standard option". So for a non-optional node, the respective axioms should contain a universal quantifier over the options for the option argument, as in the following line[14] which represents the entry points of figure 8.13. We will call such option-independent entry points *regular* ones.

$$\forall \text{ opt: Option.} \qquad \text{entries(cReq, opt)} = \text{set [\$customer, \$hotel]};$$

In the case of a mixture of optional and regular entries, the regular entries must be included in all the entry sets given for the individual options.

Also the generated axioms for the eType function may gain an universal quantifier over options, for instance:

---

[13] The motivation for the higher-order formulation will become clear in the semantics section.

[14] The surrounding box indicates again that this is a *project level* axiom generated out of pragmatic notation.

$$\forall \text{ opt: Option.} \qquad \text{eType (cReq, opt) (\$customer) = single;}$$

Fortunately, the same concept which is used for entry points can also be used to represent correspondence arrows. The only difference is that a correspondence arrow is labelled by a relationship (in SSADM-F) and points to two ECD nodes. Again, it does not make sense to have the same correspondence (to the same other target by the same relationship) twice under different cardinalities. Also options can be treated as above. So the syntax of correspondences is as follows, using a convenient sort abbreviation:

> **sortsyn** Corr = Target × Rel × Target;

> corrs: OptEvent → Set Corr;

{ES-9a} (tg1, r, tg2) ∈ corrs(oev) ⇒ tg1 ∈ admTargets(oev) ∧ tg2 ∈ admTargets(oev);
{ES-9b} ((e1, rol1), r, (e2, rol2)) ∈ corrs(oev) ⇒ related(r) = (e1, e2);

Relationships are treated in a completely symmetric way with respect to their inversion throughout this fomalization. So also the correspondences based on a relationship are required to be present in both directions. In the diagrammatic representation of ECDs, we have omitted the second, inverse names for the relationships for better readability. In this case, the translation into abstract syntax is assumed to add the inverse correspondence.

{ES-9c} (tg1, r, tg2) ∈ corrs(oev) ⇒ (tg2, inv(r), tg1) ∈ corrs(oev);

For each correspondence arrow, the syntax has also to cover two cardinality informations, for the both ends of the arrow. For this purpose, advantage can be taken from the symmetrical treatment of relationships. The function cType assigns to each correspondence arrow only one cardinality information (by convention the one for the first target argument); the second cardinality information can then be obtained from the inverse direction of the same arrow.

> cType: OptEvent → Corr → CardType;

{ES-9d} c ∈ corrs(oev) ⇒ δ (cType(oev) (c));

These few functions are sufficient to encode the information contained in an ECD. The syntax representation for ECDs is more loosely coupled with the structure of the diagram as in the case of the ER diagram. For instance, each regular correspondence (that is, a correspondence between non-optional nodes) must be included in all the result sets of corrs for all possible options. Moreover, the translation into abstract syntax is impossible for some "wrong" diagrams. A typical example of such a "mistake" in a diagram is a correspondence arrow between optional targets which belong to different options. However, the translation from an SSADM-F ECD into the abstract representation is still completely mechanical and could be carried out by a computer program.

Figure 8.16 shows the formal counterpart of the ECD for the event "customer request" (see figure 8.13 above), more examples can be found in appendix C.

```
axioms ∀ opt: Option in
entries(cReq, opt) = set [$customer, $hotel];
eType (cReq, opt) ($customer) = single;
eType (cReq, opt) ($hotel) = single;
corrs(cReq, immOff) = set [ ($customer, holds, $reservation),
        ($reservation, is_reserved_for, $customer),
        ($hotel, is_reserved_in, $reservation),
        ($reservation, reserves, $hotel),
        ($hotel, pre_booked_by, $quota), ($quota, is_for, $hotel) ];
cType (cReq, immOff) ($customer, holds, $reservation) = single;
cType (cReq, immOff) ($reservation, is_reserved_for, $customer)
        = single;
cType (cReq, immOff) ($hotel, is_reserved_in, $reservation)
        = single;
cType (cReq, immOff) ($reservation, reserves, $hotel) = single;
cType (cReq, immOff) ($hotel, pre_booked_by, $quota) = single;
cType (cReq, immOff) ($quota, is_for, $hotel) = setOf;
corrs(cReq, inqFromH) = set [ ($customer, wants, $request),
        ($request, is_requested_by, $customer),
        ($hotel, is_requested_in, $request),
        ($request, requests, $hotel),
        ($hotel, pre_booked_by, $quota), ($quota, is_for, $hotel) ];
cType (cReq, immOff) ($customer, wants, $request) = single;
cType (cReq, immOff) ($request, is_requested_by, $customer)
        = single;
cType (cReq, immOff) ($hotel, is_requested_in, $request)
        = single;
cType (cReq, immOff) ($request, requests, $hotel) = single;
cType (cReq, immOff) ($hotel, pre_booked_by, $quota) = single;
cType (cReq, immOff) ($quota, is_for, $hotel) = setOf;
endaxioms;
```

Fig. 8.16

The relatively simple abstract syntax for ECDs shows that the SSADM-F variant of these diagrams is well integrated into the syntactical framework of SSADM-F.

8.3.4 Effect Correspondence Diagrams: Axiomatic Semantics

The formal semantics for an ECD in SSADM-F is structured into two parts. In the first part, the definition of entry points is related to the classification of occurrence identifiers in the semantic reference model. The second part gives an interpretation of the correspondence relation, using standard notions from relational algebra.

Before going into the technical details of the semantics, it is useful to recall the general situation addressed by the ECDs, see figure 8.17.

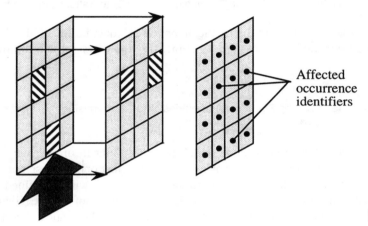

Affected occurrence identifiers

Fig. 8.17

We assume here a given (current) state of the system and an input event leading to an update of the system and therefore to a "next" state. The input event is classified by its event and option names. The update is described on the level of affected occurrences. The semantics of the Event-Entity Matrix ensures that to each affected occurrence identifier a role is assigned. Moreover, such an occurrence identifier has a fixed entity which classifies the respective occurrence in both the current and the next state (if it is present there). Since a pair of entity and role is called a target, we have now for each target a set of affected occurrence identifiers. It is convenient to define an abbreviation for this set. The following axiom defines the set formally, but does not yet express any semantic constraint.

> targetSet: State × InpEv × Target → Set OccId;

{E-9}   (i ∈ targetSet(s, ie, tg)) = (target(s, ie, i) = tg);

The semantics of an ECD addresses the affected occurrence identifiers via target sets. An entry point of cardinality type single means that the set of occurrence identifiers assigned to this target must be a singleton set. This condition cannot be generally postulated for system states, but it has to hold for the appropriate targets only if an input event is accepted. Therefore, we define a *predicate* entriesOK which tests the property that the target sets for entry points are singletons. In order to allow flexible applications of this predicate, we parameterize it by the actual set of entries and by the function which assigns the cardinality information to an entry point. This will turn out as useful below when the subset of regular entries is studied.

entriesOK: State × InpEv × Set Target × (Target → CardType) **to** Bool;

{E-10a}   entriesOK(s, ie, ets, etyp) =
                    ($\forall$ tg. tg $\in$ ets $\wedge$ etyp(tg) = single $\Rightarrow$ card(targetSet(s, ie, tg)) = 1);

For any accepted input event the predicate entriesOK must be fulfilled, where the last two arguments of entriesOK are substituted by the entry set and the function etype.

{E-10b}   acc(s, ie) $\Rightarrow$
                    let oev = optEvent(s, ie) **in** entriesOK(s, ie, entries(oev), eType(oev))
                    endlet;

There is a whole list of conditions which has to be met in order to ensure the acceptance of an input event. The entries predicate is just one of these conditions, another is for instance the correspondence predicate which will be defined below. In section 8.6, a more comprehensive definition of acc(s, ie) will be given from which axiom E-10b and several other axioms can be derived as logical theorems.

It is interesting to see that the axioms E-10a and E-10b say nothing about entry points of cardinality type setOf. The only semantics we could assign to such an entry point is that the corresponding set of ocurrences does exist, which is already specified by other axioms. So this type of entry points has no semantic meaning on the level which is studied here. However, these entry points are used in later refinements of the specification, in particular if the navigation in the database is investigated. Also chapter 10 below will show a sensible use of all types of entry points.

For the correspondence arrows, a function similar to targetSet is used, which defines for a relationship those instances which exist between affected occurrence identifiers either in the current or in the next system state. The relationship instances form a binary relationship on occurrence identifiers, which makes them ready for application of concepts from relational algebra.

targetRel: State × InpEv × Corr → OccId × OccId → Bool;

{E-11}   targetRel(s, ie, (tg1, r, tg2))(i1, i2) =
                (i1 ∈ targetSet(s, ie, tg1) ∧ i2 ∈ targetSet(s, ie, tg2) ∧
                (connected(s, r) (get(s, i1), get(s, i2)) ∨
                let s' = next(s, ie) **in** connected(s', r)(get(s', i1), get(s', i2)) **endlet**);

The semantics of the correspondence arrow can be given by standard concepts from relational algebra, similar to the optionality and degree restrictions for relationships. For an example, let the left hand node of the arrow be a "single" node of entity E, as in figure 8.18 (a). This type of correspondence frequently depends on an underlying relationship in the data model, as also shown in the figure. We have chosen the most liberal type of relationship which is available in SSADM-F in order to avoid confusion with the degree and optionality restrictions of the data model.

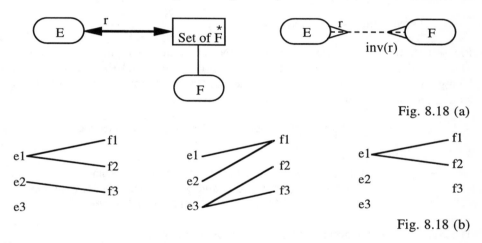

Fig. 8.18 (a)

Fig. 8.18 (b)

Figure 8.18 (b) shows three typical situations which may occur in the analysis of the target structure of an actual event. The lowercase letters correspond here to affected occurrence identifiers, the initial letter indicates whether an E or F target is assigned to these occurrence identifiers. The first situation is acceptable, since there is a one-to-one correspondence e1↔{f1, f2}, e2↔{f3}, e3↔{}. The second situation should be excluded, since e1 and e2 correspond to the same set of F-targets. Also the third situation should be excluded since the F-targets are not properly partitioned into sets: Occurrence identifier f3 does not belong to any target set. So the semantics of the ECD is exactly the same kind of constraint for the affected occurrence identifiers as it is expressed for a data model by the ER diagram in figure 8.18 (c).

Fig. 8.18 (c)

Please note that the decision how to define the details of the semantics can only be motivated by an *intuitive* understanding of the purpose of ECDs. The main source for our definition was the use of ECDs in later stages in SSADM, where the correspondence arrows are used for navigation in the database. There it would be unsuitable, for instance, to admit F-targets which are not reachable via an E-target in the example from above.

The same constructions from relational algebra which were used to define the relationship degrees and optionalities can now be used for the semantics of the correspondence. In chapter 7, the mappings INV (inverse), L-UNIQUE (left-uniqueness) and L-TOTAL (left-totality) were introduced, and the ER diagram was translated into the following constraint for an instance ρ of the relationship r, where χ is the "contained"-predicate which tests whether an occurrence is contained in the state:

$$L\text{-UNIQUE}(\rho) \wedge L\text{-TOTAL}(\chi, INV(\rho))$$

Please note that it is necessary to use the INV construct, since the crow's foot is placed at the right hand side of the relationship which is labelled with inv(r)[15]. Using this idea, we define the predicate corrOK, analogously to entriesOK. A similar parameterization as for the entries is used here.

corrOK: State × InpEv × Set Corr × (Corr → CardType) **to** Bool;

{*}   corrOK(s, ie, crs, ctyp) =
                ($\forall$ tg1, tg2, r, c. c $\in$ crs $\wedge$ c = (tg1, r, tg2) $\wedge$ (ctyp(c) = single)
                $\Rightarrow$ **let** ρ = targetRel(s, ie, c) **and** χ = λ i. i$\in$ targetSet(s, ie, tg2) **in**
                        R-UNIQUE(ρ) $\wedge$ L-TOTAL(χ, INV(ρ)) **endlet**);

The connection to the acceptance predicate is also analogous:

{E-14b} acc(s, ie) $\Rightarrow$
                let oev = optEvent(s, ie) **in** corrOK(s, ie, corrs(oev), cType(oev))
                endlet;

This definition of the corrOK predicate tests whether the relationship instances on affected occurrences have the typical properties of a left-optional one-to-many relation. Such a restriction is caused by the "single" node at the left hand side of the correspondence arrow.

However, we have seen in the informal explanations above (see figures 8.12 (a) and 8.12 (b)) that it is not yet sufficient to fix the semantics for atomic

---

[15] Due to the χ parameter, the expression is also semantically different to right-totality.

correspondence arrows. Figure 8.12 (b) shows a case where the constraints of each atomic correspondence are fulfilled, but not the implicit consequence for transitive correspondences. Therefore, the idea of the first attempt has to be transferred onto chains of correspondence arrows.

The generalization uses a generic closure operator which constructs the set of possible composed correspondence arrows, as well as a transitive extension targetRel* of the function targetRel. The detailed technical definitions for these functions (axioms E-12 and E-13) are omitted here. Based on these auxiliary constructs, the axiom {*} from above can be generalized into the following axiom E-14a.

{E-14a} corrOK(s, ie, crs, ctyp) =
$\qquad$ $\forall$ uc. uc $\in$ closure(crs, ctyp) $\wedge$ (length(uc) $\geq$ 1) $\wedge$ (ctyp(first(uc)) = single)
$\qquad$ $\Rightarrow$ **let** ρ = targetRel*(s, ie, uc)
$\qquad\qquad$ **and** $\chi = \lambda$ i. i$\in$targetSet(s, ie, π_3(last(uc))) **in**
$\qquad\qquad$ L-UNIQUE(ρ) $\wedge$ L-TOTAL(χ, INV(ρ)) **endlet**;

It has become clear from these semantic definitions that the meaning of an ECD is the definition of a predicate which tests the set of affected occurrence identifiers and their assignment to targets for structural properties.

> ***Example.*** In the case of the "customer request" event (see figure 8.13), in the "immediately offered" option, the ECD semantics is a predicate which tests the following properties: There must be one affected occurrence which is assigned to the target "customer" in "standard role", one occcurrence assigned to "hotel", and one assigned to "reservation" (in "standard role" as well). The hotel target must be connected by the "is_reserved_in" relationship to the reservation target and by the "holds" relationship to the customer target. Moreover, there may be a set of "quota" targets each of which is connected to the hotel (by the "pre_booked_by" relationship). Please note that according to the Event-Entity Matrix, some of the targets and relationship instances have to be present in the current state (customer, hotel, pre_booked_by) and some are created by the update (reservation, is_reserved_in, holds).

As it can be seen from the example, the semantics of ECDs up to now does not distinguish between optional and non-optional nodes in the ECD. This is correct, since the correspondences have to hold for all nodes, as soon as the option of the actual input is known. Obviously, the option must be determined from the information in the input event and those parts of the system state which are accessible without already knowing the option. In other words, the option must be defined, as soon as the regular entries and the regular correspondences are established. Formally, the regular entries and regular correspondences for an event are simply defined as the intersection of all entry and correspondence sets for the various options of the event.

$$regEntries: \quad Event \to Set\ Target;$$
$$regCorrs: \quad\ Event \to Set\ Corr;$$

{E-15a}   tg $\in$ regEntries(ev) $\Leftrightarrow$ ($\forall$ opt. opt $\in$ admOpts(ev) $\Rightarrow$ tg $\in$ entries(ev, opt));
{E-15b}   c $\in$ regCorrs(ev) $\Leftrightarrow$ ($\forall$ opt. opt $\in$ admOpts(ev) $\Rightarrow$ c $\in$ corrs(ev, opt));

In the example from figure 8.16 above (event "Customer Request" with options "immediately offered" and "inquired from hotel"), we have only regular entries. This was the reason for the use of universal quantifiers in the syntactic axioms.

regEntries(cReq, opt) = set [$customer, $hotel];

The regular correspondences are exactly the two triples which appear in both axioms for the corr function.

regCorrs(cReq, immOff) = set [
            ($hotel, pre_booked_by, $quota), ($quota, is_for, $hotel)];

It is intuitively correct that this part of the data model (the quota information for the hotels) is the main information source for the agency whether if can offer a reservation to a customer.

With these definitions, we can give a more precise characterization of the circumstances under which the option is selected. First, we define the obvious specialization of the eType and cType functions to the regular case.

$$regEType: \quad Event \to Target \to CardType; \qquad regEType\ \textbf{total};$$
$$regCType: \quad Event \to Corr \to CardType; \qquad\ regCType\ \textbf{total};$$

{E-16a}   regEType(ev, tg) = single $\Leftrightarrow$
                ($\forall$ opt. opt $\in$ admOpts(ev) $\Rightarrow$ eType((ev, opt), tg) = single);
{E-16b}   regCType(ev, tg) = single $\Leftrightarrow$
                ($\forall$ opt. opt $\in$ admOpts(ev) $\Rightarrow$ cType((ev, opt), tg) = single);

Now we can reuse the parameterized entriesOK and corrOK predicates to give a necessary condition for the definedness of an option: The regular part of the ECD must be fulfilled before an option can be determined.

{E-16c} δ option(s, ie) $\Rightarrow$
            let ev = event(ie) **in**
                entriesOK(s, ie, regEntries(ev), regEType(ev))
                $\wedge$ corrOK(s, ie, regCorrs(ev), regCType(ev)) **endlet**;

As in the case of the acceptance predicate, some other conditions (mainly the existence of targets in the current state) are needed to precisely characterize the definedness of option. A sufficient condition is given in section 8.6.1 below. More details about option selection are added in chapter 11.

To summarize, the axiomatic semantics of ECDs has shown that the ECDs are an integral part of system specification in SSADM-F. Due to the strong orientation of ECDs towards the data model, also the theoretical foundations of Logical Data Modelling could be reused for the ECD semantics. Also the more vague use of ECDs in original SSADM could be provided with formal foundations, but in this case the connections to other parts of the syntax and semantics are significantly weaker.

Although ECDs belong to Entity-Event Modelling, they do not cover much of the dynamic aspects of system behaviour but give a relatively static description of a single modification step. For the modelling of system dynamics, SSADM proposes another technique: Entity Life Histories.

8.4 Entity Life Histories

In this section we give an abstract syntax and formal semantics for Entity Life Histories (ELHs). Fortunately, the ELHs have a more straightforward semantics than the Effect Correspondence Diagrams and can be easily integrated into SSADM-F with only quite trivial refinements of the notation.

8.4.1 Entity Life Histories: Introduction

In a complete SSADM requirements specification, an Entity Life History diagram must be drawn for each entity to define a temporal order for the events which affect the entity. All these diagrams for all entities together give a specification of the allowed evolutions of the system state over time.

The Entity Life Histories in SSADM use a notation which has been taken from Jackson Structured Programming (JSP) and Jackson System Development (JSD). Compared to JSD, the close integration of a process description with the static data model is new. This brings SSADM rather close to object-oriented approaches like OOA [CY91, SM92], where the admitted evolutions of database objects are described by state machines. To put it simply, SSADM uses a syntax of regular expressions rather than the (equivalent) framework of finite state machines.

The notation for Entity Life Histories are the so-called *(Jackson) structure diagrams*. The complete Entity Life History for a single entity must be captured by a single structure diagram, the top node of which is labelled with the name of the entity.

The atomic units of a structure diagram are boxes which are labelled with an event name. In some cases, the event is accompanied by an option which is valid for the event or by a role which is valid for the entity the history of which is drawn. Options are surrounded by round brackets, roles by square brackets. Figure 8.19 shows three examples of such atomic boxes for Entity Life Histories (which are called *effect boxes* in SSADM). As a fourth example, a special atomic unit is included which denotes the absence of any event.

Fig. 8.19

The constructions for more complex diagrams are *sequence, selection, iteration* and *parallel life*. Figures 8.20 (a) through 8.20 (d) show how these constructions are represented graphically in SSADM.

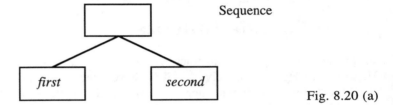

Fig. 8.20 (a)

The two boxes in the lower level of figure 8.20 (a) are placeholders for arbitrary complex structure diagrams. The sequence construction can also be applied to more than two sub-structures (as it is also the case for selection and parallel life). The intuitive meaning of a sequence construction is that this part of the entity life consists of a series of events in a linear temporal order.

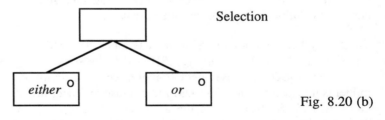

Fig. 8.20 (b)

The selection construction differs from the sequence construction only in the small circles which appear in the right upper corner of a whole level of boxes. The intuitive meaning is that for this part of the entity life there are several alternatives, one of which has to take place. As in the sequence construction more than two alternatives can be contained in a selection. However, a mixture of both constructs (that is boxes with and without small circles having a common predecessor in the tree) is not admitted.

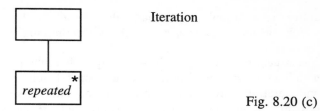

Iteration

Fig. 8.20 (c)

The iteration construction is applied to a single sub-structure. It uses the repetition asterisk which is known also from regular expressions. The meaning is here that this part of the entity life has to consist of finitely many repetitions of the entity life described in the substructure, including zero repetitions or a single repetition.

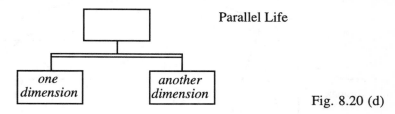

Parallel Life

Fig. 8.20 (d)

The parallel life construction is symbolized by two parallel lines in the connection of the substructures. The meaning is that this part of the entity life has to contain exactly what is described in both substructures, but in an arbitrarily mixed (interleaved) order. This construct is frequently used if an entity can evolve within two orthogonal dimensions. For instance, one branch in the ELH of a "customer" entity may show the ongoing business between a customer and the agency, and the other the possible changes of customer data, like address changes.

The SSADM standard contains an additional construction for ELHs which is intended to describe exceptional cases. This so-called "Quit-and-Resume" construction is similar to the *goto*-construct of programming languages. We do *not* cover this construct in this work because its current form in SSADM opens a way to completely unstructured descriptions. However, also an inclusion of this construct would not lead into any particular problems, except of a number of non-elegant auxiliary constructs.

Figure 8.21 below gives an example for an ELH out of the Hotel Agency example. It depicts the order of the events which may possibly affect an occurrence of the "reservation" entity. The effect boxes (leaves) of the tree correspond exactly to those lines of the Event-Entity Matrix[16] which have a non-empty entry in the "reservation" column. Some events ("customer request", "hotel reply") affect the

---

[16] See figure 8.2, and appendix B for a full version of the matrix.

entity "reservation" only in particular options. In these cases, boxes are shown which contain the event as well as the option (in round brackets).

The structure of the ELH follows a frequently found pattern. It has two main parts which are in sequential order: creation and deletion. In this example, the creation and deletion parts simply consist of an alternative between several atomic possibilities. In many cases, a third part of the ELH is a "mid-life" between creation and deletion which is empty in this example.

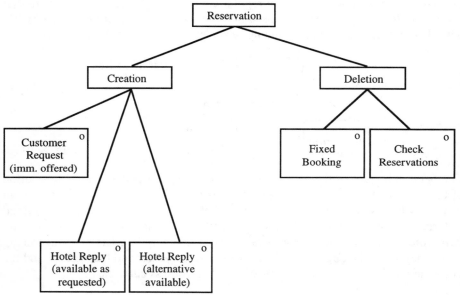

Fig. 8.21

8.4.2 Entity Life Histories: Abstract Syntax

The abstract syntax of an Entity Life History can be described by a syntax tree, as any expression of a programming language. The only particularity in SSADM is that these expressions are not written in a textual syntax, but are explicitly drawn as trees.

An ELH is simply a regular expression over a special alphabet, which is given by the effect boxes. An effect box contains an event, an option and a role (options and roles can be replaced by standard values). We use the term *effect* for such a triple and introduce a sort for effects.

    sortsyn Effect = (Event, Option, Role);

The sort Effect is the only concept in ELHs which is specific to SSADM; it was just introduced in order to apply standard concepts from formal language theory, i.e. regular expressions.

The definition of the syntax of regular expressions which appears in any textbook on formal languages can be translated easily into a SPECTRUM data declaration (see [Het93] for a detailed discussion of regular expressions in SPECTRUM). The data sort of regular expressions is polymorphic, since regular expressions can be formed over any basic alphabet.

```
data ERegExp α =
      eps                                  — — Empty regular expression
   |  atom(! α)                            — — Atomic regular expression
   |  seq2(! ERegExp α, ! ERegExp α)       — — Concatenation
   |  alt2(! ERegExp α, ! ERegExp α)       — — Alternative
   |  mrg2!(! ERegExp α, ! ERegExp α)      — — Interleaving (Merge)
   |  **(! ERegExp a);                     — — Iteration (Kleene star)
```

The new sort[17] has been called ERegExp, for "extended regular expression", since it provides one construct which is not completely standard in regular expressions, namely the interleaving (or merge) operator. However, also this operator appears frequently in application-oriented versions of regular expression syntax, for instance in Process Algebra. (A merge between two regular expressions denotes the language of all words which can be obtained by an arbitrary merge of two words denoted by its argument expressions.)

The syntax of extended regular expressions corresponds exactly to ELHs which do not use the "Quit" and "Resume" constructs. The correspondence is as follows:

Empty effect box (contains dash only)	eps
Normal effect box (event ev, option opt, role rol)	atom (ev, opt, rol)
Sequence	seq2
Selection	alt2
Parallel life	mrg2
Iteration	**

In the case of effect boxes which do not contain an option or role information, the missing option or role is replaced by the standard values. The translation of an ELH into a regular expression following these rules has the consequence that the inner nodes of the ELH tree are translated into constructor applications (sequence,

---

17   The syntax for the Kleene star is a symbolic prefix operator (since SPECTRUM does not admit postfix operators). Also the repetition of the star symbol is required by the SPECTRUM syntax.

alternative, iteration, parallel), which do not provide a place for the labels of the inner nodes. So the labels of the inner nodes are ignored; they have no semantic meaning and can also be omitted from ELHs.

For every entity, there is exactly one ELH, so the ELHs are given by a total function.

ELH: Entity → ERegExp Effect;   ELH **total**;

As an example, the ELH from figure 8.21 above leads to the following axiom.

```
ELH(reservation) =
     seq [   alt [    atom(custReq, immOff, stdRole),
                      atom(hotelReply, availAsReqd, stdRole),
                      atom(hotelReply, altAvail, stdRole)     ],
             eps,
             alt [    atom(fixedBkg, stdOpt, stdRole),
                      atom(chkResvs, stdOpt, expd)  ] ];
```
Fig. 8.22

In order to keep the formal specification simple, we have defined and used here n-ary variants of the sequence, alternative and parallel life constructs, defined by the following functions.

seq, alt, mrg: List (ERegExp Effect) → ERegExp Effect;

An application of one of these functions can be seen as an abbreviation for a cascade of the respective binary construct. All three constructs (sequence, alternative, merge) are known to be associative from formal language theory, so such a cascade may be constructed from the left or from the right hand side. A formal definition of n-ary extensions can be easily given using standard concepts from functional programming ("folding", [BW88]), but is omitted here. Moreover, the formalization has explicitly introduced an empty "mid-life" part for the ELH.

It was said above that the ELHs for a given project can be seen as a refinement of the information contained in the Event-Entity Matrix. Therefore, the information in the matrix and in the ELHs must be consistent in the sense that every atomic box present in the ELHs corresponds to a non-null entry in the matrix. This context condition is captured by the following axiom.

{ES-10}   (atom(ev, opt, rol) isPartOf ELH(e))   ⇔   (e, rol) ∈ admTargets(ev, opt);

This axiom uses an auxiliary operation on ELHs for testing whether an ELH expression is part of another ELH expression. The definition of this auxiliary operation is obvious, it can be found in section 8.7.1.

A second, less obvious context condition is a cross-consistency with the Event-Entity Matrix. We claim generally that every entity life history starts with a single creation event, proceeds with various read and modification events and close with a deletion event. The axiomatic semantics which are defined in the next subsection would be logically inconsistent with the semantics of the Event-Entity Matrix if this condition was violated[18]. We formulate this as a decidable syntactic condition. Each ELH in SSADM-F has to be composed of a "creation", a "middle" and a "deletion" part. The creation part contains those effect boxes which have a C-entry in the Event-Entity Matrix, and analogously for the deletion part and D-entries. Finally, both the creation and the deletion part describe sequences of length 1. This context condition was the reason for the auxiliary "middle" part in the formal ELH of figure 8.22.

{ES-11} ∃ CL, ML, DL: ERegExp Effect.
　　　　　ELH(e) = seq [CL, ML, DL] ∧ atomic(CL) ∧ atomic(DL)
　　　　　∧ (EEX((ev, opt), (e, rol)) = C ⇔ atom(ev, opt, rol) isPartOf CL)
　　　　　∧ (EEX((ev, opt), (e, rol)) = D ⇔ atom(ev, opt, rol) isPartOf CL);

Axiom ES-11 uses a predicate atomic to test whether a regular expression accepts only a word of length 1. This property is generally decidable; see section 8.7.1 for a criterion for this property which is adequate for practical use.

Obviously, one could think of more liberal context conditions at this place; however, the condition given here is met by most SSADM examples in the literature.

8.4.3 Entity Life Histories: Axiomatic Semantics

The ELHs prescribe a temporal order for the events accepted by the system. Therefore they only restrict the acc function in the semantic reference specification which defines under which circumstances an event is accepted by the system. The semantic definition uses standard concepts from formal language theory.

The idea of an Entity Life History is to localize the behaviour of the system, which is its reaction to a series of input events, onto the level of ocurrences. Given an occurrence identifier and a life history of the whole system over time, we can decide for each state transition whether it affects the actual occurrence identifier or not. For the local life history of the occurrence identifier, we are interested only in these state transitions where the occurrence identifier is affected (see figure 8.23).

---

[18] See chapter 9 for more information on logical consistency.

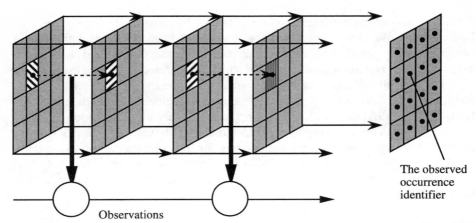

The observed
occurrence
identifier

Observations

Fig. 8.23

The relevant observations of an occurrence are the effects as they appear in the ELH. If an input event leads to a next state and affects the occurrence identifier, then the classification information into event, option and role is available (due to axioms E-1 and E-2). Moreover, axiom E-4 ensures that all observed occurrences belong to the same entity, so also the entity information is available. To simplify other axioms, we first introduce a function effect which defines the event, option, role triple for an affected identifier, using the classification functions from above.

effect: State × InpEv × OccId → Effect;

{E-17}   effect(s, ie, i) = (event(ie), option(s, ie), role(s, ie, i));

The function occHistory localizes a system life into the life of a given occurrence identifier, represented as a list of effects. Besides the occurrence identifier, an entity is given as an additional parameter to ensure that all observations belong not only to the same identifier but also to the same entity. This is necessary since the same identifier could be used for different entities (in disjoint life cycles). The function occHistory filters the system life to those event instances where the given occurrence identifier is affected (and bound to the observed entity).

occHistory: State × List InpEv × OccId × Entity → List Effect;

{E-18a}   occHistory(s, [], i, e) = [];
{E-18b}   affects(s, ie, i) ∧ idEntity(s, ie, i) = e ⇒
              occHistory(s, [ie]++ui, i, e)
                      = [effect(s, ie, i)]++occHistory(next(s, ie), ui, i, e);
{E-18c}   ¬ affects(s, ie, i) ∨ idEntity(s, ie, i) ≠ e ⇒
              occHistory(s, [ie]++ui, i, e) = occHistory(next(s, ie), ui, i,e);

An ELH defines a constraint for such occurrence lifes. Using the ELH which belongs to the observed entity, we can test whether the observed state transitions match the order given by the ELH. For this test we can use standard formal language theory which defines a test whether a given list over the basic alphabet (which is called a word there) matches a regular expression. We recall the SPECTRUM formulation of these standard definitions here.

$$\text{matches}: \quad \alpha:: EQ \Rightarrow \text{List } \alpha \times \text{ERegExp } \alpha \rightarrow \text{Bool};$$

{EA-6a} matches(u, eps) = (u = []);
{EA-6b} matches(u, atom(x)) = (u = [x]);
{EA-6c} matches(u, seq2(E1, E2)) =
        $\exists$ u1, u2. u = u1++u2 $\wedge$ matches(u1, E1) $\wedge$ matches(u1, E1);
{EA-6d} matches(u, alt2(E1, E2)) = matches(u1, E1) $\vee$ matches(u1, E1);
{EA-6e} matches(u, mrg2(E1, E2)) =
        $\exists$ w: List (Bool $\times \alpha$). map(w, λ(b, x). x) = u
                $\wedge$ matches(filter(w, λ(b, x). b), E1)
                $\wedge$ matches(filter(w, λ(b, x). $\neg$b), E2);
{EA-6f} matches(u, (**E)) =
        $\exists$ uu: List List α. u = concat(uu) $\wedge \forall$ v. (v elem uu $\Rightarrow$ matches(v, E));

The definitions for the empty and atomic expressions, the sequence and the alternative are quite trivial. For the two remaining constructs, we have chosen quite descriptive formulations:

- The definition of the "merge" (parallel life) operator encodes the following idea: A word u is a merge of two other words u1 and u2 if there is a "switching" word which adds a Boolean value to each component of u such that filtering the sequence to components which the two truth values (true and false) gives the words u1 and u2.

- The idea for the definition of the iteration (Kleene star) is as follows: The word u matches the iteration of expression E if it can be split into subwords each of which matches E. Formally the list of subwords is a list of words the sequential concatenation of which gives u[19].

The obvious idea for the semantics of Entity Life Histories is to constrain the system behaviour in such a way that all derivable occurrence histories match the regular expression given by the corresponding Entity Life History. In order to realize this idea, we have to assume a common "starting point" for the system behaviour. This is necessary since the ELHs have a defined starting point as well, and it must be ensured that all occurrence histories begin at this starting point.

---

[19] See appendix D for the exact definition of the function concat.

Therefore we define an initial system state initState which does not contain any occurrences at all.

> initState: State;

{E-19} $\neg$ bound(initState, i);

Using this initial state, the idea for the semantics can be expressed as a relatively simple mathematical formula. It assumes an accepted behaviour of the whole system, localizes it to the life of any occurrence and compares this occurrence history with the appropriate ELH.

{*}   s = next*(initState, ui) $\Rightarrow$ ($\exists$ vi. (occHistory(s, ui, i, e)++vi) matches (**(ELH(e))));

Two features of this axiom are noteworthy. First, the axiom (*) claims the occurence history to be a *prefix* of a complete life history, by introducing the variable vi which stands for the rest of the life history up to completion. This is intuitively correct since in an arbitrary intermediate state of the system behaviour also an arbitrary initial part of the single occurrence lifes is observed. It is a very common pattern in the description of dynamic behaviour to define some kind of *complete* behaviour, as the ELHs do, with an implicit extension to "approximations" of this complete behaviour.

Moreover, and maybe more surprisingly, the axiom (*) does not require the occurrence histories to match the ELH itself, but an iteration of the ELH. This is motivated by the fact that for the same occurrence identifier (which is a combination of attribute values in SSADM) several different occurrences may be created and subsequently deleted during the lifetime of the system. We have chosen this kind of semantics since it admits an occurrence to be permanently deleted form a system state without leaving any traces.

As it was already mentioned for other parts of SSADM, our intention is to give a precise characterization of the function acc. This will be possible at the end of this chapter, when all EEM documents have been formalized. The coincidence with the ELHs is one of the contributions to the acceptance test and has to be integrated there. For this purpose, a variant of the axiom from above is needed which encapsulates the test into a predicate similar to the predicates entriesOK and corrOK which were derived from the ECDs. So we give here two more refined axioms which entail the formula (*) from above. (This is also the reason why the axiom was not given a proper name above.)

historyOK: State × InpEv × OccId **to** Bool;

{E-20}   affects(s, ie, i) $\Rightarrow$ **let** e = idEntity(s, ie, i) **in**
                    historyOK(s, ie, i) =
                            ($\forall$ ui. s = next*(initState, ui) $\Rightarrow$
                                    $\exists$ vi. (occHistory(initState, ui, i, e)++[effect(s, ie, i)]++vi)
                                            matches (**(ELH(e))))
                endlet;

{E-21}   acc(s, ie) $\land$ affects(s, ie, i) $\Rightarrow$ historyOK(s, ie, i);

From the two axioms E-20 and E-21, by an inductive argument the formula (*) from above can be derived. Moreover, axiom E-20 shows a quite interesting aspect of the way how system dynamics are modelled in SSADM. The system state s in axiom E-21 can be understood as a point in time, the ui-lists are possible past histories which may have lead to the current state and the vi-list is a possible future history which will complete the prescribed life history. The next step into the future is admitted only if there is a way to complete the life history (see also figure 8.24).

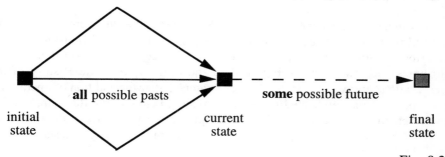

initial
state

all possible pasts

current
state

some possible future

final
state

Fig. 8.24

At a first look, it might puzzle the reader that the possibility of several alternative histories leading to the current state is covered here. This possibility is needed due to a very pragmatic reason. The universal quantification over possible pasts gives a chance for an implementation to *abstract* the past into some more compact representation. For instance, the *state indicators* which are introduced during stage 5 of SSADM based on the ELHs are such a way to represent exactly this infomation which is needed to decide on the acceptance of an input event. The same state indicator may be used, for instance, to indicate the mid-life of a "reservation" occurrence, independently of the numer of times the occurrence has been checked (negatively) for expiration. Theoretically, one could also think of an implementation which stores the whole history within the system state. In such a construction, the set of possible pasts collapses to a single one. This idea is also used in chapter 9 to show the consistency of the axioms which were introduced above.

Now the main components have been defined which determine the acceptance of an input event (acc predicate): The selection of an option, the entry-point and correspondence constraints on the target occurrences and the history constraint for each single target occurrence. However, before moving on to the synthesis of all these parts, we shortly cover another part of Entity-Event Modelling in SSADM, which is very closely connected to Entity-Life Histories: the so-called Operation Lists.

8.5 Operation Lists

During step 360 of SSADM, "Develop Processing Specification", Entity-Event Modelling is completed by three activities. The ELHs are drawn, the complementary ECDs are drawn, and operations are added onto the ELHs. Strictly speaking, operations are a part of the Entity Life History document. However, we formalize the Operation Lists as a separate document type since they are semantically independent of the ELHs.

8.5.1 Operations: Introduction

For a complete requirements specification, SSADM requires the atomic boxes in the Entity Life Histories to be enhanced by a sequence of so-called *operations* which describe the update of an occurrence of the respective entity on the level of attributes and relationships. Figure 8.25 shows the Entity Life History of the "reservation" entity in the Hotel Agency example, after the addition of operations. The operations are indicated by small numbered boxes in the diagram, and are described in a separate list. These descriptions are texts in a style similar to commands of a programming language for the manipulation of system states.

The syntax for operations is not defined in SSADM in every detail, however the main keywords are prescribed. A single operation may denote

- the inital assignment of an attribute value ("Store" operation);

- the update of an attribute value ("Replace" operation);

- the introduction of a new relationship instance to a master occurrence ("Tie" and "Gain" operations);

- the deletion of a relationship instance to a master occurrence ("Cut" and "Lose" operations).

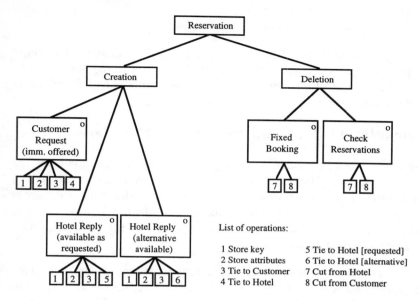

List of operations:

1 Store key	5 Tie to Hotel [requested]
2 Store attributes	6 Tie to Hotel [alternative]
3 Tie to Customer	7 Cut from Hotel
4 Tie to Hotel	8 Cut from Customer

Fig. 8.25

The distinction between "Tie" and "Gain" (and "Cut" and "Lose", respectively) is motivated by the fact that SSADM (in the later design stages) does support only one-to-many relationships. If the relationship is addressed from an entity which participates at the "many end" of a one-to-many relationship (called a "detail" occurrence in SSADM), then "Tie" and "Cut" are used. The verbs "Gain" and "Lose" apply if the occurrence is at the "single" end (a so-called master occurence).

All these operations refer to an occurrence of a specific entity, which is the one to which the actual ELH belongs. An operation can be restricted to occurrences in a particular role by placing it beneath an effect box which specifies a role (in square brackets). The creation or deletion of occurrences is not handled at the level of operations[20], however some special abbreviations are allowed for the initial assignment of keys and mandatory attributes at creation of an occurrence ("Store keys", "Store attributes").

Usually, the operations do not specify what the new value is for an attribute update. In SSADM, this information is often obvious from other documents like Function Definitions and from an informal understanding of the purpose of the system. The only formal syntax which is defined in SSADM for specifiying the new value is the "Using" clause which supplements "Store" and "Replace" operations, as in the following example:

---

[20] This does hold only for stage 3, in which we are interested here; it does no longer hold for stage 5 of SSADM.

1   Replace NumRequests Using NumRequests + 1.

For the formalized notation SSADM-F, we have decided not to support "Using" clauses as part of Operation Lists. They are clearly inferior to the possibility to integrate formal specifications for attribute values into SSADM-F, which is discussed in chapter 10 below.

8.5.2 Semantic Analysis and Refinement of Notation

The operation boxes are inserted into the diagram beneath an event box using the "sequence" construction. However, the order of the operations usually is not significant. Each operation addresses one attribute or relationship only, and there is no reason to introduce several operations for the same attribute or relationship. The list structure serves only for breaking down the update into smaller parts which refer to a single attribute or relationship.

Moreover, it does not make much sense to distinguish between "Gain" and "Tie" verbs (and "Lose" and "Cut" as well), since SSADM-F does support also many-to-many relationships. So SSADM-F provides only the "Gain" and "Lose" variant. Moreover, the SSADM-F "Gain" and "Lose" operations require the relationship identifier to be named explicitly.

Similarly, we do not distinguish in SSADM-F between "Store" and "Replace", but always use "Store". The "Store" operations have to be explicit about the addressed attribute, implicit references like "Store attributes" are not admitted.

With these modifications, the SSADM-F version of figure 8.25 differs from original SSADM only in the operations which are assigned to the numbers, as it is shown in figure 8.26.

List of operations:

1   Store attribute Reference Number
2   Store attributes Period, Number Rooms, Date Offered
3   Gain relationship Is_Reserved_For to Customer
4   Gain relationship Reserves to Hotel
5   Gain relationship Reserves to Hotel [requested]
6   Gain relationship Reserves to Hotel [alternative]
7   Lose relationship Reserves to Hotel
8   Lose relationship Is_Reserved_For to Customer   Fig. 8.26

From a systematic point of view, the operation boxes are not very well integrated into the formalism of ELHs. It is not clear what the advantage of the graphical representation is here, since the operation boxes always appear in the form of lists. The convention of using number-indexed lists makes the operation notation difficult to read and to keep consistent. The lists of operations for larger projects, however, tend to be quite difficult to handle. (As an impressive example, see the Entity Life Histories which are reproduced in [DH92].) It is also irritating to find the execution-oriented style of operations among the otherwise rather descriptive documents of Event-Entity Modelling. The only explanation for these choices in SSADM is that ELHs are used to derive process logic in stage 5. However, the operations cover an important specification aspect, that is to define which attributes and relationships are modified by an input event. This is the reason why they are included in SSADM-F.

8.5.3 Operations: Abstract Syntax

For Operation Lists in SSADM-F, we define here an abstract syntax which captures all the essential information. For this purpose, it is not necessary to refer to the tree-like syntax of ELHs. Instead, an Operation List is associated with every effect box on the ELH. Such an effect box is a triple of event, option and role.

The general situation of an operation according to the SSADM notation is as shown in figure 8.27.

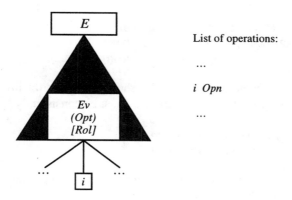

List of operations:

...

$i \; Opn$

...

Fig. 8.27

It is obvious from figure 8.27 that the whole classification scheme of event, option, entity and role is available for each operation. Three of these identifiers are found in the effect box, the name of the entity (indicated by E) is the label of the root box of the ELH.

In SSADM-F, three types of operations are admitted, one attribute operation (Store) and two operations dealing with relationship instances (Gain and Lose). The "Store"-operation refers to an attribute identifier. Each of the "Gain"- and "Lose"-operations references a relationship identifier and a target (in the sense which was defined above, as an entity plus role). Due to this similarity, a common syntax can be used for "Gain" and "Lose", with an additional tag to distinguish between them. This leads to the following syntax for operations.

> **data** Opn = attSto(! Attr) I relMod(! RMod, ! Rel, ! Target);
> **data** RMod = gain I lose;

The operation lists themselves are modelled by a function which assigns a set of operations to any quatruple of event, option, entity and role, abbreviated, as usually, as a pair of OptEvent and Target.

> OPS: OptEvent × Target → List Opn;

Obviously, the operation list should be defined if the quatruple corresponds to an effect box on the ELH. According to axiom ES-9, this is equivalent to the constraint given by the admTargets-function (which was itself derived from the Event-Entity Matrix).

{ES-12} tg ∈ admTargets(oev) ⇒ δ OPS(oev, tg);

Moreover, there are a few simple context conditions for the arguments of the operations.

{ES-13} attSto(a) elem OPS(oev, (e, rol)) ⇒ a ∈ attrs(e);
{ES-14} relMod(rm, r, (e2, rol2)) elem OPS(oev, (e1, rol1))
          ⇒ (e2, rol2) ∈ admTargets(oev) ∧ related(r) = (e1, e2);

If a relationship instance is created or deleted, this shows up within the life histories of both related entities. Obviously, these operations must be consistently specified.

{ES-15} relMod(rm, r, tg2) elem OPS(oev, tg1) ⇔
          relMod(rm, r, tg1) elem OPS(oev, tg2);

As an example, figure 8.28 shows the formal translation of the operation lists which were given in figures 8.25 and 8.26 above.

```
OPS((custReq, immOff), $reservation) =
        [ attSto(refNo), attSto(period),
        attSto(numRooms), attSto(dateOffer),
        relMod(gain, is_reserved_for, $customer),
        relMod(gain, reserves, $hotel) ];
OPS((hotelReply, availAsReqd), $reservation) =
        [ attSto(refNo), attSto(period), attSto(numRooms),
        attSto(dateOffer),
        relMod(gain, is_reserved_for, $customer),
        relMod(gain, reserves, (hotel, reqd)) ];
```

```
OPS((hotelReply, altAvail), $reservation) =
    [ attSto(refNo), attSto(period), attSto(numRooms),
    attSto(dateOffer),
    relMod(gain, is_reserved_for, $customer),
    relMod(gain, reserves, (hotel, altern)) ];
OPS(%fixedBkg, $reservation) =
    [ relMod(lose, reserves, $hotel),
    relMod(lose, is_reserved_for, $customer) ];
OPS(%chkResvs, $reservation) =
    [ relMod(lose, reserves, $hotel),
    relMod(lose, is_reserved_for, $customer) ];
```
                                                                         Fig. 8.28

Since the operations are intended to supply detail information on top of the other documents of Entiy-Event Modelling, there are several additional context conditions to ensure consistency. Examples are the following ones:

• If the Event-Entity Matrix shows a target as created by an event, the respective operation list has to contain a "Store"-operation for every primary key of the respective entity.

• If the Event-Entity Matrix shows a target as deleted by an event, the respective operation list must not contain any attribute operations at all.

• If the Effect Correspondence Diagram shows a relationship between two targets, one of which is created by an event (according to the Event-Entity Matrix), then the respective operation list for each of the targets must contain a "Gain"-operation for the relationship and the other target.

We omit the full list of context conditions here. However, all these context conditions are necessary, in the sense that if they were violated, the semantics which are assigned to operations would cause logical inconsistencies.

An interesting observation from the abstract syntax definition for operations is that one could think of several other ways of pragmatic representation for the information contained in the abstract syntax. For instance, the attribute operations could be integrated into the Event-Entity Matrix and the relationship operations into the Effect Correspondence Diagrams. Probably the best solution is, however, to keep the operations in a separate document where they are represented in form of matrices.

8.5.4 Operations: Axiomatic Semantics

The assignment of axiomatic semantics to operation lists is very similar to the way in which the semantics of the Event-Entity Matrix has been defined above. Essentially, the current and next system state are compared, where the meaning of an operation is a certain difference on the level of attributes or relationship instances.

The formal semantics of a "store" operation is quite simple. As usual, we consider a situation, where the current state is updated due to an event, and where an occurrence identifier is affected. If an attribute of the respective entity appears in a "store"-operation, it is known that the value of the attribute is defined within the new state. Since the "Using"-clauses have been excluded, no information about the precise value is available.

{E-22}   next(s, ie) = s' ∧ target(s, ie, i) = tg ∧ attSto(a) elem OPS(optEvent(s, ie), tg)
         ⟹ def(get(s', i), a));

The axiom above does only state the consequences for those attributes or which some attribute operation is given. Implicitly, SSADM assumes that "nothing else changes" (see [BMR93]). This assumption is captured by the next axiom.

{E-23}   next(s, ie) = s' ∧ target(s, ie, i) = tg ∧ ¬ (attSto(a) elem OPS(optEvent(s, ie), tg))
         ⟹ (get(s, i)@a = get(s', i)@a);

Similarly, the formal semantics of "gain"- and "lose"-operations can be defined as propositions about the connectedness of two occurrence identifiers in the current and next state.

{E-24}   next(s, ie) = s' ∧ target(s, ie, i1) = tg1 ∧ target(s, ie, i2) = tg2
         ∧ relMod(gain,r, tg2) elem OPS(optEvent(s, ie), tg1)
         ⟹ ¬ (connected(s, r) (get(s, i1), get(s, i2)))
         ∧ connected(s', r) (get(s', i1), get(s', i2));

{E-25}   next(s, ie) = s' ∧ target(s, ie, i1) = tg1 ∧ target(s, ie, i2) = tg2
         ∧ relMod(lose,r, tg2) elem OPS(optEvent(s, ie), tg1)
         ⟹ connected(s, r) (get(s, i1), get(s, i2))
         ∧ ¬ (connected(s', r) (get(s', i1), get(s', i2)));

Again, it is important to state that "nothing else changes". If no relationship operation is specified for a certain relationship, then no update of relationship instances is allowed to occur.

{E-26}   next(s, ie) = s' ∧ target(s, ie, i1) = tg1 ∧ target(s, ie, i2) = tg2 ∧
          ∧ (∀ rm. ¬ (relMod, rm(r, tg2) elem OPS(optEvent(s, ie), tg1)))
              ⇒ connected(s, r) (get(s, i1), get(s, i2))
                  = connected(s, r) (get(s', i1), get(s', i2));

This semantics clarifies that operations, as they are interpreted in SSADM-F, constitute a quite descriptive feature of the specification framework. Using this interpretation, just the name is misleading, which evokes associations to programming and execution.

8.6 EEM: The Whole Picture

At this point, the most central types of documents of the Entity-Event Modelling technique of SSADM have been formalized completely. All these documents have been connected by an axiomatic semantics to the semantic reference specification. However, during the detailed discussion only a sketch could be achieved of the way how these relatively complex specification mechanisms work together. In this final section of the chapter, a few additional semantic axioms will be presented which point out how the various parts of EEM cooperate.

The basic component of the semantic reference specification with respect to system dynamics is the function next, which resembles a state transition of the system caused by an external input event. The purpose of all documents of EEM is to provide detailed specifications for this function. Interestingly, a substantial amount of specification effort goes into a specification of the condition under which the next function is defined.

8.6.1 The Acceptance Condition

The condition under which an input event is accepted has been given the name of acc (acceptance predicate) in chapter 6. At various places during the discussion above, more special conditions have been formulated which have to be met by an input event to be successfully accepted by the system. These conditions, which are composed from all parts of EEM, are:

- An appropriate option is selected for the current state and the input event (axiom E-1).

- There is an assignment of occurrence identifiers to target names which satisfies the requirements given by the Effect Correspondence Diagram (predicates entriesOK and corrOK, axioms E-10b, E-14b).

- If an occurrence identifier is assigned to a target which is shown as read, modified or deleted in the Event-Entity Matrix, then the occurrence identifier is accessible in the current system state (axiom E–8).

- If a pair of occurrence identifiers in the current state is assigned to targets which are connected by a relationship in the Effect Correspondence Diagram, then they are connected by a relationship instance in the current system state, unless the respective relationship is shown as "gained" in the Operation Lists (axioms E-25, E-26 together with E-11 and E-14a).

- For all affected occurrence identifiers, the input event forms a legal extension of their life histories since the initialization of the system (predicate historyOK, axiom E-21).

All these conditions are necessary, and altogether they are also sufficient for the acceptance of an input event. This is captured by the following semantic axiom E-27 which integrates the various documents of EEM. The axiom consists of five conditions, each of which corresponds to an item from the list above. From axiom E-27, four other axioms can be derived (and therefore could be omitted from the specification). These axioms are: E-1, E-10b, E-14b, E-21.

{E-27} $acc(s, ie) \Leftrightarrow$
        δ option(s, ie)
  $\wedge$ **let** oev = optEvent(s, ie) **in**
        entriesOK(s, ie, entries(oev), eType(oev))
  $\wedge$ corrOK(s, ie, corrs(oev), eType(oev))
  $\wedge$ $(\forall\ i, tg.\ target(s, ie, i) = tg \Rightarrow ((i \in s) = (EEX(oev, tg) \neq C))$
  $\wedge$ $(\forall\ r, i1, i2, tg1, tg2.$
       target(s, ie, i1) = tg1 $\wedge$ target(s, ie, i2) = tg2 $\wedge$ (tg1, r, tg2) $\in$ corrs(oev)
          $\Rightarrow$ (connected(s, r)(i1, i2) = $\neg$((gain, r, tg2) elem OPS(oev, tg1))))
  $\wedge$ $(\forall\ i.\ affected(s, ie, i) \Rightarrow historyOK(s, ie, i))$ **endlet**;

Also the definedness condition for option which appears in axiom E-27 can be characterized now in a similar style. Axiom E-16c already has stated that the entry and correspondence conditions must be fulfilled for the regular part of the ECD (that is the part which can be interpreted without knowing the option). This condition has to be enhanced, similar as in E-27 above, such that all regular targets are guaranteed to be present in the current state, unless they are to be created. A similar condition is needed for regular relationships. Before giving the definedness axiom for option, we have to define formally what a regular target and a regular relationship is. In analogy to the definitions from the ECD semantics, we call a target or relationship regular, if it has to be present in the current state, independently of the option. Regularity of relationships is analogously defined, based on the Operation Lists.

      regTarget: Event $\times$ Target $\rightarrow$ Bool;
      regRel: Event $\times$ Corr $\rightarrow$ Bool;

{E-28a}　regTarget(ev, tg)　⇔　∀ opt. opt ∈ admOpts(ev) ⇒ EEX((ev, opt), tg) ≠ C;
{E-28b}　regRel(ev, (tg1, r, tg2))　⇔
　　　　　　∀ opt. opt ∈ admOpts(ev) ⇒ ¬((gain, r, tg2) elem OPS(oev, tg1));

Please note that a correspondence may be contained in the set of regular correspondences, according to the ECD, but may be shown as "gained" for one option in the Operation Lists. In this case, it cannot be required to be present before the option is selected. Based on these definitions, the definedness axiom consists of four subconditions, two of which were earlier given by axiom E-16c.

{E-29}　　δ option(s, ie) = **let** ev = event(ie) **in**
　　　　　　　entriesOK(s, ie, regEntries(ev), regEType(ev))
　　　∧　　corrOK(s, ie, regCorrs(ev), regCType(ev))
　　　∧　　(∀ tg, i. target(s, ie, i) = tg ∧ regTarget(tg) ⇒ i ∈ s)
　　　∧　　(∀ r, i1, i2, tg1, tg2. target(s, ie, i1) = tg1 ∧ target(s, ie, i2) = tg2
　　　　　　　∧ (tg1, r, tg2) ∈ regCorrs(oev) ∧ regCorr(tg1, r, tg2)
　　　　　　　　⇒ connected(s, r) (i1, i2))　　　　**endlet**;

By these axioms (in particular E-27), the acceptance predicate is specified completely. Two aspects are deliberately left open by SSADM: An exact description under which circumstances a particular option is chosen, and a prescription which individual occurrence identifiers should be assigned to a target. Both aspects are covered in SSADM only informally (by textual function descriptions). Chapter 10 below discusses a way to add a precise formal specification for these aspects on top of SSADM-F.

For a closer look at the state transition function next itself, we have to compare the current and the next state. For this purpose, we first discuss generally how two states can be compared.

8.6.2 Comparing States by Comparing Occurrences

The localization principle in the reference specification (axiom CD-2) claims that two states are equal if all the contained occurrences are equal. For the comparison of two occurrences for equality, however, no axiom has been given up to this point. The reason for this omission is that only at the end of the discussion of EEM a complete list of properties has become available by which two occurrences can be distinguished.We list here all possible observations of occurrences which have appeared. From this list, an axiom will be derived which declares two occurrences to be equal if they coincide within all the properties in the list.

- The most basic property of an occurrence is the entity it belongs to.

- Attributes have been defined for occurrences. The value of an attribute is an observation on an occurrence.

- For any occurrence (also if it is not contained in a state!) it can be observed whether it is linked by some relationship to some occurrence identifier. This comes from the fact that we can observe from a state whether two occurrences are connected (by function connected), so due to the localization principle there must be an observation on the level of occurrences capturing the same information.

- Finally, we can observe the history status of an occurrence. Again, the behaviour of a state (its acceptance of an input event) can vary depending on the preceding history of events. Due to the localization principle, this is not a property of the state, but of the occurrences it contains.

We formalize the last two observations as explicit observation functions. This improves readability of the equality axiom for occurrences.

The linkage observation can be modelled as a function which "asks" an occurrence whether it is connected by a given relationship to a given occurrence identifier. Obviously, such observations can be carried out only for occurrences which are contained in a state.

$$\text{linked:} \qquad \text{Occ} \times \text{Rel} \times \text{OccId} \to \text{Bool};$$

{E-30}   get(s, i1) = o $\Rightarrow$ linked(o, r, i2) = connected(s, r)(o, get(s, i2));

Due to this axiom, a natural implementation of occurrences includes some kind of local "link pointers" which are stored within an occurrence. However, other implementations (like separate link tables) are possible, but in these cases a proof is needed to show how the concept of occurrence can be realized adequately.

The history status observation can be modelled by defining a new sort which closely resembles the "state indicators" (SIs) which are introduced in stage 5 of SSADM. The state indicator can be observed from any occurrence which is contained in a state. Two occurrences coincide in their state indicators, iff their history tests for a new input event give the same result.

sort SI;   SI:: EQ;

histStat: Occ $\to$ SI;

{E-31}   get(s, i) = o $\wedge$ get(s', i') = o' $\Rightarrow$
          (histStat(o) = histStat(o')) = ($\forall$ ie. historyOK(s, ie, i) = historyOK(s', ie, i'));

In a natural implementation some local "status indicator field" should be present within any occurrence, as it is proposed by SSADM.

Using the additional observation functions (which are not new, but derived from existing functions), the equality of occurrences can be characterized explicitly.

{E-32} $(o = o')$ $\Leftrightarrow$ entity(o) = entity(o')

$\qquad\qquad\qquad\land\qquad$ ($\forall$ a. o@a = o'@a)

$\qquad\qquad\qquad\land\qquad$ ($\forall$ r, i. linked(o, r, i) = linked(o', r, i))

$\qquad\qquad\qquad\land\qquad$ histStat(o) = histStat(o');

For our purpose of studying state transitions, we have now found a scheme how the current and the successor state can be compared.

- First, a correspondence between the occurrences in the current and the next state has to be established, in order to localize the comparison.

- Then, for each occurrence, the four components entity, attributes, links and history status are compared, individually.

Using this guideline, we now give an informal argumentation why the axiomatic semantics gives an acceptably complete characterization for state transitions.

8.6.3 The Successor State

We apply the comparison scheme from above to a state transition, that is to the input and output of the central function next. So let us assume, as usual, that the current state is called s and the next state (by acceptance of an input event ie) is called s'.

The first step of comparison is to establish a correspondence between the occurrences in the two states. This is achieved by the use of occurrence identifiers. The local comparison is applied to those pairs of occurrences which are identified by the same occurrence identifier in both states. For the following explanations, we refer to an occurrence identifier named by i.

Already in the core specification, the affects predicate was defined to distinguish among occurrence identifiers. For non-affected identifiers, the two states coincide (axiom CE-4). For the comparison, we are interested in the case where i is affected. As it was pointed out in the section on the Event-Entity Matrix, a role is assigned to i (axiom E-2). Other consequences are that an occurrence for the identifier i is contained in either one or both of the states (axiom CE-5). If there are occurrences in both states, then they coincide in the entity (axiom E-4). Let us call the entity e and the role rol.

By the Event-Entity Matrix (axiom E-8), it is fixed whether i is bound in the current or in the next state or in both. So on the first level of comparison (bound occurrence identifiers), the next state is specified completely.

On the level of comparing individual occurrences, we restrict our attention to the case where the Event-Entity Matrix shows an "M" entry. For the occurrence bound to i in s, we use the name o, for the one in s' the name o'. Now the four components of o and o' can be compared.

- The first component of an occurrence (its entity) is required to be equal, as it was said above (axiom E-4).

- For the second component (attributes), the Operation Lists give a detailed and complete comparison. For any attribute which is relevant for the entity e, either axiom E-22 or axiom E-23 applies and fixes whether o' contains the same value for the attribute as o or whether there is an update to this attribute value. The only aspect which is left open in this specification is the new value for an updated attribute.

- Similarly, the Operation Lists define precisely and completely which updates to the linkage component of the occurrences can occur (axioms E-24, E-25, E-26).

- Finally, the history status component is also specified since it relies on the test predicate historyOK which is explicitly defined for any concrete state transition. In this case, no explicit value for the history status is given. However, it is obvious from axiom E-20 which information must be captured in the history status. It represents of the list of input events which have effected the occurrence during the past state transitions which have led from the initial state to the current state.

Finally, axiom E-30 allows us to conclude the equality of o and o' from the pairwise equality of the four components. So the EEM documents cover a complete specification of the state transition caused by an input event, besides the following aspects.

- The exact characterization of an option, depending on the system state.

- The selection mechanism for individual target occurrences.

- The new values for updated attributes.

These three aspects are discussed in chapter 10 below in more detail.

To summarize, the EEM technique of SSADM and its notations provide a well-integrated way to describe the dynamic updates of an information system on an abstract level. The formalization of the notations has led to a variant of the notations which encourages a more disciplined use than in original SSADM. In particular, for the Event-Entity Matrix and the Effect Correspondence Diagrams significant improvements could be proposed based on the semantic analysis.

8.7 EEM Project Level Translation Schemes

As in the last two chapters, this section gives a few schematic translation tables from pragmatic notations into the abstract syntax of SSADM-F. The tables cover only the Event-Entity Matrix and the event/option/role classification, which are at the center of the EEM semantics. For the other EEM documents, the translation of the diagrammatic notation was explained in all detail in the main text above.

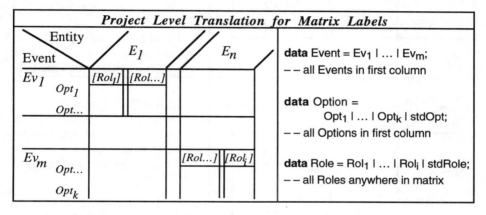

Project Level Translation for Matrix Labels

data Event = Ev_1 | ... | Ev_m;
-- all Events in first column

data Option =
    Opt_1 | ... | Opt_k | stdOpt;
-- all Options in first column

data Role = Rol_1 | ... | Rol_i | stdRole;
-- all Roles anywhere in matrix

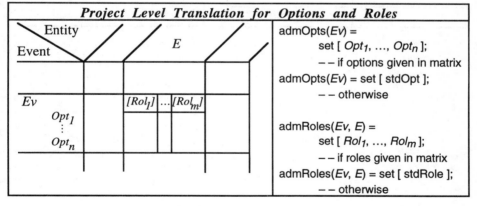

Project Level Translation for Options and Roles

admOpts(Ev) =
    set [Opt_1, ..., Opt_n];
    -- if options given in matrix
admOpts(Ev) = set [stdOpt];
    -- otherwise

admRoles(Ev, E) =
    set [Rol_1, ..., Rol_m];
    -- if roles given in matrix
admRoles(Ev, E) = set [stdRole];
    -- otherwise

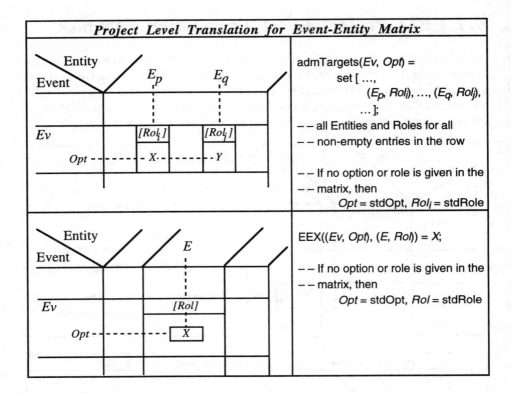

Chapter 9
Logical Consistency of SSADM-F

The last three chapters have provided a detailed formal basis for the pragmatic software specification framework of SSADM, as far as the LDM and EEM techniques are concerned. At every stage of this formalization, a clear structure and simple concepts have been emphasized, in order to keep the formal specification simple. Nevertheless, the SSADM semantics is a non-trivial algebraic specification: The axiomatic semantics alone (core specification plus D- and E-axioms) contains about 60 axioms. Given this amount of formal material, a detailed discussion of properties and consequences seems to be more fruitful than adding further details from SSADM. So the discussion of the Data Flow Modelling technique of SSADM is postponed to chapter 11 and will be kept very brief there. This chapter and the next chapter try to point out the benefits which can be achieved by the work which was presented in the preceding chapters 6 through 8.

This chapter concentrates on the question of consistency of an SSADM-F specification. In chapter 10, a more thorough integration of SSADM-F and SPECTRUM will be discussed which helps to compensate some weak points in SSADM.

Probably one of the biggest achievements by a formal foundation of a pragmatic specification notation is that the question of consistency can be addressed using techniques from mathematical logic. An SSADM-F specification is called consistent if the logical theory is consistent which is obtained by instantiating the axiomatic semantics with the formal translation of the SSADM-F specification. Logical consistency simply means that *there is a model which satisfies the axioms*. A model (in the sense of an algebraic structure) can exist only if the axioms do not contradict themselves. It can be shown *generically* that the method level specification of SSADM-F is consistent if the project level instantiation fulfils the context conditions which were formulated in the chapters 7 and 8. In this chapter we give an overview of the technical background for this proposition. We try to avoid technical details here and concentrate on the basic ideas and design decisions.

9.1 Proof of Consistency by Executable Implementation

For a relatively large and complex specification written in a descriptive style, like the SSADM-F method level specification from above, it is quite difficult to determine whether the axioms are logically consistent.

Basically, there are two approaches available to ensure consistency:

- The *deductive* approach relies on the existence of a deduction calculus for deriving logical consequences from a set of axioms. It tries to exclude any possibility to derive a contradiction.

- The *model-theoretic* approach tries to construct a model (an algebraic structure) directly. For the construction of the model the full power of mathematical constructions can be used. Afterwards it has to be proven that this model satisfies all the axioms.

Unfortunately, both approaches have serious disadvantages if practically applied to a large specification like the one we are analysing here. The deductive approach is well suited for the proof of *inconsistencies*, however it is difficult to use for the positive proof of consistency. For the very general and powerful logic of SPECTRUM, there is a provably correct deduction calculus. But there does not exist any worked-out theory for a systematic analysis of the deductive consequences of a set of axioms. Such tools currently are available only for a very restricted specification logic (essentially equational logic).

The model-theoretic approach, on the other hand, has the disadvantage that the construction of the model usually takes place outside the specification framework. As a consequence, the powerful tool of the deduction calculus for SPECTRUM cannot be used for the consistency proof.

We have decided to use a technique which combines the two approaches to consistency proofs in order to avoid the disadvantages of both. The idea is to construct a model *within the specification language itself*. This idea is not new, but it has been applied only rarely for larger examples up to now, since most specification languages do not support such a wide range of description styles as SPECTRUM.

The main requirement for the construction of a model within the specification language is a criterion which ensures for a specification that it describes (up to isomorphism) a single model. Such a criterion exists for SPECTRUM, which designates a sublanguage which is called the *executable sublanguage*. If a specification belongs to the executable sublanguage of SPECTRUM, it can be understood as a *functional program*. This means that there is a canonical construction for a mathematical model for the specification, and therefore the specification is guaranteed to be consistent.

The construction of a model within the specification language itself has the advantage that the test for satisfaction of the axioms now is a question which can be tackled completely within the formal specification framework. Once an executable specification is given, the consistency of the original axiom set can be proven by showing that the executable specification is a *refinement* of the given axioms. This means, basically, to prove that all given axioms can be derived from the axioms of the executable specification, a question for which the deduction calculus can be used. To summarize, the consistency proof for a given specification SP is carried out in two steps:

1 Executability proof:
   A new specification SP' is given which is shown to belong to the executable sublanguage.

2 Refinement proof:
   It is shown that the given specification is a consequence of the new one:
   Axioms(SP') $\Rightarrow$ Axioms(SP).

Methodically, this way of proceeding has the advantage that a second specification (SP') for the same intended meaning (here the semantics of SSADM-F) is given. As it has been pointed out in [BW85], the adequacy and correctness of any formal description can be significantly improved by describing the same facts a second time independently, and then to check the coincidence of both descriptions.

We do not go into the details of the executable sublanguage of SPECTRUM and of the refinement proof itself here. We just report the main concepts of an executable specification for the LDM and EEM parts of SSADM-F. This specification has been developed in SPECTRUM and can be found in the original text of the thesis from which this book was derived [Hus94]. The executability of the specification (step 1) has been shown by a one-to-one translation into the functional programming language Gofer [Jon93]. The refinement proof (step 2) has been carried out manually. Only the basic ideas underlying the proof are reproduced here. The proofs themselves do not provide any information which helps in understanding of the general approach. It would be an interesting and important research subject to use computer-support for carrying out these lengthy but rather trivial proofs.

In the next section, the basic ideas of the executable specification for SSADM-F and the refinement proof are outlined. For a reader who is not interested in the technicalities of formal methods, it is recommended to skip this section and to resume at the summary given at its end (subsection 9.2.3).

9.2 An Executable Specification for SSADM–F

The SSADM-F method level specification is parameterized by a so-called project level instantiation, which is obtained by mechanical translation from pragmatic SSADM notation. In order to prove consistency, we are going to describe an executable specification which is parameterized by the same parameter specifications as the axiomatic semantics from above. The abstract syntax representations and the syntactic constraints for them (the "context conditions") remain unchanged.

9.2.1 From Descriptive to Executable Specifications via Constructive Specifications

The SSADM-F specification is given in a deliberately *descriptive* style. This means that it collects various loosely related observations which are claimed to hold for any model of the specification. The whole specification does not give much information about the process how to *construct* some value, for instance a system state.

In contrast to this, for an executable specification it is important to define so-called *constructor operations* for the values of all data sorts. The observation functions are then defined by case analysis and recursion for any term built of these constructors. A good example is the sort State for system states. The last chapters have provided basically two functions which have a result value of this sort: initState and next. This means that for states different from the initial state, only a rather indirect way of construction is available. In an executable specification, a set of operations is needed to construct non-trivial states in small and simple steps. Typical constructor operations for states, as they will be introduced in the next subsection, are the insertion of a single occurrence or the introduction of a single relationship instance. In an executable specification, it is important that any sort is connected with a set of constructor operations, such that exactly those values of the sort are admitted which can be obtained by repeated application of constructor operations. This gives the *inductive definition principle* which is used for the definition of executable observation functions.

In order to explain a systematic way for the development of an executable specification from a descriptive one, we use a very small example. Obviously, the basic methodical ideas are easier to understand on the background of a trivial example than for whole SSADM-F.

Example: Time values (Descriptive Specification). We assume a very simple descriptive specification of a sort Time for time values. Two observation functions are defined for the sort, which observe the current hour and the current minute.

DS = { **enriches** Naturals;

      sort Time;
      hour, minute: Time → Nat;

      axioms ∀ t: Time **in**
      (hour(t) < 24) ∧ (minute(t) < 60);
      endaxioms; }

Please note that at this point nothing is said about the internal structure of the sort Time except that it must be able to capture the hour and minute information. The sort could be easily extended by another observation, for instance for the current second. This is exactly the style in which the specifications for SSADM-F were given above.

The further extension of the sort Time by new observations can also be prohibited in a descriptive specification using an axiom like the following:

$$(t1 = t2) \Leftrightarrow (hour(t1) = hour(t2) \wedge minute(t1) = minute(t2));$$

This axiom states that the information contained in a Time value is characterized exactly by the hour and minute observations. The SSADM-F specification does also contain axioms of this style (for instance DC-2 and E-32). Such axioms give valuable hints for an explicit definition of the sort under consideration.

We give now a more execution-oriented version for the descriptive specification. The new specification defines constructor operations and defines of the observation functions with respect to these constructors.

Example (continued): Constructive specification. The following SPECTRUM specification defines the sort Time using constructor functions.

CS = { **enriches** Naturals;

      sort Time;
      mkTime: Nat × Nat → Time;
      Time **generated by** mkTime;

      hour, minute: Time → Nat;   hour, minute **total**;

axioms ∀ h, m: Nat **in**

δ mkTime(h, m) = (h < 24) ∧ (m < 60);

t = mkTime(h, m) ⇒ hour(t) = h;

t = mkTime(h, m) ⇒ minute(t) = m;

endaxioms; }

We call the style of a specification like CS *constructive* since it is dominated by the constructors for the sorts which enable the construction of carrier sorts and therefore a model out of the specification. Each axiom of a constructive specification either gives the definedness condition for a function symbol or is part of the definition of an observation function by case analysis on constructors.

In order to show that the specification CS is a refinement of DS, we have to prove the logical implication:

$$\text{Axioms(CS)} \implies \text{Axioms(DS)}.$$

In the SPECTRUM calculus, this proof can be easily carried out by using the induction principle for Time which is available due to the **generated-by** construct.

For the proof of consistency, it is sufficient to define a constructive refinement of the descriptive specification. However, a constructive sublanguage for SPECTRUM has not been defined. The *executable* sublanguage which exists for SPECTRUM is more restrictive than constructive specifications; in particular the constructors have to be total and pairwise distinct in an executable specification. The main adavantage of the executable sublanguage is that it is quite close to existing functional programming languages and therefore gives access to specification prototyping (see section 9.3 below). This is the reason why we have given for SSADM-F not only a constructive, but also a truely executable refinement.

In the special case where all constructor operations are total, a constructive specification is executable. In this case, all sorts can be defined by **data** declarations in SPECTRUM. For those cases where the constructors are not total (like our example), a second step is necessary after the development of the constructive version.

> *Example (continued): Executable specification with partial constructors.* If truely partial constructors are to be represented in an executable specification, a simple solution is to introduce a second level of specification. First, an underlying data structure is defined which has total constructors. In a second step, the constructor functions are defined as partial functions computing a value of the underlying data structure. For the example, we use the data structure of pairs of natural numbers.

ES = {   **enriches** Naturals;

   data Pair = mkPair(! Nat, ! Nat);

   mkTime':   Nat × Nat → Pair;
   hour', minute': Pair → Nat;

   axioms ∀ h, m: Nat **in**
   mkTime'(h, m) = **if** (h < 24) ∧ (m < 60) **then** mkPair(h, m) **else** ⊥ **endif**;
   hour'(mkPair(h, m)) = h;
   minute'(mkPair(h, m)) = m;
   endaxioms; }

The specification ES differs from CS mainly in one aspect: The question of definedness of constructor values has been moved from the executable specification itself to the *correct use* of the functions given by the executable specification. The hour and minute observation functions should be applied only to values which have been constructed by mkTime, and they are required to work correctly only on such values.

A specification in the style of ES can easily be translated into an equivalent functional program. Therefore such a specification is regarded as an executable SPECTRUM specification.

Again we are interested in proving formally that ES is a refinement of CS. This is not directly obvious, since the sort of pairs of natural numbers does contain values which are not legal as time values. This problem is solved as in classical data refinement by defining a *representation predicate*. The representation predicate distinguishes those concrete values (pairs, in our case) which are representations of an abstract value (a time value). In our example, the representation predicate for a pair of numbers is:

   P(mkPair(h, m)) = (h < 24) ∧ (m < 60)

Please note that this predicate coincides only accidentially with the definedness condition for mkTime. For a different representation, quite another representation predicate would be used. (For instance, if the time values were represented by a single number counting the minutes, the predicate would be "P(n) < 1440".)

> *Example (continued): Data refinement.* In SPECTRUM, the effect of a representation predicate can be achieved by an auxiliary partial constructor which derives the abstract value from a concrete value. The representation predicate is written down as the definedness condition for this constructor.

abs: Pair → Time;
Time **generated by** abs;

$$\delta \, abs(mkPair(h, m)) = (h < 24) \wedge (m < 60);$$

All operations from EC are lifted in a schematic way to functions working on the abstract sort, using the abs function.

mkTime(h, m) = abs(mkTime'(h, m));
hour(abs(p)) = hour'(p);
minute(abs(p)) = minute'(p);

Please note that abs and these axioms are just an auxiliary construction for verification purposes. They do not belong to any of the specifications CS and ES. Let us call this "mediating specification" ABS. Within the SPECTRUM calculus, the following implication can now be easily verified:

$$Axioms(ES) \wedge Axioms(ABS) \Rightarrow Axioms(DS)$$

The technical details of this style of verification are not important here. The methodically important point is that the representation predicate is an *invariant* which holds for all pairs of natural numbers, as long as they are representations for time values.

To summarize, the following steps are necessary for establishing an executable implementation of a descriptive specification.

- For each data sort in the descriptive specification, appropriate constructor functions are sought. Partial constructors are allowed. Using these constructors, a specification in constructive style is written.

- It is formally proven that the axioms of the constructive specification imply those of the descriptive specification.

- A SPECTRUM declaration for a data structure (using **data** and **sortsyn**) is given for any sort in the constructive specification.

- For each data structure representing an abstract sort, a representation predicate is defined which is to be maintained as an invariant by all data values if they represent an abstract value.

- For each constructor and observation operation from the constructive specification, an executable version is given which works only on those data values which are representations of abstract values.

- It is formally proven that the axioms of the executable specification, together with an abstraction based on the representation predicate, imply those of the constructive specification.

If all these steps have been carried out successfully, the given descriptive specification is logically consistent, and the functional program derived from the executable specification represents a model of the descriptive specification.

9.2.2 Executable Specification for SSADM-F: Static Aspects

The executable specification for SSADM-F has been developed according to the guidelines which were explained above. We give here only an overview of the specification and point out the basic design decisions. The whole specification text (comprising more than 80 rather technical axioms) can be found in [Hus94].

The following sorts are defined in the axiomatic semantics of SSADM-F:

State, InpEv, Output, Occ, OccId, SI

The sorts InpEv and Output are discussed below in the section on dynamic aspects. For two of the remaining sorts (OccId and SI), an appropriate executable definition can be given immediately, without going through all the steps from above.

The identifier of an occurrence in SSADM is the composed value of its primary key attributes. We use this to represent the sort OccId by a composition of attribute values. An occurrence identifier is realized in the executable specification by a finite set of (attribute, value)-pairs.

sortsyn OccId = Set (Attr × AttrVal);

The sort SI (state indicator) formalizes the history status of an occurrence. In the executable specification, each occurrence carries with it the whole list of events by which it was affected since system initialization. So the history status is simply a list of effects. (An effect is the relevant classification of an input event).

sortsyn SI = List Effect;

This is a quite inefficient way of realization, compared to the state indicator values which are proposed by stage 5 of SSADM. However, the purpose of this executable specification is only to demonstrate the consistency of the axioms. Efficiency questions are completely ignored here.

For the remaining two sorts State and Occ, the two-step machinery from above (constructive specification plus executable specification) has to be applied.

The Constructive Specification of SSADM-F

The first step towards an executable version is to find appropriate constructor functions for the sorts State and Occ, such that all observations can be defined recursively over the constructor terms.

As it was explained in section 8.6.2, an occurrence contains information about its entity, its attribute values, its relationship links, and its history status. For the entity and attribute information and the history status, the respective observation functions are already declared in the SSADM-F specification.

entity:	Occ → Entity;	entity **total**:
def:	Occ × Attr → Bool;	– – Test whether the attribute is defined
. @ .:	Occ × Attr → AttrVal;	– – Attribute value
histStat:	Occ → List Effect;	histStat **total;**

For the link information, it is convenient to use the function linked which was defined at the end of chapter 8 (axiom E-30). It tests whether an occurrence is linked by a relationship instance to some occurrence identifier.

linked:	Occ × Rel × Occld → Bool;	linked **total;**

The constructor operations for occurrences now have to provide the information which is observed by these functions. If an occurrence is created, only its entity must be known.

crea:	Entity → Occ;	crea **total;**

A freshly created occurrence has undefined attribute values, it has no relationship links and an empty history status. The following axioms are examples for the style in which the observation functions are defined for each constructor[1].

{PC-2a}	entity(crea(e)) = e;
{PC-3a}	a ∈ attrs(e) ⇒ def(crea(e), a) = false;
{PC-5a}	linked(crea(e), r, i) = false;
{PC-6a}	histStat(crea(e)) = [];

The constructor sto stores an attribute value into an occurrence, provided the attribute belongs to the entity of the occurrence and the value obeys the domain restriction. For this constructor, we show the definedness condition, as an example for the axioms.

---

[1] See [Hus94] for the complete specification. The numbering of axioms is consistent with the order which is used there. Therefore the axioms are not numbered continuously here.

sto: Occ × Attr × AttrVal → Occ;

{PC-1a} δ sto(o, a, v) = a ∈ attrs(entity(o)) ∧ dom(e, a)(v);

By link, an occurrence gets a relationship link to another occurrence. Since the entity of the linked occurrence is not given as an argument (but only its identifier), we define this as a total operation for occurrences. On the level of states, a restriction about the entities related by a relationship will be added. Links are removed by the operation unlink.

link, unlink: Occ × Rel × OccId → Occ;   link, unlink **total**;

Finally, there is a way to record an input event within an occurrence. The input event is represented by its effect (which is a triple of Event, Option and Role). The purpose of the recEff constructor is that the effect is appended to the actual history status.

recEff: Occ × Effect → Occ;   recEff **total**;

Now the list of constructor operations for occurrences is complete; a generation axiom can be given.

Occ **generated by** crea, sto, link, unlink, recEff;

In the axioms dealing with occurrences, the observation function ident frequently appears which obtains the occurrence identifier from an occurrence.

Based on the definition of occurrence identifiers as sets of (attribute, value)-pairs, the frequently used ident function can be defined as a derived operation. The ident function simply filters the attribute values of an occurrence to the primary key attributes.

In the same style, constructor and observation functions for the sort State can be defined. Some of the constructors are quite obvious, since a state essentially is a collection of occurrences.

initState: State;   -- Initial (empty) state
put: State × Occ → State;   -- Insertion of an occurrence
del: State × OccId → State;   -- Deletion of an occurrence

The corresponding observation functions on the level of occurrences are already declared in the descriptive specification:

bound: State × OccId → Bool; bound **total**;
                                        -- Test for membership in state
get: State × OccId → Occ: -- Retrieval of anoccurrence

Interestingly, we need two additional constructors for states which correspond to the insertion and the removal of a new relationship instance between two occurrences.

est: State × Rel × OccId × OccId → State;
                                    – – Adding a relationship instance
rem: State × Rel × OccId × OccId → State;
                                    – – Removing a relationship
                                    – – instance

    State **generated by** initState, put, del, est, rem;

The two constructors est and rem seem not to be necessary at first sight, since the link and unlink operations already admit the creation of relationship instances between occurrences. However, in order to realize the requirement of *referential integrity* (axiom D-2), we have to guarantee for all system states that the links for all contained occurrences point only to occurrences which are contained in the same state. This is possible only if we provide an operation to introduce the relationship on the level of states, where it can test the presence of the respective occurrences before creating the links. Similarly, the "establish" operation can ensure that in any system state for each relationship instance a consistent inverse relationship instance exists (axiom D-3).

Using this concept, we specify that the insertion into the system state "strips" all link information from the occurrence. This is captured by the following axiom which uses an auxiliary operation to remove the links.

{PC-11a} s = put(s', o) ⇒ get(s, i) = **if** ident(o) = i **then** stripLks(o) **else** get(s', i) **endif;**

The link and unlink operations are now used only locally in the specification of states where they formally describe the effect of an est operation. If an occurrence is observed after it was involved in an est operation, the same occurrence is obtained as by an appropriate link operation. Unfortunately, a complex case analysis is needed to describe this in a constructive style. We show these axioms here to demonstrate the difference in readability between a descriptive and an operational specification style.

{PC-11c} s = est(s', r, i1, i2) ∧ i1 ≠ i2 ⇒
        get(s, i) = **if** i = i1
                        then link(get(s', i1), r, i2)
                        else if i = i2
                                then link(get(s', i2), inv(r), i1)
                                else get(s', i) **endif endif;**

{PC-11d} s = est(s', r, i', i') ⇒
        get(s, i) = **if** i = i'
                then link(link(get(s', i'), r, i'), inv(r), i')
                else get(s', i) **endif**;

The observation function connected for relationship instances can be derived easily from the get and linked observation functions:

{PC-12}   related(r) = (entity(o1), entity(o2)) ⇒
        connected(s, r)(o1, o2) =
            if contained(s)(o1) ∧ contained(s)(o2)
                then linked(o1, r, ident(o2))
                else false **endif**;

The constructive specification does cover only these relatively atomic constructors and observation functions. The complex observations which are given by the various OK-predicates for data integrities (relDegreeOK, relOptionOK, relExclOK, attrOptionOK) have been excluded here. The reason is that they are defined in the descriptive specification by an explicit formula. If all the quantifiers in the formula are transformed into exhaustive tests on the (always finite) system state, then an executable version of the predicates is obtained, which does not pose any consistency problems.

Constructive vs. Descriptive Specification

Many of the axioms of the descriptive specification can be formally deduced as theorems of the constructive specification from above. Obviously the axioms for the OK-predicates (D-4, D-5, D-6, D-10) have to be omitted, since the OK-predicates themselves are omitted. And, for the moment, also the axioms dealing with system dynamics (E-axioms) are postponed (see subsection 9.2.2 below).

Most of the proofs are quite trivial; only for a few of them an induction on the generation principles for the sorts State and Occ are needed. The most complex proofs are those which show that the realization of relationship instances by local occurrence links is equivalent to the state-global view expressed by the est, rem and connected operations (for instance axiom D-3).

The axiom CD-2 serves particular attention, since it *cannot* be proven within the constructive specification. The following axiom is equivalent to CD-2:

{CD-2'}   ∀ i1, i2. get(s, i1) = get(s', i2) ⇔ s = s';

This axiom says that two system states are equal if and only if they contain the same occurrences. This restriction is too strong to be covered by the axioms of the constructive specification. For instance, the constructive specification admits

models in which the deletion of an occurrence does not lead back to the same state
as before the deletion, but to a state in which some information has been added to
record the deletion. The get-operation then evaluates the information on deleted
occurrences (due to axiom PC-10c), so the two states cannot be distinguished by
get-observations. Fortunately, the axiom CD-2 (and the similar axiom E-32) can be
treated independently of the other axioms. The executable specification below
demonstrates that these "closure axioms" are consistent with the rest of the
descriptive specification.

Executable Specification

In order to reformulate the constructive specification for the static aspects of
SSADM-F in truely executable form, the sorts Occ and State are defined by simple
data structures. A system state can be represented, by consequent fulfilment of the
localization principle, as a finite mapping of occurrence identifiers to occurrences[2].

> **sortsyn** State = Map OccId Occ;

An occurrence is now identified with a quatruple giving its entity, attribute, link and
history status.

> **data** Occ =
>   occ(! entity: Entity, ! attm: AttrMap, ! links: Set (Rel × OccId),
>   ! histStat: List Effect);

The attribute component of an ocurrence is defined here as a finite mapping of
attribute names to attribute values.

> **sortsyn** AttrMap = Map Attr AttrVal;

As it was already explained earlier, occurrence identifiers in SSADM can also be
seen as compositions of attribute values. Therefore, in the executable specification
the same sort is used for occurrence identifiers as for the attribute component of an
occurrence. The identifier of a given occurrence can now be simply obtained by
filtering its attribute component to key attributes.

> **sortsyn** OccId = AttrMap;

Interestingly, now the axiom CD-2, which was problematic on the constructive
level, is obtained from a simple general property for finite mappings. The closure
axiom E-32 for occurrences is a trivial consequence of these definitions, too.

---

2   See appendix D (basic specifications) for the exact definition of the generic sort constructor for
    finite mappings.

Based on these definitions, it is relatively simple to give explicit definitions of all operations from the constructive specification. The axioms of the constructive specification are theorems of the executable specification; all the proofs for this fact are quite technical but simple.

9.2.2 Executable Specification for SSADM-F: Dynamic Aspects

The dynamic change of an information system specified in SSADM-F is captured by the semantic functions acc (acceptance of an input event) and next (successor state). These functions use the sorts InpEv and Output. For the sort Output, no refinement is needed, since no observation functions are given for this sort. The sort InpEv needs a closer examination.

Input Events

The information contained in an input event has been specified rather loosely in the axiomatic semantics by the abstract classification functions event, option and role. The event function classifies an input event by its event name; option gives the selected option for an input event and a system state, and role gives the role for any affected identifier.

This is a very abstract view of an input event. A realistic setting for information systems includes some user interaction component which translates a command or menu activation issued by the user into such an abstract classification. However, the specification of this part of a system is *not* part of Entity-Event Modelling in SSADM. For an executable specification of Entity-Event Modelling, the simplest solution is just to *assume* the whole classification (event, option, roles) to be given. This approach is adequate for the Entity-Event Modelling and helps to keep the executable specification on a quite abstract level. In chapter 10 below, an extension of SSADM-F is sketched which specifies also essential parts of the processing of user input (option selection and target identification).

So the information of an input event which is relevant for this chapter consists of an event, an option, and a target assignment to occurrence identifiers. Two additional aspects are important:

- Since in the executable specification the system states are generated by constructor functions, only finite system states are admitted. (This question was left open in the semantics.) Therefore, an input event can affect only a finite number of occurrence identifiers. So the target mapping (which was an arbitrary function with possible infinite domain in the semantics) can be replaced here by a finite structure showing all the affected occurrence identifiers with their targets. To ease execution, we use a list here.

- Since at several points in the semantics updates to attribute values are prescribed, it is useful to assume the new values for such updates to be given within the input event. For this purpose, we include an attribute/ value mapping within the elements of the list.

Therefore we use the following simple data structure for an input event:

> **data** InpEv = inp(! inpOptEv: OptEvent, ! inpTargets: List InpTg);
> **sortsyn** InpTg = OccId × Target × AttrMap

Obviously, a number of "context conditions" are required for such an explicit input event to fit into the semantics of a given project instantiation. However, we do not give these quite technical axioms here (for details see [Hus94]).

On top of this concrete realization for InpEv, all the semantic functions for the specification of system dynamics can be specified easily. For instance, the affects predicate just tests whether the given identifier is mentioned in the input target list. If the identifier occurs in the current state, it is moreover tested whether the entity information in the input data structure and in the system state coincide.

Acceptance Predicate

Some of the semantic axioms can be obtained by a simple transliteration which replaces quantifiers by appropriate higher-order functions. Typical such higher-order functions are all and ex which implement a search on a finite list. As an example, the transliteration of the acceptance condition according to axiom E-27 gives the following axiom PX-30. The executable axiom contains the same information as its descriptive origin, but is definitely less readable.

{PX-30} $acc(s, ie) =$ **let** $oev = optEvent(s, ie)$ **and** $ut = inpTargets(ie)$ **in**
> $entriesOK(s, ie, entries(oev), eType(oev))$
> $\land$ $corrOK(s, ie, corrs(oev), cType(oev))$
> $\land$ $(all(ut, \lambda(i, tg, am).\ affects(s, ie, i) \Rightarrow$
> > $(bound(s, i) = (EEX(oev, tg) \neq C))))$
> $\land$ $(all(ut, \lambda(i1, tg1, am1).\ all(ut, \lambda(i2, tg2, am2).$
> > $allSet(corrs(oev), \lambda(tg1', r, tg2').\ tg1 = tg1' \land tg2 = tg2'$
> > $\Rightarrow (connected(s, r)(get(s, i1), get(s, i2)) =$
> > > $\neg((gain, r, tg2)\ elem\ OPS(oev, tg1)))))))$
> $\land$ $(all(ut, \lambda(i, tg, am).\ affects(s, ie, i) \Rightarrow historyOK(s, ie, i)))$ **endlet**;

Such a transliteration can be applied only to a small part of the axioms (essentially the acceptance predicate and the OK-predicates). The state transition function, for instance, is defined in a completely new way in the executable specification. In these more complicated cases, a quality control effect is achieved by giving a second independent specification and relating it with the original specification.

State Transition

The basic idea for an executable version of the state transition function next is to split the update into six phases:

> creOccs, estRels, modOccs, remRels, delOccs, updHist:
> State × InpEv → State;

These six phases are:

- Creation of new occurrences for all input targets for which the Event-Entity Matrix contains a "C" entry.

- Introduction of new relationship instances for those correspondences between input targets for which the Operation Lists contain a "Gain" operation.

- Update of attribute values for those input targets for which the Operation Lists contain a "Store" operation.

- Removal of those relationship instances between input targets for which the Operation Lists contain a "Lose" operation.

- Deletion of those occurrences which are associated to an input target for which the Event-Entity Matrix contains a "D" entry.

- Recording of the actual effect in the history status of all affected occurrences.

Each of these six phases can be defined as a step of "interpretation" for some data structure. For the occurrence operations, the list of input targets is interpreted stepwise (three times for creation, update and deletion). For the relationship instance modifications, the set of correspondences (out of the ECDs) can be used as a guideline, together with the operation lists. The next operation is just a composition of these six phases.

{PX-40}   next(s, ie) =
>   **if** acc(s, ie)
>   **then**   updHist(delOccs(remRels(modOccs(estRels(creOccs(
>   s, ie), ie), ie), ie), ie), ie)
>   **else** ⊥ **endif**;

As an example for the style in which the individual phases are described, we show here the first of the six phases, which is the creation of occurrences. Similar definitions are given for the other five phases (see [Hus94]).

{PX-31a} creOccs(s, inp(oev, [])) = s;
{PX-31b} creOccs(s, inp(oev, [(i, (e, rol), am)]++ut)) =
        let s' = **if** EEX(oev, (e, rol)) = C
               then put(s, attrOps(crea(e), OPS(oev, (e, rol)), am))
               else s **endif in**
        creOccs(s', inp(oev, ut)) **endlet**;

This completes the sketch of an executable specification for whole SSADM-F. The executable axioms imply all semantic axioms for SSADM-F (including the dynamic aspects in C-1, CE-4, CE-5 and the E-axioms). The formal proof for this fact was carried out manually – mechanical proof support is urgently needed for this type of proof.

Semantic Concepts Particular to the Executable Specification

Two aspects should be mentioned in which the executable specification differs significantly from the concepts which were explained for the axiomatic semantics.

The first difference is the treatment of life histories. In the semantics of Entity Life Histories (8.4.3), the life of an occurrence identifier from system initialisation up to the current system state was considered. Such a life history was required there to be a prefix match of the *iteration* of the respective ELH. In the executable specification, the history status of an occurrence identifier is always a prefix match of the *bare* ELH (without iteration). The general situation is sketched in figure 9.1, where "C" marks the creation and "D" the deletion of a new occurrence for identifier i. Please note that the identifier may be reused several times.

History of occurrence identifier i

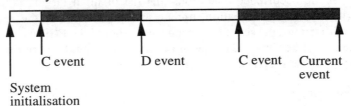

            C event   D event   C event   Current
                                              event
System
initialisation   Fig. 9.1

There is a context condition for ELHs (axiom ES-11) which says that the life cycle of an occurrence always begins with a "C" event and ends with a "D" event. This axiom ensures that the composition of the individual life histories always is a prefix match of the iterated life of the respective entity. (According to axiom E-20, the entity under consideration is always the entity of the currently existing occurrence, older life cycles are only included in the occurrence life if they refer to the same entity, see axiom E-18.)

A second difference comes from the decision to include the selected option directly in the input data structure. This is necessary in an executable specification, since the details of the selection of the apropriate option are left open in SSADM-F, as it was described in chapter 8. Chapter 10 below will introduce a more precise specification for the function option, which fits into the general semantic framework and allows us to remove the option information from the input data structure. At the current point, however, options are part of the input event, and the option function is total. Therefore the axiom E-29, which expresses the definedness condition for option, cannot be proven yet.

9.2.3 Executable SSADM-F: Summary

As it was shown above, a complete executable specification for the semantics of SSADM-F (LDM and EEM) is available, which is a refinement of the descriptive specification in chapters 6 through 8. This means that the descriptive method level specification for SSADM-F is consistent, as long as its parameter requirements (context conditions) are fulfilled.

From the Software Engineering point of view, the consistency proof is one of the essential benefits from using a formal foundation. The "context conditions" for SSADM-F, as they were given in chapters 7 and 8, are a mathematically founded consistency criterion for the pragmatic notation. A close inspection of the conditions shows even that they can be checked mechanically for a given project level specification. So the consistency proof can be carried over fully automatically to an arbitrary number of concrete specifications of any size. The analysis provided by this set of conditions fairly exceeds the amount of cross-consistency checking which is available in current CASE tools supporting methods like SSADM. Theoretically founded context conditions as they were given here for SSADM-F could form a sound basis for the development of improved CASE tools which ensure a thorough consistency of an SSADM-F specification.

It is also instructive to compare the style of the executable but abstract specification (for example the axioms PX-31 and PX-40 which were given in section 9.2.2 above) with the descriptive specification from the chapters 6 through 8. A specification for SSADM-F in a language like VDM, Z or SETL would be very similar in style to the SPECTRUM executable specification. It is the impression of the author that the descriptive approach leads to a much better separation of concerns and to simpler axioms. The descriptive axioms are easier to check for intuitive correctness, but the executable axioms can be checked simply for missing cases. So the *combination* of a descriptive and an executable specification, together with a check of the refinement relation, seems to be a good technique for improving the quality of specifications. The author has found many mistakes in older versions of the descriptive specification during the process of constructing the executable refinement.

9.3 Logical Prototying of SSADM-F Specifications

By the executable specification for SSADM-F, also some kind of prototyping tool is available. Please note that this notion of prototyping does not have a counterpart in current software development practice. Prototyping by the executable SSADM-F specification is a *logical* prototyping, which should be clearly distinguished from user interface prototyping as it is proposed by original SSADM, and from prototypes which are built to test the practicability of technical solutions. Logical prototyping corresponds to an activity which is carried out by system analysts to evaluate the specification against toy cases.

For the topic of specification prototyping, it should be kept in mind that the executable specification for SSADM-F does not cover any concepts of a user interface. It assumes the complete information about an input event to be given in a rather abstract form. An input event is simply a data structure providing the event identifier, the option identifier and a list of descriptions for all targets. However, this has the advantage that the refined specification, although being executable, still remains rather abstract.

In order to explore the possibilities of logical prototyping, a machine-executable program has been derived from the executable specification. Since currently there is no interpreter available for the executable sublanguage of SPECTRUM, the executable specification has been transformed manually into a program in the functional programming language Gofer [Jon93] which is a dialect of Haskell [HJW92]. Also the project level specification for the Hotel Agency example (appendix C) has been transformed into a Gofer program; and the instantiation of the parameterized specification could be simulated in Gofer as well (by a Gofer project file). The translation into Gofer is a relatively obvious transliteration[3], so the Gofer program resembles all details of the SPECTRUM specification.

Gofer is a very powerful prototyping language in which relatively complex programs can be formulated in a quite compact way. The price to be paid for this is a relatively low but still acceptable execution speed. In order to improve the quality of the sample SSADM-F specification, most of the context conditions for SSADM-F have been reformulated as Gofer programs. Interestingly, these programs still have uncovered a number of inconsistencies in the Hotel Agency example. The amount of errors uncovered in this exercise was astinishing, geven the fact that this example is quite small and was carefully prepared as a demonstration for a

---

3   Essentially, all functions have been "curried" to higher-order functions, for a better compliance with the powerful standard library of Gofer.

semantically sound specification. Based on this experience, a serious improvement of specification quality can be expected for larger practical projects using a mechanical check of semantic context conditions.

The dynamic semantics of an SSADM-F specification can be prototyped with Gofer as well. For this purpose, concrete values for input events have to be constructed. Figure 9.2 shows a simple example of such an input event in Gofer notation.

```
ie1:: InpEv
ie1 = Inp (AddHotel,StdOpt)
              [(mkMap [(HotelNo,(Number 100))], (Hotel,StdRole),
              mkMap[(HotelNo, (Number 100)),
                  (HotelName,
                      (Strg "Golden Anchor")),
                  (HotelAddress,
                      (Strg "Main St., Scenario City")),
                  (Price, (Number 100))])]
```

Fig. 9.2

Figure 9.2 shows an "add hotel" event to introduce a new hotel to the Hotel Agency. The hotel has been given here the name "Golden Anchor" and the hotel number 100. Please note that this explicit syntax is oriented towards the abstract notions of the semantics and is unsuitable as a direct user interface. For instance, the hotel number (100) appears twice in the input event: As a hotel identifier in the target item and as an attribute value supplied for the update operations.

Using this syntax for input events, a detailed *scenario* for the use of the information system can be constructed. A scenario is simply a sequence of input events which is intended to be executed sequentially, starting with the initial system state. In figure 9.3, a very simple scenario for the Hotel Agency is shown. It starts with the input event of figure 9.2 to introduce a hotel. Subsequently, a quota is added for this hotel, a customer is introduced and a reservation is issued for the customer and the hotel. After the definition of each input event, the new system state is computed using the semantic function next which incorporates the full semantic machinery of SSADM-F (LDM and EEM).

```
-- A simple scenario for the Hotel Agency example

-- The initial state
s0:: State
s0 = initState
```

```
-- First event: Registration of a hotel
ie1:: InpEv
ie1 = Inp (AddHotel,StdOpt)
                [(mkMap [(HotelNo,(Number 100))], (Hotel,StdRole),
                mkMap[(HotelNo, (Number 100)),
                        (HotelName,
                                (Strg "Golden Anchor")),
                        (HotelAddress,
                                (Strg "Main St., Scenario City")),
                        (Price, (Number 100))])]

-- The state after registration of the hotel
s1:: State
s1 = next s0 ie1

-- Second event: Addition of a quota
ie2:: InpEv
ie2 = Inp (AddQuota, StdOpt)
                [(mkMap [(HotelNo,(Number 100))], (Hotel,StdRole),
                initMap),
                (mkMap [(HotelNo,(Number 100)),
                        (AvailDate, (Date 1 6 94))],
                (Quota,StdRole),
                mkMap[(HotelNo, (Number 100)),
                        (AvailDate, (Date 1 6 94)),
                        (NumAvail, (Number 10))])]

s2:: State
s2 = next s1 ie2

-- Third event: Registration of a new customer
ie3:: InpEv
ie3 = Inp (NewCust,StdOpt)
                [(mkMap [(CustNo,(Number 1))],
                        (Customer,StdRole),
                mkMap[(CustNo, (Number 1)),
                        (CustName, (Strg "Jim Smith")),
                        (CustAddress,
                                (Strg "Main St., Faraway City")),
                        (CreditCardInfo, (Strg "Valid Card"))])]
```

```
s3:: State
s3 = next s2 ie3

-- Fourth event: Customer request, immediately offered
ie4:: InpEv
ie4 = Inp (CustReq,ImmOff)
            [(mkMap [(CustNo,(Number 1))],
                    (Customer,StdRole),
            mkMap[(DateLastReq, (Date 21 5 94))]),
            (mkMap [(HotelNo,(Number 100))], (Hotel, StdRole),
                    mkMap[]),
            (mkMap [(HotelNo,(Number 100)),
                    (AvailDate, (Date 1 6 94))],
            (Quota, StdRole), mkMap[(NumAvail, (Number 9))]),
            (mkMap [(RefNo, (Number 1000))],
                    (Reservation, StdRole),
            mkMap[(RefNo, (Number 1000)),
                    (Period,
                            (ValPair (Date 1 6 94) (Date 1 6 94))),
                    (NumRooms, (Number 1)),
                            (DateOffer, (Date 21 5 94))])])]

s4:: State
s4 = next s3 ie4
```

Fig. 9.3

With the help of such a scenario, the specified behaviour of an information system can be tested against the intuitive requirements. The interactive Gofer system can be used to inspect various aspects of the system state and to check integrity conditions. However, the completely symbolic execution of this simulation requires quite powerful computing equipment. For instance, for the computation of the last state (s4) in the small scenario of figure 9.3, the Gofer system performs 326518 reduction steps, which gives a response time of roughly one minute on a SUN SPARCstation 10 computer. So the current interpreter for SSADM-F can be seen only as a first prototype. But if a convenient user interface for the definition of scenarios was added, and the interpreter itself was optimized carefully, an interesting analysis tool for SSADM-F specifications could be obtained. The main advantage of this kind of analysis is that the SSADM-F specification is directly executed using the abstract semantic concepts, so any unexpected situation can be traced back immediately to the specification and its axiomatic semantics.

Chapter 10

Formal Extensions for SSADM-F

On the background of the detailed formal foundation for SSADM-F (LDM and EEM parts), we will now study the borders of SSADM-F to both the formal and the pragmatic world of Requirements Engineering. Chapter 10 discusses how an SSADM-F specification can be supplemented with parts formulated in plain SPECTRUM. Chapter 11 gives an impression how the transition from the more informal technique of Data Flow Modelling (DFM) into EEM can be supported by formal foundations. Both chapters do not present their topics in full detail, but concentrate on the basic ideas[1].

10.1 Combining Pragmatic and Formal Specifications

The semantic analysis of EEM has shown clearly that this technique puts its main emphasis on the decomposition of the dynamic behaviour of complex states. Each of the detail aspects in EEM is small enough to be represented in an easily understandable way. Generally, an SSADM-F specification says *which* part of the system is updated due to which stimulus, but it does not say much about the algorithms for finding out the affected parts and *what* the new values are for these parts. This is relatively natural for the specification of information systems, in which the algorithmic component often is quite trivial. In contrast, classical formal

---

[1] Therefore the axioms in this chapter do no longer carry systematic axiom numbers.

specification concentrates on defining the mathematical relationship between the input and output values of functions. In this chapter we show how this complementarity can be used for adding onto SSADM-F a precise and formal way to specify the algorithmic aspects of information system dynamics. The material presented in this chapter is based on SSADM-F notation, it does not have a direct counterpart in the official SSADM method.

10.1.1 Alternatives for a Formal Extension of SSADM-F

In several aspects SSADM-F shows deficiencies which can be compensated by formal specifications. One such aspect was already identified during the discussion of Logical Data Modelling (section 7.4.3), where Entity Descriptions in SSADM-F were enhanced by SPECTRUM sort declarations for a precise and flexible description of data domains for attribute values.

During the discussion of Entity-Event Modelling (chapter 8), a whole set of open questions has appeared: The identification of target occurrences, the selection of an (event) option and the determination of updated attribute values are not covered in SSADM-F. By an extension with plain SPECTRUM specifications, this missing information can be added to an SSADM-F specification. We call this way to combine pragmatic and formal specifications a *local formal extension*, since in this approach the formal specification is split into several small pieces which are added locally at those places where the SSADM-F specification is insufficient. This kind of integration is discussed below in sections 10.2 through 10.4 below in detail.

But there is also another kind of combinations of SSADM-F and SPECTRUM specifications, which we call *global formal extensions*. In a global extension, the formal specification is a larger specification document which is put besides the SSADM-F specification. By referring to the abstract syntax of SSADM-F, this formal specification can further constrain the information systems which are models of the SSADM-F specification. In this approach, logical axioms can be used to express global properties which cannot be easily captured in the diagrammatic representations which always show a projection of the system onto one aspect. We discuss global formal extensions first, concentrating on one particularly important kind of global formal extensions.

10.1.2 Formal Data Integrities

In the area of Logical Data Modelling, it can be useful to specify *formal data integrities* in the form of predicates on the system state. In the Hotel Agency example, good candidates for such data integrities are the temporal conditions given in the informal description. For instance, the informal description (section 3.5) says that "if a customer does not use the services ... for a whole year, the customer is removed from the [customer] list". This means that the system state never is allowed to contain a customer record for which the "date of last request" attribute value differs from the actual date more than a year. This can be seen as an integrity condition of the system state, similar to the "standard integrities" which are derived from the degree and optionality restrictions in the ER diagram. Like the "standard integrities", also the "custom-made" integrities are best formulated as SPECTRUM predicates on system states (OK-predicate). If we call the combination of all these integrities (standard and custom-made) OK, the following two formulae express the requirement that the integrities hold for each system state, excluding intermediate states during the processing of an input event.

OK (initState);
OK (s) $\wedge$ next(s) = s' $\Rightarrow$ OK (s');

These formulae can be added as axioms to the SSADM-F method level specification. But one should be aware of the fact that this step may destroy the logical consistency of the specification. So ideally, these axioms should be formally proven as *theorems* of an extended SSADM-F specification.

The global specification of the OK predicate is composed from the standard integrity conditions (relDegreeOK, relOptionOK, relExclOK, attrOptionOK) and a number of freely formulated predicates which capture conditions like the example above (only active customers on the list). This example for a "custom-made" integrity condition can be formulated as a simple SPECTRUM axiom:

custExpirationOK(s) =
    $\forall$ o. contained(s)(o) $\wedge$ entity(o) = customer
        $\Rightarrow$ diff(dateAttr(o @ dateLastReq), today(s)) $\leq$ 365;

The axiom assumes a SPECTRUM sort Date with a few standard functions.

| today: | State $\rightarrow$ Date; | **total;** |
| diff: | Date $\times$ Date $\rightarrow$ Nat; | $--$ Date difference in number of days |

The actual date (today) is computed out of the system state. This can be easily achieved by a standard event which takes place at the end of each day and stores the new date in the system state. In order to integrate this concept into the general structure of the system state we assume for the rest of this chapter a special entity sysData to be added to the entities. For the entity sysData there is always a single occurrence present in the state which has among others an attribute for the actual date. The today function can now be understood as an ordinary lookup of the system state.

Please note that the SPECTRUM definition of the custExpirationOK predicate needs the function dateAttr to convert an attribute value of the method level sort AttrVal into a value of the project level sort Date. Only those attribute values can be

converted which belong to the data domain of dates. For each domain defined in the
ATTRVAL specification, such a conversion can be defined, following the scheme
which is demonstrated here for the domain "nat".

> natAttr: AttrVal → Nat;
> δ natAttr(v) = nat(v);
> natAttr(natural(n)) = n;

The function natural in the last axiom is the constructor function which embeds the
sort Nat into the method level sort AttrVal (see section 7.4.3).

The technical overhead of conversion functions is the price which has to be paid for
the generic specification of the attribute access mechanism in SSADM-F. If specific
sorts (like Date) are to be used instead of the generic sorts (like AttrVal), somewhere
a conversion is needed. Alternatively, the whole definition of data integrities can be
formulated on the level of generic sorts, which means to give up the sort concept of
SPECTRUM and its standard sorts. This technical problem is caused by the strong
sort system of SPECTRUM, it could only be avoided by using a specification
language with a more flexible sort system (like "dependent types")[2].

The formal data integrities do not replace any part of the SSADM-F specification,
they just encode additional constraints which have been derived from an informal
problem analysis. So this is an example how a fusion of pragmatic and formal
specification can be used exactly for those issues where the expressiveness of
pragmatic methods is insufficient.

One could also think of global formal extensions for the dynamic aspects of an
SSADM-F. For instance, free SPECTRUM text can be used to add detail information
to the update of a system state caused by an input event. This would give a formal
counterpart to the so-called "Function Definition" technique of SSADM. However,
for these relatively complex aspects of a system it is advisable to make use of the
structuring mechanisms provided by Entity-Event Modelling in SSADM-F, and to
add formal text only locally to the specification. This is discussed in the next
section.

10.2 Extensions for Entity-Event Modelling

The purpose of formal extensions is to specify those aspects of an information
system which are not yet covered by Entity-Event Modelling (EEM). These aspects
become quite obvious in an analysis of the input events, as they are used in the
executable specification from chapter 10.

---

[2]   See section 10.3.3 below for a further discussion of this topic.

10.2.1 Input Data and Input Events

The input events in an SSADM-F scenario for the executable specification contain plenty of information one would not expect to be entered into the system from outside. We distinguish here between *input data* which is information actually entered into the system and the *input event* which is used for classifying the event in the sense of Entity-Event Modelling[3]. The formal extensions provide a way to describe how an input event is derived from input data.

> *Example.* In an SSADM-F scenario, an input event for a customer request for which an immediate reservation can be offered (see figure 9.3), the following information has to be given:
> - Event (custReq)
> - Option (immOff)
> - A list of records, each of them giving an occurrence identifier (key attributes) for the following entities:
>   - Customer
>   - Reservation
>   - Hotel
>   - Quota

Formally, we assume the same sort definition for input events as in the executable specification.

> **data** InpEv = inp(! inpOptEv: OptEvent, ! inpTargets: List InpTg);
> **sortsyn** npTg = OccId × Target × AttrMap;

In contrast to this rich structure, the input data for an event provides less information. The input data for the example from above contains the customer number and the hotel number, but not the reservation number, which should be generated by the system. Also the option, which encodes whether there is sufficient quota for the customer's request, should definitely not be input to the system, but be determined by the system itself.

> *Example.* For the "customer request" event in the Hotel Agency example, the following input data is appropriate:
> - Event (custReq)
> - Customer number
> - Hotel number
> - Period for which reservation is requested
> - Number of rooms

---

[3] Input data is closely connected with the so-called *IO Structures* in SSADM, but we have chosen a different name to indicate that we do not stress the interaction aspect here.

Formally, we treat input data as a tuple consisting of the event (as an identifier) and a number of input data items. The data items have a name by which they can be retrieved from the input data structure and a value which may be restricted to some domain. Due to these properties, we reuse the mechanism of attributes and attribute values for this purpose. In most cases, the input data items correspond naturally to attributes. If this is not the case, the sorts Attr and AttrVal have to be extended appropriately.

sortsyn InpData = Event × DataItems;
sortsyn DataItems = Map Attr AttrVal;

Obviously, there are context conditions for input data. The information which data items are expected for a given event is encoded in a new SSADM document. In original SSADM, the so-called *IO structures* serve for this purpose. For the formalization, we use a simplified version of IO structures. For each event , a *list of input items* has to be defined. In the abstract syntax to every event a set of attribute names and domain restrictions is assigned.

inpItems: Event → Set (Attr × Domain);

For the example from above, we have the following project level definition within this abstract syntax[4], which is a formal encoding of the informal description of input data from above.

```
inpItems(cReq) =
        set [(custNo, nat), (hotelNo, nat), (period, pair(date, date)),
               (numRooms, nat) ];
```

The remains of this section describes a function expandInp which mediates between the simple input data and the more explicitly structured input events. It transforms an input data value (event plus data items) into an InpEv value, using information from the system state.

expandInp: State × InpData → InpEv;

10.2.2 Expanding Input Data Into Input Events

We structure the expansion into four steps. The definition of these steps quarantees that the expansion process uses information from the system state only in a

---

[4]   As in the previous chapters, the surrounding box indicates that this is an example from the project level (Hotel Agency) specification. The other specification fragments belong to the method (meta-)level.

restricted way, following constraints which are defined in the EEM documents. The four steps are:

- Identification of regular target items:

  A regular target is one for which the affected identifiers can be identified without knowing the actual option. The regular targets describe a view of the state which shows only a subset of the final targets.

- Selection of option:

  Based on the state view given by the regular target items and the input data, it is decided which option is to be used for further processing.

- Identification of all targets:

  Based on the option and the input data, the complete list of target items is defined.

- Determination of attribute values:

  Finally, from the input data and the view of the state through the target items, new values for attribute updates may be derived.

The input event resulting from the expansion consists of the given event, the option computed in the second step, and a list of target items, which is obtained through the other three steps. The identification of regular targets computes a preliminary list of target items, which is the information available to determine the option. The full list of target items is then computed by a function which differs from its regular counterpart only in an additional option parameter. The determination of attribute values is a final transformation of the list of target items.

idfyRegTgs:	Event × DataItems × BoundIds → List TgItem;
selOpt:	Event × DataItems × View → Option;
idfyTgs:	OptEvent × DataItems × BoundIds → List TgItem;
attrVals:	OptEvent × DataItems × View × List TgItem → List TgItem;

Particular attention has to be paid to the access to the system state. Each stage of the expansion process is allowed to access only a specific part of the information in the system state, controlled by the EEM documents. The sorts BoundIds and View have the purpose to "insulate" necessary information from the system state. The sort BoundIds contains the simple information which identifiers are already bound for which entity. This information (and nothing besides it) is needed for the creation of unique new identifiers.

sortsyn BoundIds = Entity $\rightarrow$ Set OccId;
boundIds: State $\rightarrow$ BoundIds;

i $\in$ boundIds(s)(e) $\Leftrightarrow$ (bound(s, i) $\wedge$ entity(get(s, i)) = e);

The function boundIds reduces a given state to the information about bound identifiers which can be passed to the target identification functions.

The sort View contains a value of sort State, which is a projection of the current state into a small part which contains exactly those ocurrences which can be addressed through a given list of input targets and a number of correspondences on them. In addition, the view contains the information which target is assigned to an occurrence.

sortsyn View = State $\times$ (Occ $\rightarrow$ Target);

view: State $\times$ List TgItem $\times$ Set Corr $\rightarrow$ View;

(s', f) = view(s, ut, crs) $\wedge$ bound(s', i) $\Leftrightarrow$
        bound(s, i) $\wedge$ (isTg(ut, i) $\vee$ entity(get(s, i)) = sysData);
(s', f) = view(s, ut, crs) $\wedge$ o' = get(s', i) $\wedge$ o = get(s, i) $\Rightarrow$
        entity(o') = entity(o) $\wedge$ (o' @ a = o'@ a) $\wedge$ histStat(o') = histStat(o)
  $\wedge$ (linked(o', r', i') = (linked(o, r', i') $\wedge$ isTg(ut, i'))
  $\wedge$ (getTg(ut, i), r, getTg(ut, i')) $\in$ crs);
(s', f) = view(s, ut, crs) $\Rightarrow$ f(o) = getTg(ut, ident(o));

This formal definition of the view uses two auxiliary functions which are defined for the executable specification. These functions realize a convenient access to the list of input items and the target information contained in them.

isTg: List InpItem $\times$ OccId $\rightarrow$ Bool;
                – – Test for appearance in target list
getTg: List InpItem $\times$ OccId $\rightarrow$ Target;
                – – Target information from target list

The expansion function is defined as a composition of the four steps from above, using the appropriate views onto the system state. First the function option is defined for a system state and input data using the regular targets and regular corespondences.

option(s, (ev, d)) =
        selOpt(d, view(s, idfyRegTgs(ev, d, boundIds(s)), regCorrs(ev))));

Based on the option information, the full list of input targets and the new attribute values can be defined.

```
expandInp(s, (ev, d)) =
    let oev = (ev, option(s, (ev, d))) in
    let ut = idfyTgs(oev, d, boundIds(s)) in
        inp(oev, attrVals(oev, d, view(s, ut, corrs(oev)), ut))
    endlet  endlet;
```

In the discussion of the details of the expansion and of formal extensions used in it, the "customer request" event in the Hotel Agency serves as an example. The best orientation aid for the expansion process is the Effect Correspondence Diagram. Therefore figure 10.1 below recalls the ECD for the example event.

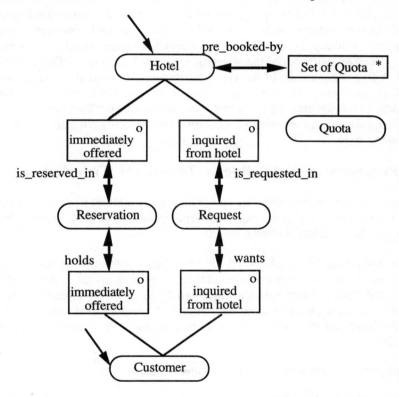

Fig. 10.1

Before entering an individual discussion of the four expansion steps, we concentrate on a common structural problem which appears when the two-level specification of SSADM-F is to be combined with plain SPECTRUM text.

10.3 Interfaces between SPECTRUM and SSADM-F

In chapter 5 above, it was argued that the best way to provide a formal foundation for a pragmatic notation is to use a *two-level* approach, where the syntax and the semantics of the pragmatic notation are formalized on a meta-level (method level), and the translation of project-specific information into the formal framework is kept as a completely separate and relatively trivial step (project level).

Unfortunately, the extension of a pragmatic notation with freely formulated formal text does not fit very well into such a two-level approach. The basic problem is here that the formal additions are specific for the individual project specification, but nevertheless need access to all of the semantic concepts which are defined on the meta-level. A first phenomenon of this type was already discussed above in section 10.1.2, where meta-level attribute values had to be converted into individual attribute sorts. In this section, we show that there are several problems of this type with a common cause, and we propose a solution by switching partially to a one-level translation style.

10.3.1 Problems in Extending a Two-Level Translation

As an introduction to the problems, we start with a naïve attempt to deal in a two-level style with the first step of the expansion from input data to input events. This first step is the identification of regular targets.

In an ECD (see figure 10.1), additional identification information is needed for every entry point and for every correspondence arrow. For instance, the regular "customer" and "hotel" entry points in figure 10.1 can be easily identified since their key attributes are given as input data items[5]. A method-level syntax in the spirit of SSADM-F for the identification of entry points is the following higher-order function.

> entrySpec: OptEvent × Target → DataItems × OccId → Bool;

The "entry specification" function associates a predicate to each entry point (which is a target). This predicate, in turn, decides for an identifier whether it is an actual

---

[5]   In original SSADM, this information can be attached as an annotation to the entry arrows. This feature has been omitted in chapter 8, for the sake of a systematic structure of the semantics. The identification specifications discussed here can be seen as a more powerful replacement for the annotations.

entry for the target. For the "customer request" example, the following lines could be included in the project level specification[6].

```
entrySpec((cReq, opt), $customer)(d, i) =
        (selMap(d, custNo) = idAttr(i, customer, custNo));
entrySpec((cReq, opt), $hotel)(d, i) =
        (selMap(d, hotelNo) = idAttr(i, hotel, hotelNo));
```

The example uses an auxiliary function idAttr. This is not problematic, since the idAttr function can be easily defined as a new observation function for occurrence identifiers. An SSADM-F occurrence identifier essentially is composed from attribute values, so we can get the values of primary key attributes from it:

$$\text{idAttr:} \qquad \text{OccId} \times \text{Entity} \times \text{Attr} \rightarrow \text{AttrVal};$$
$$\delta\, \text{idAttr(i, e, a)} = (a \in \text{primaryKeys(e)});$$

The assumption of such a function (which technically needs a few more axioms) does not destroy consistency, since in the executable specification occurrence identifiers are realized as finite mappings from attributes to attribute values which gives an obvious implementation for idAttr.

A more important observation is that the "project level" specification from above (in the box) does not keep separate the project and method levels. The sorts OccId and DataItems (of i and d) belong to the method level, so they should not appear in a project level specification. The use of these sorts in the project level specification could be avoided if a pre-defined set of higher-order functions was available (and defined on meta-level). On the project-level, these functions could be simply composed to achieve the desired specification. In such an attempt to improve the approach, the project level specification reads like the following two lines.

```
entrySpec((cReq, opt), $customer) =
        inpItem(custNo) isEqual tgAttr(customer, custNo);
entrySpec((cReq, opt), $hotel) =
        inpItem(hotelNo) isEqual tgAttr(i, hotel, hotelNo);
```

This is the same kind of solution as it was used in chapter 7 to describe the domain restrictions for attribute values by a language of predefined domain expressions. However, this solution does not give a direct interface between the SSADM-F notation and plain SPECTRUM text. Instead, the SSADM-F (method level) specification is extended by a new syntax which tends to mirror constructs of

---

6   The identifier opt is here understood as universally quantified, as it was proposed in section 8.3.3.

SPECTRUM. For instance, the method level expressions from above use a strange higher order function of name isEqual with the following signature:

isEqual: (Dataltems × Occld → AttrVal) × (Dataltems × Occld → AttrVal)
                   → (Dataltems × Occld → Bool);

The purpose of this complex construction is just to simulate equality which is readily available in the specification language.

So none of the two attempts to specify the entry identification is quite satisfactory. Moreover, the already mentioned difficulty of converting between the meta-sort AttrVal and the individual attribute sorts can appear in less trivial identification conditions as well, which even further complicates the situation.

Therefore, we propose another solution here which uses a one-level translation instead of the two-level paradigm, but in a very disciplined way.

10.3.2 One-Level Translation as Interface Generation

The problem of an adequate combination of meta-level and project-level information can be solved by admitting a mixture of both levels within well-defined boundaries. In order to explain the basic idea, we recall here the general structure of an SSADM-F specification from chapter 6.

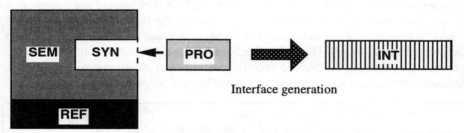

Interface generation

Fig. 10.2

As it is clear from the figure, the general separation of project and method level specifications remains unchanged. What now is added, is an additional translation from the project level specification into on *interface specification* (INT) which provides a project-level access to method-level concepts. The interface specification can be mechanically generated out of the project level information. So one could imagine here a similar preprocessor like the translator from SSADM-F diagrams to SPECTRUM project level translations, which additionally generates the interface specification.

The purpose of the interface specification is, at its name indicates, to mediate between the formal SSADM-F specification and its extensions (EXT) which can be

written in plain SPECTRUM. The complete specification of the information system
is obtained from the instantiated SSADM-F specification, on top of which the
interface specification and the extensions are added, as shown in figure 10.3.

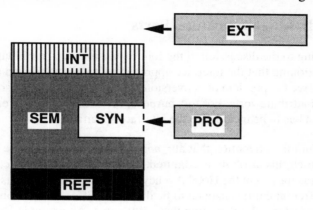

Fig. 10.3

As an example for an interface specification, we consider here the input data for the
event "customer request". The discussion of target identification above has shown
that the input data has to be accessed in the formal extensions, for instance to obtain
the customer number or hotel number which are entered into the system. In an
appropriate interface specification, a specific data structure for the input data of each
event is generated which provides a specialized access function for each input data
item. For the event "customer request", the following SPECTRUM **data** declaration
is generated (using the information given in the abstract syntax through the function
inpItems):

> **data** InpData_cReq = inpData_cReq(
>   ! inp_cNo: Nat, ! inp_hNo: Nat, ! inp_period: (Date × Date),
>   ! inp_numRmsReq: Nat);

This is the surface which is offered to formal extensions of the Hotel Agency
specification. The interface itself consists in a translation function which converts
the method-level sort InpData into the project-specific sort InpData_cReq, provided
the given input data belongs to the right event.

> inpVal_cReq: InpData → InpData_cReq;
> δ inpVal_cReq(ev, d) = (ev = cReq);
> inpVal_cReq(ev, d) =
>   inpData_cReq(natAttr(selMap(d, custNo)), natAttr(selMap(d, hotelNo)),
>   periodAttr(selMap(d, period)), natAttr(selMap(d, numRooms)));

It is important that all interface specifications are just simple abbreviations which
encapsulate a number of conversions from method level to project level and
backwards. The interface specifications should be designed always in such a way

that they do not contribute to the semantics themselves. This way, the
disadvantages of one-level translations which were mentioned in chapter 5 above
(in particular missing semantic precision) can be avoided completely.

10.3.3 Individual Attribute Sorts

Before returning to the discussion of the four expansion steps for input data, it may
be worth mentioning that the interface approach as it was introduced above is also
sufficient to solve the problem of conversion between the meta-level sort AttrVal and
the individual attribute sorts. For this purpose, for each attribute in each entity an
access function has to be included in the interface specification.

We use the naming convention that attr_*aname* refers to the attribute *aname* in all
entities for which this attribute is admitted, as long as the domains coincide in all
these entities (as they to in the Hotel Agency example). If the domains for the same
attribute in different entities happen to be different, different function names must
be chosen, for instance by including the entity name. An example for an attribute
selection function in the interface specification is the following:

> attr_numRoomsAvail: Occ → Nat;
> attr_numRoomsAvail(o) =
>   **if** entity(o) = quota **then** natAttr(o@numRoomsAvail)) **else** ⊥ **endif**;

Again, the interface specification just introduces convenient abbreviations for the
SPECTRUM formulation of formal extensions.

10.4 SPECTRUM Extensions for SSADM-F

Using the mechanism of an interface specification, an adequate solution for the
formal specification for the four steps in the expansion of input data to input events
can be given. We discuss here shortly each of the four steps. The two target
identification steps, in form of the functions idfyTgs and idfyRegTgs, differ only in
the option parameter, so we discuss these two steps together.

10.4.1 Target Identification

Entry Specification

The identification of entry points can now be handled through the interface
specification. For each entry point, a function is included in the interface
specification. For the "customer" entry in the "customer request" event, the
signature is as follows:

> entrySpec_cReq_customer: InpData_cReq × OccId_customer → Bool;

The function entrySpec_cReq_customer takes the SPECTRUM sorts for the input data and for the entities (see below) as arguments. Formal extensions in plain SPECTRUM can now be added for this function to describe the entry specification.

The connection to the axiomatic semantics is established by a single axiom in the interface specification. Please note that also this axiom can be generated schematically from the information in the EEM documents.

$$(i, \$customer, am) \text{ elem idfyRegTgs(cReq, d, bound)} \Rightarrow$$
$$\text{entrySpec\_cReq\_customer(inpVal\_cReq(d), idVal\_customer(i))};$$

The sort OccId_customer and the function idVal_customer in the examples are also part of the interface specification. For each entity (like "customer"), the information about its primary keys is translated into a SPECTRUM sort representing identifiers for the entity.

data OccId_customer = occId_customer(! id_cNo: Nat);

Similar to the input events, there is a conversion function in the interface specification by which the entity-specific identifier sort can be obtained out of a method-level value of sort OccId.

idVal_customer: OccId $\rightarrow$ OccId_customer;
idVal_customer(i) = occId_customer(idAttr(i, customerNo));

Using all these schematic extensions in the interface specification (INT), the formal extension (EXT) can be written quite simply. Please note that only this extension specification has to be provided by the specifier. So the identification of the "customer" entry can be specified by the following single line in the formal extensions:

entrySpec_cReq_customer(inpd, icust) = (id_ cNo(icust) = inp_cNo(inpd));

This specification quite clearly expresses the condition that the key attribute value (id_cNo) has to be equal to the value given in the "customer number" input item (inp_cNo). In this solution, the condition is written in plain SPECTRUM; for instance, the equality operation used here is the standard equality of the specification language.

Correspondence Specification

In a quite similar style, the correspondence arrows from the ECD can be equipped with an interface to a formal specification. We demonstrate this for the correspondence between the "hotel" target and the "quota" targets in figure 10.1. Besides the entry specification predicates, the interface specification also contains "correspondence specification predicates". A correspondence specification is a predicate for two occurrence identifiers, which has the input data as an additional argument.

> corrSpec_cReq_preBookedBy:
>   InpData_cReq × OccId_hotel × OccId_quota → Bool;

In the Hotel Agency, quotas are identified by a hotel number (the same attribute as it is used to identify hotels) and by a date. Exactly those quotas should correspond to the given hotel, which coincide in the hotel number attribute with the hotel and whose dates lie within the period given by the input data. So the correspondence specification involves the test whether a date is in a given period. In a realistic setting, there will be a library of auxiliary specifications available for such things as dates or periods. We show here a small part of such a specification, to illustrate the fact that entry and correspondence specifications may use arbitrary systems of abstract data types written in SPECTRUM.

```
corrSpec_cReq_preBookedBy (inpd, ihotel, iquota) =
        (id_hNo(iquota) = id_hNo(ihotel)) ∧
        (start(inp_period(inpd)) before id_avDate(iquota)) ∧
        (id_avDate(iquota) before end(inp_period(inpd)));
    start, end:    (Date × Date) → Date;   – – start and end date of a period
    start(d1, d2) = d1;
    start(d1, d2) = d2;
    . before .:    Date × Date → Date;     – – comparison of dates
    (d1, m1, y1) before (d2, m2, y2) =
        (y1 < y2) ∨ ((y1=y2) ∧ ((m1 < m2) ∨ ((m1=m2) ∧ (d1 ≤ d2))));
```

New Identifiers

In the ECD of figure 10.1, the "request" and "reservation" targets have not been discussed yet. These targets have a special role since new identifiers should be automatically created for them. This is a quite frequent situation in information systems, for which today's database systems offer specialized solutions (like sequence generators). Also in the formal specification, we provide a specialized concept for this. This feature can be even covered completely in a two-level style, without using an interface specification.

In the abstract syntax, a function newIdTgs is introduced which lists the targets for which a new identifier is to be created.

> newIdTgs: OptEvent → Set Target;
> newIdTgs(oev) ⊆ (admTargets(oev) \ entries(oev));

In the running example, the corresponding project level specification is obvious:

> newIdTgs(cReq, immOff) = set [$reservation];
> newIdTgs(cReq, reqFromH) = set [$request];

The semantics of the newIdTgs set can be described on the method level by two axioms. The first axiom relies on the BoundIds parameter of the identification phase, which is a function giving the set of bound identifiers for an entity.

$$(i, tg, am) \text{ elem idfyTgs}(oev, d, bound) \land tg \in \text{newIdTgs}(oev) \land tg = (e, rol) \Rightarrow$$
$$\neg (i \in bound(e));$$

A second axiom states that in the case where several target items exist for the same target ("set-of" targets), all the chosen new identifiers are pairwise different.

$$(i1, tg, am) \text{ elem idfyTgs}(oev, d, bound)$$
$$\land (i2, tg, am) \text{ elem idfyTgs}(oev, d, bound)$$
$$\land tg \in \text{newIdTgs}(oev)$$
$$\Rightarrow i1 \neq i2;$$

Since all the semantic axioms for target identification were formulated conditionally, it is necessary to state in addition that all needed target items are actually present in the result of the target identification function. For this purpose, the functions entriesOK and corrOK can be reused.

10.4.2 Option Selection

The selection of an option takes place on the basis of the input data items and the previously identified regular target items. In contrast to the identification phase, the option selection has to deal with a statically unknown number of parameters. In the "customer request" example, for each quota occurrence which lies within the requested period, a target item is passed as a parameter to the option selection. So the number of these target items is limited by a number known only at runtime. Moreover, the option selection does not get the list of target items directly as a parameter, but only a view on the system state which is derived from it. The signature of option selection is:

selOpt: Event × DataItems × View → Option;

Informally, the option for the example event can be selected according to the following condition:

"The option is 'immediately available' iff all the occurrences for the target '$quota' show a number of available rooms which is less or equal than the requested number of rooms and if these occurrences together cover the whole requested period."

We are looking now for an adequate mechanism to express this rule as a
SPECTRUM axiom on top of the SSADM-F specification. Since the option selection
conditions often are relatively complex, the mechanism of an interface specification
is used here again. The following signature for option selection in the "customer
request" case is part of the interface specification:

selOpt_cReq: InpData_cReq × View → Option;

The axiom establishing the connection from interface to meta-level is quite simple:

selOpt(cReq, d, vw) = selOpt_cReq(inpVal_cReq(d), vw);

A convenient abbreviation can be defined (also on the method level) to obtain the
set of occurrences which has been selected by the preceding identification step for a
given target. The necessary information for this purpose is contained in the view,
which has been defined above as a tuple of a (reduced) state and a target
assignment.

tgOccs: View × Target → Set Occ;
o ∈ tgOccs((s, f), tg) ⇔ contained(s)(o) ∧ f(o) = tg;

Using these preparations and the attribute selection functions in the interface
specification, the option selection for the example can be formulated in SPECTRUM
relatively simply.

---

selOpt_cReq(inpd, vw) = immOff ⇔
         (∀ o. o ∈ tgOccs(vw, $quota) ⇒
                 attr_numRoomsAvail(o) ≤ inp_numRmsReq(inpd))
     ∧   (∀ dt. (start(inp_period(inpd)) before dt) ∧
                 (dt before end(inp_period(inpd))) ⇒
                         ∃ o. o ∈ tgOccs(vw, $quota) ∧ attr_availDate(o) = dt);

This axiom captures almost literally the informal description of the option criterion
which was given above.

The formal definition of the option condition shows clearly that a descriptive
specification style is valuable also for the formal extension of SSADM-F
specifications. However, in order to get an executable variant of the extended
specification, all these specifications have to be reformulated in an executable style.

10.4.3 Attribute Values

In the executable specification for SSADM-F, each target item carries a component
of sort AttrMap which was not yet covered by the above specifications. By this
attribute mapping for any attribute of an affected occurrence a value can be given.

In the logical prototype for SSADM-F, this value is assigned to the attribute in the successor state. There may be several target items for the same target, like the "quota" occurrences in our running example, which require individual attribute values. In the example, the new available number of vacant rooms must be determined individually for each date of the booking period. So the function for the determination of the attribute values transforms a list of target items into a list of target items, where the updates are computed for each target item separately. The information available for this computation are the input data items and the view onto the system state through the full list fo target items:

> attrVals: OptEvent × DataItems × View × List TgItem → List TgItem;

In the "customer request" example, the following attributes are updated:

- In the single "customer" target, the actual date is entered as a new "date of last request". This is used to prevent the removal of the customer from the system for the next year.

- In the "request" or "reservation" target, also the actual date is entered. In the case of a request, this is only for documentation purposes, in the case of the reservation it marks the beginning of the 10 days period in which the reservation stays valid.

- If a reservation is created ("immediately offered" option), then in all "quota" targets the number of available rooms is re-adjusted.

The Operation Lists in SSADM-F contain the information that these attributes are modified. However, they do not contain a specification for the new value. This missing information[7] is added now.

The step of attribute value determination has been given the name attrVals above.

> attrVals: OptEvent × DataItems × View × List TgItem → List TgItem;

A few semantic properties of the attrVals function are obvious. The following three axioms state that the attribute maps in the target items are empty beforehand, that the attrVals function does not change other information in the target lists than the attribute maps, and that for each attribute appearing in the operation lists set a new value is defined.

---

[7] In original SSADM, there exist "using"-clauses in the operation lists which serve for specifying the new value. However, the approach described here is more precise and more powerful.

(i, tg, am) elem idfyTgs ⇒ am = initMap;

(i, tg, am) elem attrVals(oev, d, vw, ut) ⇔ ∃ am'. (i, tg, am') elem ut;

(i, tg, am) elem attrVals(oev, d, vw, ut) ⇒
           (inMap(am, a) = (attSto(a) elem OPS(oev, tg)));

For each updated attribute, a function symbol and a semantic axiom are contained in the interface specification. For instance, the update of the "date last request" attribute in the "customer" target gives the following function and axiom:

upd_cReq_customer_dateLastRequest:
    InpData_cReq × View × OccId → Date;

(i, $customer, am) ∈ attrVals(cReq, d, vw, ut) ⇒
    selMap(am, dateLastReq) =
           upd_cReq_customer_dateLastReq(inpVal_cReq(d), vw, i);

Please note that the generated function symbol has an additional OccId parameter. This parameter is not necessary in the case of a target which appears only once, but it is needed for "set-of" targets to individualize the update values. Since the new value is parameterized with the identity of the target, it may depend for instance on "old" attribute values of the target occurrence before the update. An example of such a situation is the update of the "number of available rooms" attribute in the "quota" occurrences. The function symbol and the axiom are introduced in the interface specification following the same scheme as for the first example.

upd_cReq_immOff_quota_numRoomsAvail:
    InpData_cReq × View × OccId → Nat;

(i, $quota, am) ∈ attrVals((cReq, immOff), d, vw, ut) ⇒
    selMap(am, numRoomsAvail) =
    upd_cReq_immOff_quota_numRoomsAvail(inpVal_cReq(d), vw, i);

For these two examples, now extension axioms (in plain SPECTRUM) are given. Only the two lines of code in the boxes below have to be actually supplied by the specifier. In the case of the "date last request" update, the new value is simply the actual date which can be read from the system state.

```
upd_cReq_customer_dateLastRequest(inpd, (s, f), i) = today(s);
```

The function today was already introduced at the beginning of this chapter (section 10.1.2). It accesses the sysData occurrence which we assume to be contained in every system state and which remains visible also in every view of the state.

For the more interesting "number of available rooms" update, the project level specification makes use of the additional OccId parameter. We use the name self to refer to this parameter, since it provides the update of a quota occurrence with information about its "self", that is about the identity of the updated occurrence.

```
upd_cReq_immOff_quota_numRoomsAvail((inpd, (s, f), self) =
    attr_numRoomsAvail(get(s, self)) − inp_numRmsReq(inpd);
```

The access to attributes and input data items was already explained above. So the formula just encodes the fact that for each "quota" target item, the old value of the "number of available rooms" attribute is obtained from the system view and the new value is given by subtracting the rooms which were given away to the customer on his or her request.

10.5 Perspectives for Formally Extended Pragmatic Specifications

This chapter again has introduced some additional technical machinery. It is useful to recall what the "surface" of the proposed technique is which is presented to a specifier. Under ideal machine support, all the technical axioms in the interface specifications are generated automatically, and only the material which was shown in boxes throughout this chapter has to be entered manually. This information is a compact and nevertheless precise representation of the information one would like to add onto an SSADM-F specification. The Effect Correspondence Diagram gives a good central document for getting an overview of all this detailed material. A good user interface of a tool supporting formally extended SSADM-F could for instance provide a "pop-up" access to the detail specifications through pointing at various pieces of an ECD.

An SSADM-F specification with formal extensions can be seen as a complete specification for the pure functionality of an information system (still leaving out dialogue design). So an interesting question is how this formal basis can be used for the development of provably correct programs. A definite answer to this question can be found only through practical experiments. But the impression of the author is that a straightforward application of classical program verification to the complex mixture of automatically generated and user-defined specifications will cause many practical problems. A more promising way to derive correct software from formally extended SSADM-F specifications could be to fix a sublanguage of the user-specified SPECTRUM parts, similar to the executable sublanguage of SPECTRUM, for which the various new functions get executable on the background of executable SSADM-F. For such extensions of SSADM-F, there is some hope for an implementation which can be proven to be correct *generically* for each instantiation, on the basis of the techniques which were shown in chapter 9. The investment in the correctness proof for such a generic information system generator would be acceptable, since then the verification work can be reused for several instantiations. However, it should be kept in mind that the design of a reasonably efficient information system is still a complex and creative task, so the automatic generation of an efficient and semantically correct information system will remain a real challenge for a long time.

Chapter 11
The SSADM Technique "Data Flow Modelling"

This chapter covers the third main technique in SSADM. The central notation of Data Flow Modelling is the Data Flow Diagram (DFD), a notation which was introduced rather early in the history of Systems Analysis [DeM79] and which is currently one of the most popular Requirements Engineering techniques in practice. Since Data Flow Diagrams are considered in SSADM as a quite informal tool, a rather loose specification of the semantics of Data Flow Diagrams is given and its relationships to the more detailed techniques of LDM and EEM are worked out.

11.1 Data Flow Diagrams in SSADM

This chapter contains significantly less formal material than chapter 8 on EEM. The reason for this is that, in SSADM, Data Flow Diagrams are used as an almost informal notation. DFDs serve in SSADM for a preliminary analysis the results of which form the basis for a detailed requirements specification within the EEM technique. Therefore it is quite adequate for the DFM technique to have a rather loose and simple semantics which does not yet fix the details of the required system. The formal treatment of DFM is a study of the question to which degree the borderline between informal and formal description can be supported with formal methods.

Figure 11.1 shows a typical example for a DFD in SSADM notation, which is composed of *external entities*, *processes*, *data stores* and *data flows*. For the purposes of a general explanation of DFM, we ignore here a number of special notations in SSADM[1].

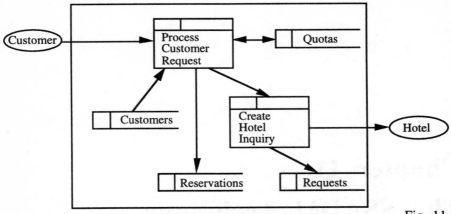

Fig. 11.1

A rectangle in a DFD (see figure 11.2 (a)) is called a *process* because it represents some function which takes input, reads and modifies some part of the system state and produces output. Generally, a process is completely independent of the event-oriented update functions as they were discussed in chapter 8. Processes in Data Flow Diagrams are drawn early in the analysis of requirements, as a simple means to represent and discuss functionality without giving a detailed specification.

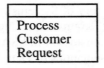

Fig. 11.2 (a)

Figure 11.2 (b) shows the symbol used for a *data store*. A data store represents a part of the system state. It is used as a simple reference to parts of the system state before a detailed structure of the system state is provided by Logical Data Modelling. After a Logical Data Model has been developed, the data stores are associated with specific parts of the data model by a *Logical Data Store/ Entity Cross Reference*.

Fig. 11.2 (b)

The third kind of node in a DFD is an oval called *external entity*, see figure 11.2 (c). An external entity is used as a source or sink for data flows which enter or

---

[1]   For instance, we do not care about the numbering scheme for processes and data stores.

leave the system. Usually, the border of the system is shown in the diagram explicitly as a frame outside of which the external entities are placed (see figure 11.1). One could think of external entities as input and output facilities of the system. The identifier given in the oval is relevant only for documentation purposes, it can used to indicate the person or technical device from which information is gathered or to which it is transferred. Despite of the appearance of the word "entity", the meaning is completely independent of the meaning of "entity" which was defined in Logical Data Modelling!

Fig. 11.2 (c)

Finally, the building blocks of a DFD are connected with directed arrows representing *data flows*. Some forms of data flow connections are excluded. For instance, a data flow arrow cannot be drawn between two data stores. In contrast to most other DFD approaches, SSADM (in version 4) allows a data flow to connect two external entities. However, such data flows are interesting only for documentation purposes, they are not relevant for the specification of the functionality of the system itself. For this reason, we do not cover these data flows in our formal treatment. In the following, we will require the simple rule that each data flow must either start in or lead to a process box.

Data Flow diagrams can be defined in a *hierarchical* manner in SSADM, as in most other variants of the DFD approach. This means that a part of a large DFD can be collapsed into a single process box, showing only the data flows which cross the border of the subdiagram. For instance, the DFD in figure 11.3 is meant as a subdiagram of a larger DFD. It covers only a small part of the functionality of the Hotel Agency example. For the sake of brevity, we do not include the notation of hierarchical DFDs here in our formalization.

The procedural guidelines of SSADM prescribe Data Flow Diagrams to be drawn at several places during the analysis of requirements. Essentially, the functionality of the current system is captured first by a *Current Physical DFD*. Then this data flow diagram is *logicalized* into the functional essence of the system under consideration (*Current Logical DFD*). After a detailed comparison of several alternatives (*Business System Options*), the *Required System Logical DFD* is drawn, which is then used as a basis for the detailed specification with the EEM technique. All these diagrams follow the same syntax, and the transformation from one into another does *not* follow rules which could be captured by a formal semantics. SSADM does give detailed methodical guidelines for a systematic construction of these various diagrams, but the transformations are based on common sense and on an intuitive interpretation of the identifiers given in the diagram. So our formalization covers the general concepts of a DFD, but it does not distinguish between the various stages in which a DFD may be drawn.

11.2 Formalization of Data Flow Diagrams

For the formal treatment of Data Flow Diagrams, we proceed in three steps. First, a general concept for the syntax and semantics of a DFD is proposed which is not related to any of the other techniques at all. This is the topic of the current section 11.2. In a second step (section 11.3), Data Flow Modelling is brought together with the static system structure (Logical Data Modelling) as it was formalized in chapter 7. Finally (section 11.4), the specification of system dynamics by Entity-Event Modelling is integrated with the DFD semantics.

11.2.1 Data Flow Diagrams: Abstract Syntax

As for all abstract syntax specifications, this section defines the parameter requirements for the formalization of a Data Flow Diagram. For the sake of simplicity, DFDs are assumed to be "flat" (non-hierarchical). A formalization of hierarchical DFDs could be easily added on top of the specifications given here. The syntax formalization is similar in its style to the formalization of ER diagrams in chapter 7.

The basic building blocks of a DFD are described by (meta-level) sorts, which are refined for any project-level DFD by data declarations. For each node type in a DFD, a sort is introduced.

      sort Proc, DataStore, ExtEnt;   Proc, DataStore, ExtEnt:: EQ;

The identifiers used in a data declaration on method level can be chosen as mnemonic abbreviations of the identifiers given in the DFD. Besides the three node types, also for the data flows a sort is introduced, in analogy to the relationship names in an ER diagram. Since the DFD (as in figure 11.1) does not provide identifiers for data flows, a new unique identifier has to be invented for each data flow. Then also the data flow names can be represented as a data declaration.

      sort Flow;   Flow:: EQ;

As an example, consider the following variant of the DFD in figure 11.1 which additionally contains flow names. The chosen names for the data flows are composed from an indicator for the kind of flow (input, output, read or write) and an abbreviation for one of the involved nodes.

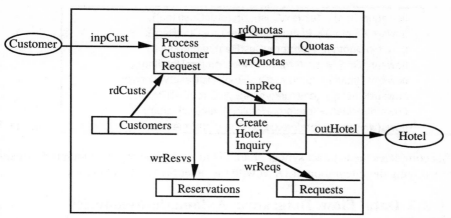

Fig. 11.3

A systematic translation of figure 11.3 into data definitions for the four syntactic sorts is shown in figure 11.4.

```
data Proc = procCustReq | creaHotelInq;
data DataStore = customers | reservations | requests | quotas;
data ExtEnt = extCustomer | extHotel;
data Flow =
        inpCust | rdQuotas | wrQuotas | inpReq | wrResvs | rdCusts |
        wrReqs | outHotel;
```

Fig. 11.4

As in the case of the ER diagram, the information about the start and the end of a data flow can be represented by a simple function which associates a pair of nodes to a flow name. But since there are three different kinds of nodes, a supersort of all DFD nodes must be constructed for this purpose.

```
data DFDNode = ext(! ExtEnt) | prc (! Proc) | dst( ! DataStore);

flows:        Flow → (DFDNode, DFDNode);        flows total;
```

There is a simple context condition for the flows function, which states that either the starting or ending point of a flow has to be a process node[2].

```
flows(fl) = (n1, n2) ⇒ is_prc(n1) ∨ is_prc(n2);
```

The obvious translation of figure 11.3 into axioms for the flows function is demonstrated by figure 11.5.

---

[2]   As it was said above, we omit here any flows between external entities only.

```
flows(inpCust) = (ext(extCust), prc(procCustReq));
flows(rdQuotas) = (dst(quotas), prc(procCustReq));
flows(wrQuotas) = (prc(procCustReq), dst(quotas));
flows(inpReq) = (prc(procCustReq), prc(creHotelInq));
flows(wrResvs) = (prc(procCustReq), dst(reservations));
flows(rdCusts) = (dst(customers), prc(procCustReq));
flows(outHotel) = (prc(creaHotelInq), ext(extHotel));
flows(wrReqs) = (prc(creaHotelInq), dst(requests));
```

Fig. 11.5

This completes the abstract syntax of a DFD in a very basic form which is sufficient for studying the integration of DFM with the other SSADM techniques.

11.2.2 Data Flow Diagrams: Axiomatic Semantics

The formal semantics of Data Flow Diagrams has been addressed by several authors [Sho88, FD89, TP89, FKV91, PvKP91, Fra92, SFD92, NW93, LPT94][3]. However, in most of these approaches (except of [PvKP91, LPT94]), the DFDs are seen as the basic paradigm for specifying the dynamics of the system. The central question is there how *control flow* can be specified. By "control flow" we mean any conditions for the activation order of processes. In one group of approaches, the control flow is derived from the causality relation given by the DFD, such that a framework like Petri nets or stream-processing functions can be used. Another group of approaches extends DFDs with additional notation for an explicit representation of control flow.

All these approaches seem to be not fully adequate for DFDs as they are used in SSADM. The system dynamics are defined in SSADM by Entity-Event Modelling and not by Data Flow Modelling, which is a superior replacement of control-extended DFDs for information system applications. Also the approaches which derive the control flow from the data flow do not fit very well into the framework of SSADM, since the basic system architecture in such an approach is a distributed, communication-oriented network. SSADM, however, aims at a sequential system architecture during requirements analysis and tries to leave concurrency issues to the implementation level as far as possible[4]. A DFD in SSADM does not even specify a causality relation between processes. In a situation like in figure 11.6, where two processes are connected by a data flow, it may be very well the case that

---

[3]   See also section 3.1.2.

[4]   Obviously, there are applications where the physical distribution of data has such a prominent role that it appears already in the requirements specifications. But in such applications, communication and synchronization must be handled on the level of Entity-Event modelling, too. So also in these cases, a concurrency-oriented semantics for DFDs is not very useful.

an activation of the "second" process P2 is the cause for an activation of the "first" process P1 (in order to obtain data needed for the processing).

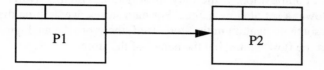

Fig. 11.6

So for a pure DFD as it is given by the abstract syntax from above, only very little can be said about the semantics. At this point, a formal semantics can be given only for a *single* process (since no causality is involved in DFDs directly). This first semantics covers only a description of the input, output and accessed state part for a process[5]. As DFDs are not yet related to any description of transformed data, even this specification must be kept quite loose. In the following sections, this semantics will be refined into a more specific one, including also a special treatment for process-to-process flows.

For a pure DFD, two sorts are introduced to represent the data which flows in a DFD (input, inter-process flows and output) and values for the possible states of data stores.

    sort DFData, DState;

The semantics of a DFD process is a function which takes all the input data on all input flows to the process and reads all the data stores from which a data flow goes into the process. Its result is output data for all output flows from the data store and an updated state for each data store to which the process sends a data flow. It is convenient to compose all input data into a single value of sort DFData, and analoguously also the output data, read stores and written stores. So the process simply takes a pair of data and state and delivers a pair of data and state. We use two functions, as in the EEM semantics.

    trans: DState × Proc × DFData → DState;
    outp: DState × Proc × DFData → DFData;

    δ outp(s, p, dd) $\Rightarrow$ δ trans(s, p, dd);

As far as possible, we would also like to formalize the rules how the values on the data flows are composed. The following four functions are auxiliary definitions working on the abstract syntax of a DFD. For instance, the prcInput function puts together all data flows which lead into a process coming from an external entity or

---

[5]   For the composition of data flow diagrams, techniques from the literature could be added, like the SAC approach from [PvKP91].

another process. These are the data flows on which the process expects explicit data values. An analogous function exists for the output flows. The result of these functions is a composition of the only information which is available about the individual flows: a set of flow names. For data stores, we assume that the access may include some navigation in the store itself, therefore the analoguous functions do not collect the flow names, but the names of the stores.

$$prcInput, prcOutput: \; Proc \rightarrow Set \; Flow;$$
$$fl \in prcInput(p) \Leftrightarrow$$
$$(\exists \; p'. \; flows(fl) = (prc(p'), prc(p))) \vee (\exists \; ee. \; flows(fl) = (ext(ee), prc(p)));$$
$$fl \in prcOutput(p) \Leftrightarrow$$
$$(\exists \; p'. \; flows(fl) = (prc(p), prc(p'))) \vee (\exists \; ee. \; flows(fl) = (prc(p), ext(ee)));$$

$$prcRead, prcWrite: \quad Proc \rightarrow Set \; DataStore;$$
$$ds \in prcRead(p) \Leftrightarrow (\exists \; fl. \; flows(fl) = (dst(ds), prc(p)));$$
$$ds \in prcWrite(p) \Leftrightarrow (\exists \; fl. \; flows(fl) = (prc(p), dst(ds)));$$

Using these four auxiliary functions, one would like to specify that the input and output data fulfil some structural conditions. In the example above, it is natural that the data flowing from the customer to the "Process Customer Request" box comprises information about the requested hotel, the customer number, the number of requested rooms and the requested period of time. Similarly, one would like to fix that the "Reservations" store really corresponds to "reservation" entities in a system state. Unfortunately, such information cannot be described precisely at this point because it is not yet syntactically contained in the Data Flow Diagram. In the next section, appropriate annotations will be included for this purpose. However, we can give already a very loose specification for such conditions which can be refined later. The specification is loose in the sense that we simply introduce a predicate which tests whether some actual input data matches a condition which can be derived from the set of input or output flows, and correspondingly for the data store values.

$$ioTest: \qquad DFData \times Set \; Flow \rightarrow Bool;$$
$$dstTest: \qquad DState \times Set \; DataStore \rightarrow Bool;$$

$$\delta \; trans(s, p, dd) \Rightarrow$$
$$ioTest(dd, prcInput(p)) \wedge dstTest(s, prcRead(p) \cup prcWrite(p));$$
$$s' = trans(s, p, dd) \Rightarrow dstTest(s', prcWrite(p));$$
$$dd' = outp(s, p, dd) \Rightarrow ioTest(dd', prcOutput(p));$$

The ioTest function provides a "hook" to constrain the input and output of a particular process further. Please note that the first two axioms follow the idea that a data store which is to be updated by the process must also be read by it. This is obviously necessary for each kind of update different to the simple creation of a new data record.

From a practical viewpoint, the semantics given here is not very fruitful. Obviously this kind of axiomatic semantics is so abstract that it does not contribute to the specification of a concrete project. In fact, the semantics are not (yet) connected to the reference specification, and so they formally do not constrain information systems at all. Nevertheless, this semantics *is* adequate for the DFDs which are drawn in the early phases of requirements engineering in SSADM (like the *Current Physical Data Flow Diagram*). The fact that the semantics do not constrain the models of the system is just a consequence of the informality of these steps.

11.3 Integration between DFM and LDM

It is a logical next step to connect a data flow diagram with the Logical Data Model of the system. This is also proposed by SSADM as a rather early activity in requirements analysis (in step 140 "Investigate Current Data"). For a formal connection to LDM, the abstract syntax and the axiomatic semantics of DFDs are extended.

11.3.1 Data Flow Descriptions

For inter-process flows and flows between processes and external entities, the flow arrows are annotated with information on the data flowing. In SSADM, to each arrow of a DFD a list of identifiers can be attached. In order to reuse existing terms, we assume that a data flow arrow is annotated with a set of attribute identifiers (and domain restrictions). The abstract syntax is quite obvious.

$$flowDescr: \quad Flow \rightarrow Set\,(Attr \times Dom);$$

The flow description is not required for those arrows which involve data stores, since a data store itself represents a kind of data structure. This gives the the following context condition.

$$\delta\,flowDescr(fl) \Leftrightarrow (\forall\,from,\,to.\,fl = (from,\,to) \Rightarrow \neg\,(is\_sto(from) \vee is\_sto(to));$$

For the sample DFD, adequate flow descriptions are shown in figure 11.7.

```
flowDescr(inpCust) =
          set [ (custNo, nat), (hotelNo, nat), (numRooms, nat),
                (period, pair(date, date)) ];
flowDescr(inpReq) =
          set [ (custNo, nat), (hotelNo, nat), (numRooms, nat),
                (period, pair(date, date)) ];
flowDescr(outHotel) =
          set [ (numRooms, nat), (period, pair(date, date)) ];
```

Fig. 11.7

The axiomatic semantics of the flow description is just a refinement of the loosely specifed function ioTest. If a concrete data value flowing along the arrow is given, it can be decided whether it carries a binding for all the attributes given in the annotation. Formally, we refine the sort DFData here into a mapping of attribute identifiers to attribute values.

> **sortsyn** DFData = Map Attr AttrVal;

This definition has the advantage that it easily covers the composition of several data items into a single value. The function ioTest checks a (composed) data value against a flow description.

> ioTest(am, sf) =
> $(\forall$ fl, a, d. (fl $\in$ sf) $\wedge$ (a, dom) $\in$ flowDescr(fl) $\Rightarrow$
> defMap(am, a) $\wedge$ dom(selMap(am, a)));

11.3.2 Logical Data Store / Entity Cross Reference

Analogously, also the data stores can be connected with the definitions used in LDM. In SSADM it is proposed to produce a Logical Data Store / Entity Cross Reference. This cross reference is a table which associates to each data store a part of the ER diagram. For the example DFD used here, the cross reference table is as shown in figure 11.8.

Data store	Logical Data Structure
Customers:	Customer
Reservations:	holds is_reserved_in Customer ⤙- - -◅ Reservation ▻- - -⤚ Hotel is_reserved_for reserves
Requests:	wants is_requested_in Customer ⤙- -◅ Request ▻- - ⤚ Hotel is_requested_by requests
Quotas:	pre_booked_by Hotel ⤙- - -◅ Quota is_for

Fig. 11.8

Such a cross reference table is represented by an abstract syntax which consists of two functions. One gives the set of entities for a data store, the other one the set of relationships.

DEX: DataStore → Set Entity;   DEX **total**;
DRX: DataStore → Set Rel;   DRX **total**;

We skip the obvious context conditions here. The translation of the correspondence table from figure 11.8 into the abstract syntax notation is shown in figure 11.9.

DEX(customers) = set [customer];
DRX(customers) = set [];
DEX(reservations) = set [customer, reservation, hotel];
DRX(reservations) =
        set [holds, is_reserved_for, reserves, is_reserved_in];
DEX(requests) = set [customer, request, hotel];
DRX(requests) =
        set [wants, is_requested_by, requests, is_requested_in];
DEX(quotas) = set [hotel, quota];
DRX(quotas) = set [pre_booked_by, is_for];

Fig. 11.9

The idea of the axiomatic semantics for such a correspondence table is to refine the function dstTest in the DFD semantics towards a structural condition on system states. For this purpose, the sort DState of state values for data stores is refined into a fragment of a system state, as it was defined in LDM. By a fragment of a system state we mean a part which is not necessarily closed in the sense of referential integrity, but may contain links into other parts of a system state. We have chosen to represent the state fragments by mappings from occurrence identifiers to occurrences. This is exactly the representation of system states from the executable specification. Please note that we could have defined a "semantically pure" refinement of DState as well, which is closed under referential integrity. But this had led to a more complex semantics in the next section, without giving better insight into the way the integration works.

sortsyn DState = Map Occld Occ;

We use for the state DState the same functions as for the sort State, since the definition of DState coincides with the implementation of State in the executable specification.

Based on the refinement of DState, the test whether a data store fulfils the description given in the correspondence table consists of a test whether all occurrences and relationship instances are listed in the table. Please note that the axiom which claims this test predicate to hold for any process activation was already given above (in 11.2).

dstTest(s, sd) =
        ($\forall$ o. contained(s)(o) $\Rightarrow$ $\exists$ ds. (ds $\in$ sd) $\wedge$ (entity(o) $\in$ DEX(ds)))
    $\wedge$ ($\forall$ r, i1, i2. connected(s, r)(i1, i2) $\Rightarrow$ $\exists$ ds. (ds $\in$ sd) $\wedge$ (r $\in$ DRX(ds)));

The semantics we have given up to now for DFDs is a completely static one. DFDs are interpreted as a semi-formal equivalent to function signatures in an axiomatic specification language. For each process, just structural conditions on its input and output are required. Process-to-process flows are not interpreted specifically; the interpretations of the following two DFDs are equivalent, as long as the flow description for flow 2.1 and flow 2.2 are both equal to the flow description of flow 1.

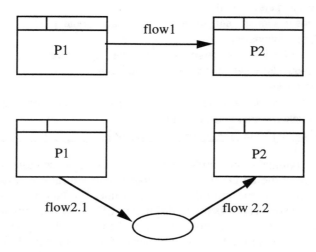

Fig. 11.10

So in the static view, process-to-process flows are just a diagrammatical abbreviation for showing that process P2 is able to accept the kind of output which is produced by P1. This interpretation differs clearly from the complex DFD semantics in most of the literature. However, the simpler interpretation seems to be perfectly adequate for the use of DFDs in SSADM. In the opinion of the author, the simple use which is made of DFDs in SSADM (as a preliminary informal tool and *not* as a design tool) is definitely superior to the approaches which try to derive a system design from DFDs (as classical Structured Analysis/ Structured Design).

11.4 Integration between DFM and EEM

In SSADM, there exists only a loose coupling between the results of Data Flow Modelling and the more refined specification by Entity-Event Modelling. In fact, SSADM does not require Data Flow Diagrams to be part of a complete requirements specification, and it does also not enforce any consistency rules between DFM and EEM documents. However, at the borderline between the two techniques (step 330 "Derive System Functions"), a number of hints are given how to obtain a starting point for EEM out of the Required System Logical DFDs. In this section, a formally based explanation for this step is given.

11.4.1 Derivation of System Functions

The term of a "function" is not defined very precisely in SSADM. A function is a group of services of the system which satisfies the needs of a particular kind of users (user role). Since we do not cover Dialogue Design in this book, we identify a function with the processing caused by an input event. In original SSADM, a function may comprise several types of input events. SSADM moreover distinguishes between user-initiated update functions, system-initiated update functions and enquiry functions. For our purposes, we concentrate on user-initiated update functions. System-initiated updates can be subsumed for a formal definition by something quite similar to a user-initiated function, since the passing of time can be seen as a special kind of input event. Enquiry functions have been excluded throughout this book.

A textbook on SSADM describes the derivation of user-initiated functions from DFDs as follows:

> "Firstly, systematically select the inputs from the external entities in the DFM. Next identify the processing which takes place as a consequence of each input. This is often contained in a single elementary process. These are user-initiated functions."
>
> [DCC92, p. 146]

This text points out how an input event and the processes in a data flow diagram are connected. Each input event is identified by a data flow into the system; the processing activated by the input event is the set of processes "which takes place as a consequence of the input". This gives a reasonable interpretation to process-to-process flows: Exactly those processes are included in the processing activated by an input which are directly or indirectly connected by data flows to the process receiving the stimulus.

For a formal treatment, it is convenient to order the set of activated processes according to the data dependencies. So we require a *list of (elementary) processes* to be associated to an event. (This implicitly excludes the case of a cyclic data dependency among activated processes.) An abstract syntax for expressing this is a function which maps an event (plus option) onto a list of processes[6].

    processes: OptEvent → List Proc;

Several context conditions are necessary for the processes function. The most important one expresses the closure condition with respect to process-to-process flows:

---

[6]   A "regular" process assignment depending only on the event can be defined analoguously.

up = up1++[p]++up2 ∧ flow(fl) = (prc(p), prc(p')) ⇒ p' elem up2;

The DFD which was used as a running example in this chapter can be connected to EEM by the following two project level axioms:

processes(custReq, immOff) = [procCustReq];
processes(custReq, inqFromH) = [procCustReq, creaHotelInq];   Fig. 11.11

For a semantic integration between DFM and EEM, we first have to address the issue that a DFD process works only on a particular fragment of the system state and not on the global system state which is used in the EEM semantics (next function). To integrate DFM, functions are needed to select a fragment out of a system state which matches the description of the data stored read by the process. Similarly, the fragment corresponding to the written data stores has to be replaced in the system state, see figure 11.12.

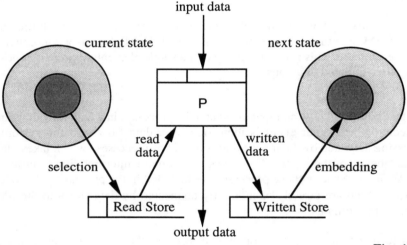

Fig. 11.12

The selection and embedding functions can be defined simply due to the decision to associate arbitrary fragments of the system state with the data stores. The disadvantage of this relatively rough definition is that the list of relationships in the correspondence table (DRX function) cannot be used to constrain the access to relationship instances. We base the selection and embedding simply on the entities in the correspondence table. However, the formalisation is precise enough to explain the idea.

select: State × Set Entity → DState;
embed: State × Set Entity × DState → State;

get(select(s, se), i) = o $\Leftrightarrow$ (get(s, i) = o $\wedge$ entity(o) $\in$ se);
get(embed(s, se, ds), i) = o $\Leftrightarrow$
    (entity(o) $\in$ se $\wedge$ get(ds, i) = o) $\vee$ (entity(o) $\notin$ se $\wedge$ get(s, i) = o);

The remaining definition of the integration is standard functional programming. Readers which are not interested in details can directly skip from here to subsection 11.4.2.

The select and embed functions are used to "lift" the DFD semantics onto the level of conventional system states as given in the reference specification. We use the names ltrans and loutp for the lifted variants of the two functions fixing the DFD semantics.

ltrans: State $\times$ Proc $\times$ DFData $\rightarrow$ State;
ltrans(s, p, am) =
      let sr = DEX*(prcRead(p)) **and** sw = DEX*(prcWrite(p)) **in**
          embed(s, sw, trans(select(s, sr), p, am)) **endlet**;

loutp: State $\times$ Proc $\times$ DFData $\rightarrow$ DFData;
loutp(s, p, am) = outp(select(s, DEX*(prcRead(p)), p, am));

The auxiliary function DEX* appearing here is simply the additive extension of DEX (data store-entity cross-reference) to sets of data stores. It is needed since all read and written data stores are composed in our approach.

Finally, the lifted transition function is iteratively applied to all processes given by the processes list. The output produced by any process in the list is collected together with the initial input (assuming a composition function "+++" for DFD data) and the collection is made available to all later processes. Each process then gets its appropriate input (including data communicated from earlier processes) by a filter function on this collected data[7].

trans*:   State $\times$ List Proc $\times$ DFData $\rightarrow$ State;

trans*(s, [], am) = s;
trans*(s, [p]++up, am) =
      pnext*(pnext(s, p, filterInp(am, prcInput(p))), up, am+++loutp(s, p, am));

The next function of the remantic reference specification now can be seen as equivalent to the composed processing of the associated DFD processes.

next(s, expandInp(s, ev, d)) = trans*(s, processes((ev, option(s, ev, d), d);

---

7   For simplicity, we ignore name clashes between attributes in different data flow descriptions.

This definition uses the expansion step from input data to input events which was defined in chapter 10 and passes the list of input data items to the DFD semantics as initial input flow. This is possible since the sorts DFData and DataItems (from chapter 10) are equal. Obviously, as a context condition it is necessary that the structure of the input data items coincides with the input flow description of the DFD processes. In the example, this is the case due to the equality:

> flowDescr(inpCust) = inItems(cReq);

Obviously, the same construction can be applied to integrate the DFD output with the output function out of the semantic reference specification.

11.4.2 Consistency between EEM and DFM

The first impression of the integration between EEM and DFM is that Data Flow Modelling can completely replace EEM, since it gives an explicit definition for the next function. However, the whole machinery of Data Flow Modelling relies on the semantics of elementary DFD processes for which no specification mechanism has been provided above. In classical Structured Analysis, the elementary processes are specified in detail (by so-called *mini-specifications*), and also SSADM contains the document type of *Elementary Process Descriptions* (EPDs) for this purpose. If formally based DFDs would be used as the basis of a detailed system specifications, the EPDs had to be extended towards a formal definition. Basically, this could be done following the ideas which were explained in chapter 10. In fact, the individual project team can decide whether it will specify details on the level of Data Flow Modelling or Entity-Event Modelling without leaving the framework of SSADM. Our decision to leave out a formal counterpart of EPDs is based on the fact that the literature on SSADM clearly considers the DFM documents as quite informal and preliminary, in contrast to a detailed specification by EEM.

Given this situation, where DFDs exist but the elementary processes are not specified in detail, also the question of consistency between the DFM and the EEM specification is not difficult to answer. The DFM specification can be understood here as a very loose specification of the part of the system state which is read and modified by the update caused by an input event. So the main source for inconsistency is between data store access in DFM and the Entity-Event Matrix in EEM. The following context conditions postulate these two ways of access to the system state to be consistent, based on the Logical Data Store/ Entity Cross Reference:

> EEX(oev, (e, rol)) $\in$ set [C, M, D] $\Rightarrow$
> $\exists$ p, ds. p elem processes(oev) $\land$ ds $\in$ prcWrite(p) $\land$ e $\in$ DEX(ds);

> EEX(oev, (e, rol)) = R $\Rightarrow$
> $\exists$ p, ds. p elem processes(oev) $\land$ ds $\in$ prcRead(p) $\land$ e $\in$ DEX(ds);

We state it as a conjecture that these context conditions already express the essential consistency condition between DFM and EEM. A detailed proof could be carried out by showing that the executable mode of chapter 9 fulfils the DFM axioms under these assumptions.

To summarize, Data Flow Modelling has turned out as a technique which somehow overlaps with EEM, but which is very well integrated into the general semantic framework of SSADM. In particular, it is quite interesting that DFM can be used on several levels of integration, from a very abstract and informal "stand-alone" semantics through an integration with LDM only, up to a complete integration with LDM and EEM.

Chapter 12
Summary and Outlook

In this final chapter, the achievements of this work are summarized and evaluated. As an outlook, several possible ways for applications and for further related research are indicated.

12.1 Summary

Basically, the work reported in this book is a demonstration that the two worlds of Software Engineering, the pragmatic and the formal world, are not at all as unrelated as many people seem to believe. For the two representatives, SSADM and SPECTRUM, a very close connection has been established which enables improvements for both the formal and the pragmatic method and even opens a way to combine the two specification paradigms.

The specific aim of this work was to give a precise semantic foundation for the pragmatic method SSADM. The framework of a formal specification language has been used successfully as a *meta-language* to define a generic semantics for the pragmatic method. This has led to a semantic specification of manageable size and clear structure.

The various notations of SSADM have turned out as differently well suited for formalization. The notations in Logical Data Modelling (ER-diagrams and entity descriptions), for instance, could be given a formal semantics quite easily, since they are already based on a solid mathematical background. Other techniques (for instance the Event-Entity Matrix and Operation Lists) could be formalized adequately only after a slight refinement of the pragmatic notation. As a result, not the original SSADM method was formalized, but a more rigorous and at some places simplified version, which was called SSADM-F throughout this work. However, the original "look and feel" of all studied SSADM document types could be kept in the formalized variant SSADM-F.

The semantic analysis has shown that SSADM, despite of its complexity, is a well-designed method which can be explained on the background of a simple semantic model. In particular the integration of the various notations on the basis of a central data model is convincing.

Due to the chosen approach of meta-specification, the semantics of SSADM-F is available in form of an ordinary SPECTRUM specification, which is parameterized by a representation of the documents specifying a concrete project. Therefore, standard techniques from the SPECTRUM framework could be applied to prove the consistency of the semantics. This proof is valid only if a number of parameter requirements is fulfilled by the concrete project. This list of conditions, which can be seen as "context conditions" for the syntax of an SSADM-F specification, is a novel contribution to the pragmatic method. No other complete set of consistency conditions for SSADM is known to the author.

Finally, the formal semantics has been laid out in such a way that at several places a combination of formal and pragmatic notations can be used. Such a hybrid SSADM-F/ SPECTRUM specification is a true formal specification many parts of which are presented in SSADM notation. The formal language is used only at those places where the expressiveness of the diagrammatic notations in SSADM is insufficient for a precise description.

12.2 Evaluation

This book tries to contribute to two areas of Software Engineering. It claims to constitute progress in the theory of program specification and a step towards practically applicable specification frameworks.

12.2.1 Theoretical Achievements

From the theoretical point of view, the most interesting contribution seems not to be the detailed specification of SSADM-F, but the general approach of analysing a pragmatic specification method by axiomatic formalization. This can be developed into a useful general analysis tool for arbitrary notations. In this respect, the basic feasability of a proof of consistency is of particular value.

The choice of SPECTRUM as a meta-language was motivated to a substantial amount by the author's interest in an evaluation of the language for a complex and highly abstract application case. Generally, the performance of SPECTRUM as a meta-language for specification formalisms is quite good. Many of the features of the language turned out as helpful for the description of a generic and compact meta-specification. In particular, higher-order functions and parametric polymorphism could not be removed from the specification without significant loss of readability. The consistency proof has also shown that a truly formal specification language with a defined deduction calculus is superior to the general language of mathematics as a meta-language. The SPECTRUM framework has provided the methodical background for the consistency proof (construction of an executable refinement via a constructive specification). The proof itself has turned out as mathematically trivial, but technically tedious, so that mechanical proof support can be of great help.

The only significant drawback of SPECTRUM as a meta-language is that there is no way to loosen its strong sort discipline. This has led into a quite unsatisfactory situation at those points where freely formulated SPECTRUM specifications are combined with an SSADM-F specification. In these cases, the generation of a large set of conversion functions is needed to embed ordinary SPECTRUM specifications into the meta-level framework. Although the generation of conversions can be completely automatized, a mechanism would be desirable here which fits better into the general meta-specification approach. For this purpose, a specification language with several levels of sorts is needed. The minimal requirement is a language which supports *subsorts* and automatic conversions like OBJ [FGJ+85]. But it would also be interesting to study languages which provide a layered approach to sort universes, as the languages based on mathematical type theory.

12.2.2 Practical Applications

From a more practical viewpoint, one can consider various scenarios where the formal foundations for SSADM (or an improved variant of it) could be used.

Scenario 1: Black-Box Application of SSADM-F

The notations of SSADM-F together with its consistency conditions can be simply used as a refined and more rigourous replacement for SSADM. In this style, SSADM-F can be applied *without any reference to formal methods*. The only difference to SSADM recognizable by users of the notations is that the syntax and its context conditions are more restrictive and that cross-document consistency is strictly enforced. For an application where a thoroughly analysed specification of an information system is necessary, SSADM-F seems to be one of the few methods which are applicable to large systems and simultaneously offer a significant degree of precision.

Scenario 2: SSADM-F with Minor Formal Extensions

The second scenario aims at the development of an information system which is conventional in most aspects but contains a few particularly critical aspects, like a collection of complex algorithms or an absolutely inevitable semantic data integrity condition. In such a case, SSADM-F can be applied for the conventional part of the system as in scenario 1. For the critical parts (*and only for those*) the techniques which were presented in chapter 10 can be used to add an ordinary SPECTRUM specification. The interesting point is here that SSADM-F admits a *local* addition of formal precision for specific purposes. In a development team this means that only a few members of the team have to be familiar with formal methods; for most of the team members an education in SSADM is sufficient. To achieve this effect, it is not always necessary to provide a full SSADM-F specification containing all documents from Event-Entity Modelling. For instance, consider a case where the only requirement which needs a formal specification is an integrity condition for the system state. Here it is sufficient to use the LDM part of SSADM-F and to formulate the data integrity as a predicate on top of this specification. The specification of system dynamics can then be carried out at an arbitrary level of precision, within SSADM-F or any other formal or informal specification framework.

Scenario 3: Hybrid SSADM-F/ SPECTRUM Specification

In the most sophisticated case of application, a completely formal specification may be needed for an information system. The author was involved in practical attempt to formally specify a medium-sized toy example of an information system [SNM+93, CHL95]. This experiment has led to the clear conclusion that for the more conventional parts of an information system (like the data model), a formal specification can greatly benefit from the embedding of semi-formal techniques like ER-diagrams. SSADM-F now provides a quite systematic way towards a complete formal specification, if all formal extensions are added (following chapter 10). The advantage is here that the full methodical support of SSADM is available. The detailed specification of processing (steps 330 and 360) now also includes the writing of formal specifications at those places where original SSADM requires informal text. This gives a completely formal specification without leaving the methodical context of SSADM.

At this point, it is interesting to review the requirements for the development of safety-critical systems as they have been fixed during the last years in many countries. The following citation is from the German "Criteria for the Evaluation of Trustworthiness of Information Technology Systems":

"For assurance level Q6, the following documentation shall be provided by
the sponsor: [...]
Informal, semi-formal and formal hierarchically structured specification of
the system components to be valuated with all the documents necessary to
check the formal proof of consistency of the model and the specification."

[GIS89]

If a system is specified within SSADM-F and all formal extensions are added in a
style which cannot introduce additional inconsistencies (for instance, as explicit
definitions on top of the abstract executable specification), then these requirements
are fulfilled. The interesting aspect is here that the requirement for the consistency
proof of the formal specification *can be fulfilled generically* by (a worked out
version of) the SSADM-F consistency proof. So for safety-critical systems, an
approach similar to SSADM-F may be also reasonable under economic
considerations.

12.3 Outlook

Despite of the amount of technical material which is contained in this work, many
questions remain open and many further refinements of the general approach would
be feasible.

12.3.1 Improvements

The most important need for SSADM-F is *tool support*. A complete workbench for
SPECTRUM is currently under development[1]. It will integrate syntax test and
configuration control components with an interactive tactical theorem prover. This
will provide adequate support for all method level activities for SSADM-F. In
particular the consistency proof for the method level SSADM-F specification
should be carried out with the help of a theorem prover, in order to get a truely
reliable formal foundation.

For the development of SSADM-F specifications for a concrete project, another
type of tools is needed. Here a user interface in the style of current CASE tools
would be most useful, with graphical editors for the diagrammatical notations of
SSADM-F and a central repository to store the abstract representation of the
documents. Depending on the application scenario (from the list above), the needed
tool support can be further differentiated:

- For scenario 1 developments (black box use of SSADM-F), a modified variant
  of an existing CASE tool would be optimal. For a large project, a multi-user

---

[1]   The prototype of the development environment is named CSDM (Correct Software
Development Munich); it is developed at the Ludwig-Maximilians-Universität in Munich.

repository and project management functions are particularly valuable. The necessary modification with respect to SSADM are a few changes in the notations (mainly in the Event-Entity Matrix, the Effect Correspondence Diagrams and the Operation Lists) and a realization of the consistency checks. A generic CASE tool like *Maestro II*[2] could provide a good platform here. Also for scenario 2 developments, this kind of support is adequate, as long as the formal specification parts are relatively small.

- Projects for which a scenario 3 development (completely formal specifications) is undertaken typically will be much smaller than projects in scenario 1. Therefore less support for large-scale project would be acceptable, in favour of good integration with the SPECTRUM tools. For such projects, the central repository can be replaced by ordinary SPECTRUM files. The best basis for such a project is the SPECTRUM development workbench, into which graphical editors should be integrated for editing SSADM-F documents, together with an automatic translation into SPECTRUM code and an automatic generation of the interface specification. The prototype tool for the SAZ method [SAZ94] follows this idea, combining the graphical editors of the *System Engineer*[3] tool with the CADiZ workbench for Z specifications.

In the context of formal specification, it is also an important aim to reach a *formal verification* of programs. The SSADM-F specification framework provides a necessary prerequisite for verification by a precise formulation of the properties which are to prove for an implementation of the system. But the task of verification still remains extremely complex, due to the sophisticated architectures (database systems, transaction monitors, user interface toolboxes) which are used in the realization of large information systems. In the opinion of the author, only two options seem realistic here.

- In a scenario 2 development, where only a local and complex algorithm is specified formally, this specification can be treated separately by a formal development to reach a verified implementation in an executable language. In many cases, it will be possible to integrate a reformulation of the algorithm directly into the system, in a similarly fashion as its formal specification was added onto the SSADM-F specification.

- On the basis of the executable specification of SSADM-F, a *generic* implementation on top of a standard architecture for information systems could be attempted. This means *application generator verification* (in analogy to compiler verification). Obviously, much additional research is needed to provide

---

[2] Maestro II is a trademark by Softlab GmbH. There exists already an SSADM instance for Maestro II.

[3] System Engineer is a product by Learmonth and Burchett Management Systems (LBMS).

a good formal description of existing implementation platforms. However, for relational database systems with their solid theoretical foundation, this seems to be not completely unrealistic. A first attempt to specify parts of the INGRES database is for instance [BFG87].

12.3.2 Transfer

Some of the achievements of this work are not restricted to SSADM. In particular, the general approach of meta-level specification should be transferrable also to any other pragmatic methods, if its notations and informal meaning are described in sufficient detail. However, for methods which aim at another class of software (like embedded systems or real-time systems), a completely different semantic reference specification can be needed, which might be more difficult to handle than the simple conceptual specification of an information system.

As an example, let us consider the basic steps in transferring the ideas to one of the modern object-oriented approaches to systems analysis. As an example, we use "Object-Oriented Analysis" (OOA) introduced by Coad and Yourdon [CY91].

Formal Foundations for OOA: A Sketch

The general structure of a system is given in OOA by the *object model* which has close similarities to an ER diagram and therefore can also be modelled by the same approach. The term of an occurrence is renamed into *object* and entities are now called *classes*. A significant addition to classical ER modelling are the concepts of *aggregation* and *inheritance*. The axiomatic semantics can be easily extended to accommodate also these features. For instance, an inheritance relation between entities could be added to the SSADM-F semantics by a meta-level definition according to the following idea:

> inherits: $\text{Entity} \times \text{Entity} \to \text{Bool};$
>
> $\text{inherits(entity(o1), entity(o2))} \Rightarrow \text{attrs(o2)} \supseteq \text{attrs(o1)};$

In an object-oriented approach, the objects do not only contain data-valued attributes (as the occurrences in SSADM), but also local procedures which are often called *methods*. OOA uses the name *services* here. Due to the availability of higher-order functions in SPECTRUM, also this seems not to be a principal problem. Services can be understood as attributes of a particular (functional) sort, and so they can be handled by the same general approach.

Another local property of an object is described by a *state transition diagram* for a class. This concept has close similarities to the Entity Life Histories in SSADM, and again the basic approach can be reused.

However, there remains one topic which is significantly different to SSADM and which may lead to a thorough revision of the concepts. This is the description of system dynamics by *interaction of objects*. An OOA object, in contrast to an SSADM occurrence, is not passive, but may actively cause new events as a response to some input event. One idea is to model this by some kind of "internal" events which are used only for describing the way the system reacts onto a single input event. Another idea is to switch to another reference specification which inherently contains a concept of communication. The main problem with these approaches is that the order of internal events caused by an input event is not fixed statically. So a large degree of *nondeterminism* comes into the semantics. Nondeterminism can basically be handled within axiomatic specifications [Hus93], but the integration of nondeterminism into such a powerful specification framework as SPECTRUM is an unsolved problem.

Towards a Formally Founded Modelling Toolbox

From the brief sketch above it is quite obvious that the same concepts appear in several pragmatic methods. So a long-term aim could be to give general formal specifications for concepts like an object-structured system state or object lifecycles. Ideally, the formal semantics of a pragmatic method then would consist in a composition of several pre-produced methodical concepts, together with a description of the syntactic and semantic particularities of the approach under consideration. Such a systematic study of methods could lead to a clear and detailed recognition of the similarities and differences among pragmatic methods. Results of this kind would be very valuable also for the education in software development methods.

In this sense, the work presented in this book represents a small step towards the long-term aim of a general mathematically based theory of software development.

Appendix A
Glossary

This glossary contains important terms both from SSADM and SPECTRUM. Most of the SSADM definitions have been adapted from [Eva92]. The *italic* font marks words which are glossary entries.

Attribute. An *attribute* is an identifier which is associated with an *entity*. For each attribute of an entity, a name for a data *domain* is defined. An attribute of an entity is to be interpreted as a function mapping *occurrences* of the entity onto values of the involved data domain. An attribute is called *optional*, if an undefined value for the attribute is permitted.

Axiom. An *axiom* in SPECTRUM is an expression of Boolean sort which is part of a specification. The axioms of a specification use the *function symbols* which are defined in the *signature* part of the specification or in the signature part of *primitive* specifications.

Data Flow. A *data flow* is an arrow drawn in a *Data Flow Diagram*. It connects a *process* with *external entities*, with *data stores* or with other processes, in order to represent the input and output for the process.

Data Flow Diagram. A *Data Flow Diagram (DFD)* consists of *external entities*, *processes*, and *data stores* which are connected by *data flow* arrows. The purpose of a DFD in SSADM is to represent basic functionality of a system in a structured way without giving a detailed specification.

Data Store. A *data store* is one of the building blocks for a *Data Flow Diagram*. It represents a part of the system state which is read or updated by the *processes* to which it is connected by *data flow* arrows.

Degree (of a *relationship*). A degree is a classification which restricts the number of *occurrences* of an *entity* being associated by a particular *relationship*. The following cases are distinguished, how an entity E can participate in a relationship to another entity F:

- If there is no restriction about the number of occurrences of entities E and F, the relationship is called *many-to-many* (n:m).

- If only one ocurrence of entity E can be associated with a given occurrence of entity F, but arbitrary many occurrences of entity F can be associated with a given occurrence of entity E, the relationship is called *one-to-many* (1:m). In this case the entity E is called the "master" in the relationship, and the entity F is called the "detail".

- If, additionally, one and only one occurrence of the entity E can be associated with an occurrence of entity F, the relationship is called *one-to-one* (1:1).

By default, in all three cases an occurrence of entity E has to be associated with at least one occurrence of entity B and vice versa, unless the relationship is declared to be *optional* for one or both of the participating entities.

DFD. See *Data Flow Diagram*.

Domain. A set of possible values from which any *attribute* of an *occurrence* may take its actual value.

ECD. See *Effect Correspondence Diagram*.

Effect. Any update of the system state caused by an event instance is described by its local *effects* to single *occurrences*. An effect specifies the changes for a given entity occurrence and its relationship associations.

For a given *entity* of the occurrence under consideration, an effect is classified by a triple consisting of the actual *event*, the actual *option* and the *role* (of the occurrence). Role and option information may be omitted in simple cases. An effect is further described as a composition of *operations*. The operations performed on a single entity occurrence can be read from the leaf of the *Entity Life History* of the entity which is labelled with the event and (possibly) the option and role.

Effect Correspondence Diagram. An *Effect Correspondence Diagram (ECD)* is a diagrammatical representation of the structure of the portion of the database which is affected by any instance of an *event*. The ECD contains the names of the involved *entities*, together with information on the multiplicity of *ocurrences* for these entities and the access paths within the database to identify the affected parts. *Options* and *roles* are used for a further distinction of event and entity.

ELH. See *Entity Life History.*

Entity. An *entity* is an identifier, which is to be interpreted as a set of elements which are called the *occurrences* of the entity. Seen as abstractions from real-world things, all occurrences of the entity have the same characteristics and conform to the same rules. SSADM does only take care of entities which are candidates for components of the system data base.

Entity Life History. An *Entity Life History (ELH)* is a diagram of a tree-like shape which refers to a single *entity*. It contains (in its leaves) *event* names (possibly further specified by *options* and *roles*), which describe some *effect* on an occurrence of the entity under consideration. The tree-structure of the diagram (Jackson structure) enables an interpretation as a a set of admitted sequences of events. During system specification, the leaves are augmented with *operations*, which give a detailed description of the effect caused by the event.

Event. An *event* is an identifier which is interpreted as a property of transformations of the system state. The admitted state transformations (event instances) are disjointly classified by the event identifiers. An event is further specified by the *Effect Correspondence Diagram*, the *Event/ Entity Matrix* and by the *operations* contained in several *Entity Life Histories.*

Event/ Entity Matrix. The *Event/ Entity Matrix* gives a compact overview describing which occurrences are affected by an event instance and in which way. The overview is given as a matrix, indexed by *event* and *entity* identifiers. The matrix entries show a rough classification of the type of update (creation, modification, deletion).

In SSADM-F, the Event/ Entity matrix is refined into a form which also covers *option* and *role* information.

External Entity. An *external entity* is one of the building blocks for a *Data Flow Diagram*. It represents a source for input data or a sink for output data of the system.

Formality. A *technique* of a *method* is called *formal*, if it relies only on the syntactical form of the used artifacts, and not on the particular choice of identifiers. A method is called formal, it all its techniques are formal. A method with a significant of formal as well as informal techniques is called *semi-formal.*

Function.
a. In SSADM, a *function* is a user's view of a piece of system processing. [Eva92]
b. In SPECTRUM, *function* is often used as a short form for *function symbol*.

Function symbol. A function symbol in SPECTRUM is declared in the *signature* of a specification together with *sort symbols*. The declaration gives an identifier for the function symbol and its sort expression, which often involves the cartesian products ($\times$) and function space ($\rightarrow$) constructions. Any *model* of the specification associates with the function symbol a mathematical function, which corresponds to the interpretation of the sort expression and which is required to be monotonic with respect to the underlying approximation order on carrier sets. Function symbols are used in the *axioms* of a specification.

Key. A *key* is an *attribute* whose value uniquely identifies a specific *occurrence* of an *entity*. [Eva 92]

Mapping. In SPECTRUM, the word *mapping* is used for a special kind of *function symbols* the interpretation of which is not required to be continuous. In the *signature* syntax, mappings are indicated by using the keyword **to** instead of the function arrow ($\rightarrow$).

Method. A (software development) *method* is a notational and procedural framework to be used by humans for producing computer software. It consists of three parts:

- A set of *notations*, which define the syntax of artifacts (texts, tables, diagrams, forms), which are to be produced when carrying out the method.

- A set of *techniques*, which encapsulate a number of notations together with basic *technical steps* of analysis and transformation for artifacts which are written in these notations.

- A set of *procedural guidelines*, which define an order for applying the technical steps.

Model. The semantics of a SPECTRUM *specification* is defined as the class of models of the specification. A model is a many-sorted algebra, which associates with each *sort* (expression) a carrier set and with each *function* (symbol) a continuous function working on the appropriate carrier sets. Moreover, non-monotonic functions are admitted as the interpretation of *mappings*. For details see [BFG+93].

Notation. See *Method*.

Occurrence. An *occurrence* is a single element belonging to the set described by an abstract *entity*. The state of an information system is a collection of occurrences.

Operation.

    a. In SPECTRUM, the word *operation* is frequently used as a synonym for *function*, which is an abbreviation for *function symbol*. Typically, function symbols with a symbolic or an infix syntax are addressed as *operations*.

    b. In SSADM, an operation is a discrete piece of processing which constitutes, together with other operations, an *effect*, i.e. a modification of the system state [Eva 92, adapted]. An operation always refers to one single occurrence of an entity. Possible operations are:

- creation of an *occurrence*

- changing the values of one or more *attributes* in the occurrence

- deletion of an ocurrence

- establishment of a *relationship* association with another occurrence

- removal of a relationship association with another occurrence.

    During Requirements Specification in SSADM, the creation and deletion operations are not yet shown, but in Logical Database Process Design they appear exlicitly.

Option (for *event*). An *option* is an identifier which is used as an additional qualification for a specific *event*. The specification of an actual state transformation caused by an event instance is split into subcases by an option. The classification of an event instance by an option may depend on the actual state of the system.

Optional Attribute. An *attribute* of an *entity* is called *optional*, if it is allowed that some *occurrence* of the entity may have no defined value for the attribute.

Optionality (of *relationship*). In a *relationship* R relating *entity* E to entity F, R is called *optional* for F, if *ocurrences* of entity E can exist which are not related through R to an occurrence of entity F. Analogously, the relationship R may be optional for F. In the graphical representation, the optionality of R for E is expressed by dashing the part of the R line attached to the E node. A non-optional relationship is called "mandatory".

Pragmatism. A *method* is called *pragmatic* if its *notations*, *techniques* and *procedural* guidelines are derived from significant practical experience and if its usefulness in practical applications has been proven.

Process. A *process* is one of the building blocks for a *Data Flow Diagram*. The semantics of a process is the transformation of the system state, where the *data flows* coming into the process from a *data store* represent a read access to parts of the state, the data flows going from the process to a data store represent updates to parts of the state. Other input and output data for the transformation are represented by data flows from and to *external entities* and other processes.

Relationship. A *relationship* is an identifier to which a number of *entities* are associated. In SSADM, a relationship is always associated with two entities, and therefore is called *binary*. A relationship is to be interpreted as a mathematical relation between the sets of occurrences which are denoted by the entities involved.

Requirements Specification. A software requirements specification is „a document containing a complete description of *what* the software will do without describing *how* it will do it.“ [Dav90, p.17]

Role. A *role* is an identifier which is sensible only if connected with a specific *entity* and a specific *event*. It is used to partition the set of occurrences of the entity into subclasses which are updated differently by instances of the given event.

Semi-formal. See *Formality*.

Signature. The *signature* is the part of a SPECTRUM specification which contains declarations of *sort symbols* and *function symbols*. The other main constituents of a SPECTRUM specification are *axioms*.

Sort Symbol. A *sort symbol* is declared in the *signature* part of a SPECTRUM specification. A sort symbol is an identifier, which is to be interpreted in any *model* of the specification as a set of values. Sort symbols are used mainly in the *function* declarations in specifications, to ensure that the arguments and results of functions in the model belong to specific sets of values.

A special case are here sort constructors for polymorphic sorts which can be understood as functions producing new sorts if provided with appropriate argument sorts. For a clear distinction between sort names and sort parameters for sort constructors, the sort parameters are always named by greek letters in this work, by convention.

Strict. In SPECTRUM, a *function symbol* f can be declared to be *strict*. This means that the mathematical function associated with f in any model yields an undefined result if it is given an undefined argument.

Strong. In SPECTRUM, a *mapping symbol* m can be declared to be *strong*. This means that the mathematical function associated with m in any model yields a defined result for any (defined or undefined) argument.

Technique. See *Method*.

Total. In SPECTRUM, a *function symbol* f can be declared to be *total*. This means that the mathematical function associated with f in any model yields a defined result if it is given a defined argument.

Appendix B

"Hotel Agency" –
An SSADM-F Specification

This appendix contains the detailed SSADM-F documents for the small example which was informally introduced in chapter 3. Appendix C contains the formal representation of these documents in the SPECTRUM abstract syntax for SSADM-F. As in the main text, mainly Logical Data Modelling (LDM) and Entity-Event Modelling (EEM) are covered here. For Data Flow Modelling (DFM), only a single Data Flow Diagram (the Context Diagram) is given. Examples of diagrams of lower levels are given in chapter 11.

B.1 DFD Documents

B.1.1 Level 0 Data Flow Diagram (Context Diagram)

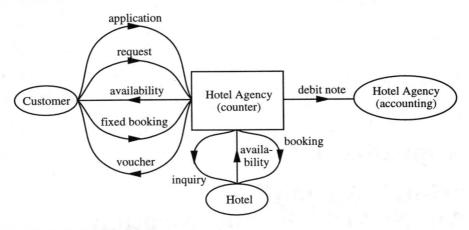

B.2 LDM Documents

B.2.1 Entity-Relationship Diagram

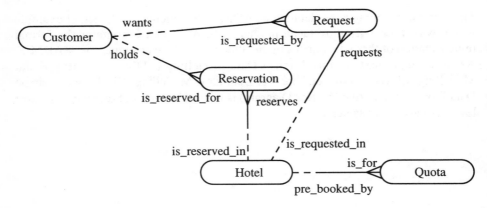

B.2.2 Entity Descriptions

SSADM-F Extended Entity Description

Entity name   Customer

Attribute name	Mandatory	Prim. Key	SPECTRUM Domain
Customer number	√	√	nat
Customer name	√		str
Customer address	√		str
Credit card info	√		str_in(16)
Date last request	√		date

SSADM-F Extended Entity Description

Entity name   Request

Attribute name	Mandatory	Prim. Key	SPECTRUM Domain
Reference number	√	√	nat
Period of time	√		pair(date, date)
Number of rooms	√		nat
Date req. hotel	√		date

SSADM-F Extended Entity Description

Entity name   Reservation

Attribute name	Mandatory	Prim. Key	SPECTRUM Domain
Reference number	√	√	nat
Period of time	√		pair (date, date)
Number of rooms	√		nat
Date off. customer	√		date

SSADM-F Extended Entity Description

Entity name   Hotel

Attribute name	Mandatory	Prim. Key	SPECTRUM Domain
Hotel number	√	√	nat
Hotel name	√		str
Hotel address	√		str
Room price	√		amount

SSADM-F Extended Entity Description

Entity name   Quota

Attribute name	Mandatory	Prim. Key	SPECTRUM Domain
Hotel number	√	√	nat
Available date	√		date
Num. rooms avail.	√		nat

B.3 EEM Documents

B.3.1 Event-Entity Matrix

Event \ Entity	Customer	Request	Reservn	Hotel [reqd.]	[alt.]	Quota
Customer Request						
immed. offered	M		C	M		M
inquired fr. hotel	M	C		M		R
Hotel Reply						
available as reqd.	M	D	C	M		M
altern. available	M	D	C	M	M	M
not available	M	D		M		
Fixed Booking	M		D	M		
Check Reservns.	M		D	M		M
Check Customers	D					
New Customer	C					
Add Hotel				C		
Remove Hotel				D		D
Add Quota				M		C
Remove Quota				M		D

B.3.2 Effect Correspondence Diagrams

Event New Customer:

Event Add Hotel:

Event Remove Hotel:

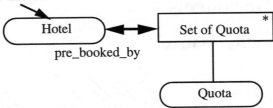

Event Add Quota / Event Remove Quota:

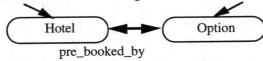

Event Customer Request:

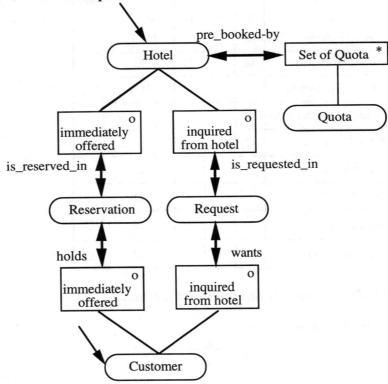

Event Hotel Reply:

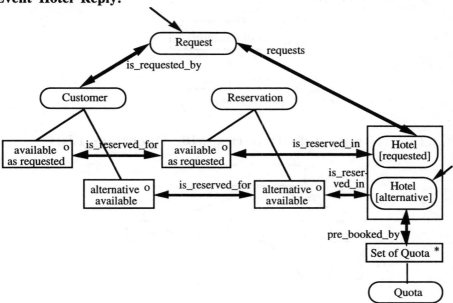

Event Fixed Booking:

Event Check Reservations:

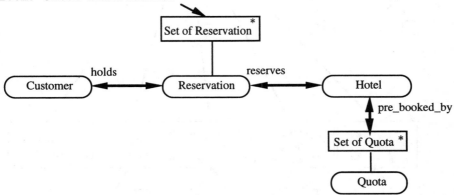

Event Check Customers:

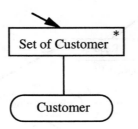

B.3.3   Entity Life Histories with Operation Lists

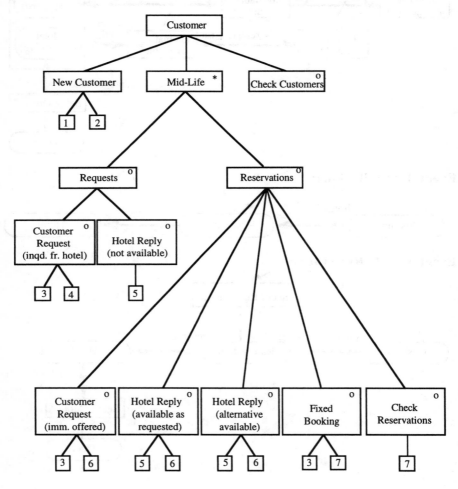

List of operations:

1 Store attribute Customer number
2 Store attributes Customer name, Customer address, Credit card information
3 Store attribute Date last request
4 Gain relationship Wants to Request
5 Lose relationship Wants to Request
6 Gain relationship Holds to Reservation
7 Lose relationship Holds to Reservation

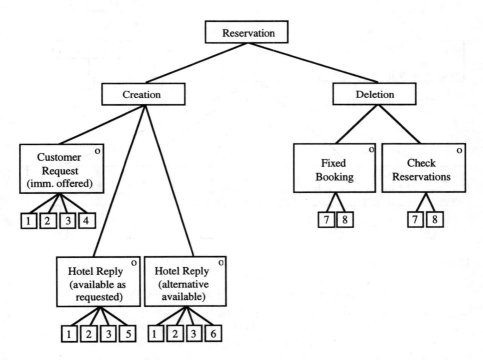

List of operations:

1 Store attribute Reference Number
2 Store attributes Period, Number Rooms, Date Offered
3 Gain relationship Is_Reserved_For to Customer
4 Gain relationship Reserves to Hotel
5 Gain relationship Reserves to Hotel [requested]
6 Gain relationship Reserves to Hotel [alternative]
7 Lose relationship Reserves to Hotel
8 Lose relationship Is_Reserved_For to Customer

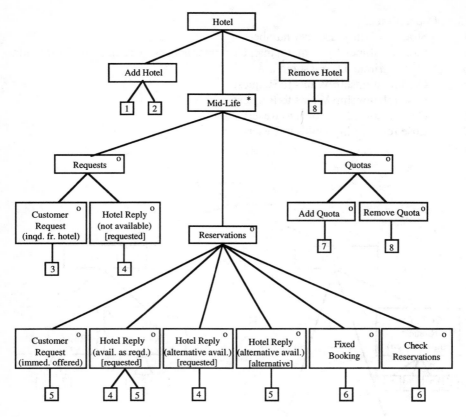

List of operations:

	1	Store attribute Hotel Number
	2	Store attributes Hotel Name, Hotel Address, Price
	3	Gain relationship Is_requested_in to Request
	4	Lose relationship Is_requested_in to Request
	5	Gain relationship Is_reserved_in to Reservation
	6	Lose relationship Is_reserved_in to Reservation
	7	Gain relationship Pre_booked_by to Quota
	8	Lose relationship Pre_booked_by to Quota

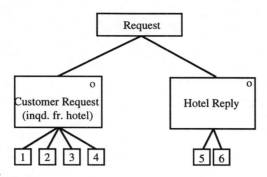

List of operations:

1. Store attribute Reference Number
2. Store attributes Period, Number Rooms, Date Inquired
3. Gain relationship Is_requested_by to Customer
4. Gain relationship Requests to Hotel
5. Lose relationship Is_requested_by to Customer
6. Lose relationship Requests to Hotel [requested]

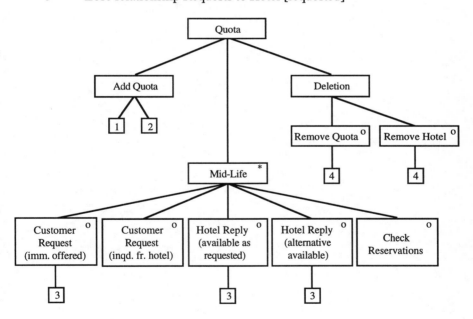

List of operations:

1. Store attributes Hotel number, Date, Number Available
2. Gain relationship Is_for to Hotel
3. Store attribute Number Available
4. Lose relationship Is_for to Hotel

Appendix C

SPECTRUM Translation of the "Hotel Agency" Specification

This section contains the same information as appendix B (sections B.2 and B.3), but in the SPECTRUM abstract syntax for SSADM-F. This is a project level specification by which the parameterized SSADM-F specification can be instantiated.

C.1 Translation of LDM Documents

C.1.1 Entity-Relationship Diagram

```
HA_ERD = {
        data Entity = customer | reservation | request | hotel | quota;
        data Rel = holds | is_reserved_for | wants | is_requested_by
                | is_reserved_in | reserves | is_requested_in | requests
                | pre_booked_for | is_for;

        inv:                    Rel → Rel;
        related:                Rel → Entity × Entity;
        multiple, optional:     Rel → Bool;

        axioms
        inv(holds) = is_reserved_for;          inv(is_reserved_for) = holds;
        inv(wants) = is_requested_by;          inv(is_requested_by) = wants;
```

inv(is_reserved_in) = reserves;   inv(reserves) = is_reserved_in ;
inv(is_requested_in) = requests;   inv(requests) = is_requested_in;
inv(pre_booked_for) = is_for;   inv(is_for) = pre_booked_for;

related(holds) = (customer, reservation);   related(is_reserved_for) =
                                  (reservation, customer);
related(wants) = (customer, request);   related(is_requested_by) =
                                  (request, customer);
related(is_reserved_in) = (hotel, reservation);   related(reserves) =
                                  (reservation, hotel);
related(is_requested_in) = (hotel, request);   related(requests) =
                                  (request, hotel);
related(pre_booked_for) = (hotel, quota);   related(is_for) = (quota, hotel);

multiple(holds) = false;   optional(holds) = true;
multiple(wants) = false;   optional(wants) = true;
multiple(is_reserved_in) = false;   optional(is_reserved_in) = true;
multiple(is_requested_in) = false;   optional(is_requested_in) = true;
multiple(pre_booked_for) = false;   optional(pre_booked_for) = true;

multiple(is_reserved_for) = true;   optional(is_reserved_for) = false;
multiple(is_requested_by) = true;   optional(is_requested_by) =
                                  false;

multiple(reserves) = true;   optional(reserves) = false;
multiple(requests) = true;   optional(requests) = false;
multiple(is_for) = true;   optional(is_for) = false;
endaxioms; }

C.1.2 Entity Descriptions

ATTRVAL = { − − Attribute values for Hotel Agency; enhanced version of figure 7.11
     strict total;
     enriches Naturals + String;

     data AttrVal = natural(!natval: Nat) | string(!strval: String)
            | boolean(!boolval: Bool)| dateYear(!day, !month, !year: Nat)
            | money(!beforePt, !afterPt: Nat) | valPair(! val1, ! val2: AttrVal);
     sortsyn Domain = AttrVal → Bool;

     nat, bool, str: Domain;
     nat_in: Nat × Nat → Domain;
     str_in: Nat → Domain;
     date, amount: Domain;
     pair: Domain × Domain → Domain;

axioms ∀ n, n1, n2: Nat; d1, d2: Domain; v: AttrVal **in**
nat(v) = is_natural(v);
str(v) = is_string(v);
bool(v) = is_boolean(v);
nat_in(n1, n2) (v) = is_natural(v) ∧ (n1 ≤ natval(v)) ∧ (natval(v) ≤ n2);
str_in(n) (v) = is_string(v) ∧ (length(s) = n);
date (v) = is_dateYear(v)
      ∧ (1 ≤ day(v)) ∧ (day(v) ≤ 31) ∧ (1 ≤ month(v)) ∧ (month(v) ≤ 12);
amount (v) = is_money(v) ∧ (0 ≤ afterPt(v)) ∧ (afterPt(v) ≤ 99);
pair(d1, d2)(v) = is_valPair(v) ∧ (d1(v) ∧ d2(v));
endaxioms; }

HA_ED = {
    strict total;
    enriches HA_ERD + SET + ATTRVAL;
    data Attr = custNo I custName I custAddress I creditCardInfo I dateLastReq
           I refNo I period I numRooms I dateInq I dateOffer
           I hotelNo I hotelName I hotelAddress I roomPrice
           I availDate I numAvail;

    attrs, mandatory, primaryKey: Entity → Set Attr;

    axioms
    attrs(customer) =
        set [custNo, custName, custAddress, creditCardInfo, dateLastReq];
    mandatory(customer) =
        set [custNo, custName, custAddress, creditCardInfo, dateLastReq];
    primaryKey(customer) = set [custNo];
    dom(customer, custNo) = nat;
    dom(customer, custName) = str;
    dom(customer, custAddress) = str;
    dom(customer, creditCardInfo) = str_in(16);
    dom(dateLastReq) = date;

    attrs(request) = set [refNo, period, numRooms, dateInq];
    mandatory(request) = set [refNo, period, numRooms, dateInq];
    primaryKey(request) = set [refNo];
    dom(request, refNo) = nat;
    dom(request, period) = pair(date, date);
    dom(request, numRooms) = nat;
    dom(request, dateInq) = date;

    attrs(reservation) = set [refNo, period, numRooms, dateOffer];
    mandatory(reservation) = set [refNo, period, numRooms, dateOffer];
    primaryKey(reservation) = set [refNo];

```
dom(reservation, refNo) = nat;
dom(reservation, period) = pair(date, date);
dom(reservation, numRooms) = nat;
dom(reservation, dateOffer) = date;

attrs(hotel) = set [hotelNo, hotelName, hotelAddress, roomPrice];
mandatory(hotel) = set [hotelNo, hotelName, hotelAddress, roomPrice];
primaryKey(hotel) = set [hotelNo];
dom(hotel, hotelNo) = nat;
dom(hotel, hotelName) = str;
dom(hotel, hotelAddress) = str;
dom(hotel, roomPrice) = amount;

attrs(quota) = set [hotelNo, availDate, numAvail];
mandatory(quota) = set [hotelNo, availDate, numAvail];
primaryKey(quota) = set [hotelNo, availDate];
dom(quota, hotelNo) = nat;
dom(quota, availDate) = date;
dom(quota, numAvail)= nat;
```
endaxioms; }

C.2 Translation of EEM Documents

C.2.1 Event-Entity Matrix

HA_EEX1 = { **strict**;
    enriches SET;

      data Event = custReq I hotelReply I fixed Bkg I chkResvs I chkCusts I newCust
             I addHotel I remHotel I addQuota I remQuota;
      data Option = stdOpt I immOff I inqFromH I availAsReqd I altAvail I notAvail;
      data Role = stdRole I remvd I notRemvd I expd I notExpd I reqd I altern;

      admOpts: Event → Set Option;   admOpts **total**;
      admRoles: Event × Entity → Set Role;   admRoles **total**;

      axioms ∀ ev: Event **in**
      admOpts(custReq) = set [immOff, inqFromH];
      admOpts(hotelReply) = set [availAsReqd, altAvail, notAvail];
      admOpts(fixed Bkg) = set [stdOpt];
      admOpts(chkResvs) = set [stdOpt];
      admOpts(chkCusts) = set [stdOpt];
      admOpts(newCust) = set [stdOpt];
      admOpts(addHotel) = set [stdOpt];

```
        admOpts(remHotel) = set [stdOpt];
        admOpts(addQuota) = set [stdOpt];
        admOpts(remQuota) = set [stdOpt];

        admRoles(ev, customer) = set [stdRole ];
        admRoles(ev, request) = set [stdRole];
        admRoles(ev, reservation) = set [stdRole ];
        admRoles(custReq, hotel) = set [stdRole ];
        admRoles(hotelReply, hotel) = set [reqd, altern];
        admRoles(fixedBkg, hotel) = set [stdRole];
        admRoles(chkResvs, hotel) = set [stdRole];
        admRoles(addHotel, hotel) = set [stdRole ];
        admRoles(remHotel, hotel) = set [stdRole];
        admRoles(ev, quota) = set [stdRolel;
    endaxioms; }

HA_EEX2 = { strict;
        enriches EEX_AUX;

        admTargets:      OptEvent → Set Target;
        EEX:             OptEvent × Target → AccessType;

        axioms
        admTargets(custReq, immOff) = set [$customer, $reservation, $hotel, $quota];
        admTargets(custReq, inqFromH) = set [$customer, $request, $hotel, $quota];
        admTargets(hotelReply, availAsReqd) =
                set [$customer, $request, $reservation, (hotel, reqd), $quota ];
        admTargets(hotelReply, altAvail) =
                set [$customer, $request, $reservation, (hotel, reqd),
                (hotel, altern), $quota];
        admTargets(hotelReply, notAvail) = set [$customer, $request, (hotel, reqd)];
        admTargets(%fixedBkg) = set [$customer, $reservation, $hotel];
        admTargets(%chkResvns) = set [$customer, $reservation, $hotel, $quota];
        admTargets(%chkCusts) = set [$customer];
        admTargets(%newCust) = set [ $customer ];
        admTargets(%addHotel) = set [$hotel ];
        admTargets(%remHotel) = set [$hotel, $quota];
        admTargets(%addQuota) = set [$quota, $hotel];
        admTargets(%remQuota) = set [$quota, $hotel];

        EEX((custReq, immOff), $customer) = M;
        EEX((custReq, immOff), $reservation) = C;
        EEX((custReq, immOff), $hotel) = M;
        EEX((custReq, immOff), $quota) = M;
        EEX((custReq, inqFromH), $customer) = M;
```

```
EEX((custReq, inqFromH), $request) = C;
EEX((custReq, inqFromH), $hotel) = M;
EEX((custReq, inqFromH), $quota) = R;
EEX((hotelReply, availAsReqd), $customer) = M;
EEX((hotelReply, availAsReqd), $request) = D;
EEX((hotelReply, availAsReqd), $reservation) = C;
EEX((hotelReply, availAsReqd), (hotel, reqd)) = M;
EEX((hotelReply, availAsReqd), $quota) = M;
EEX((hotelReply, altAvail), $customer) = M;
EEX((hotelReply, altAvail), $request) = D;
EEX((hotelReply, altAvail), $reservation) = C;
EEX((hotelReply, altAvail), (hotel, reqd)) = M;
EEX((hotelReply, altAvail), (hotel, altern)) = M;
EEX((hotelReply, altAvail), $quota) = M;
EEX((hotelReply, notAvail), $customer) = M;
EEX((hotelReply, notAvail), $request) = D;
EEX((hotelReply, notAvail), (hotel, reqd)) = M;
EEX(%fixedBkg, $customer) = M;
EEX(%fixedBkg, $reservation) = D;
EEX(%fixedBkg, $hotel) = M;
EEX(%chkResvs, $customer) = M;
EEX(%chkResvs, $reservation) = D;
EEX(%chkResvs, $hotel) = M;
EEX(%chkResvs, $quota) = M;
EEX(%chkCusts, $customer) = D;
EEX(%newCust, $customer) = C;
EEX(%addHotel, $hotel) = C;
EEX(%remHotel, $hotel) = D;
EEX(%remHotel, $quota) = D;
EEX(%addQuota, $quota) = C;
EEX(%addQuota, $hotel) = M,
EEX(%remQuota, $quota) = D;
EEX(%remQuota, $hotel) = M;
endaxioms; }
```

C.2.2   Effect Correspondence Diagrams

HA_ECD = { **strict**;
    enriches ECD_AUX;

entries:	OptEvent → Set Target;
corrs:	OptEvent → Set Corr;
eType:	OptEvent × Target → CardType;
cType:	OptEvent → Corr → CardType;

axioms ∀ opt: Option **in**
entries(custReq, opt) = set [$hotel, $customer];
entries(hotelReply, availAsReqd) = set [$request];
entries(hotelReply, altAvail) = set [$request, (hotel, altern)];
entries(hotelReply, notAvail) = set [$request];
entries(fixedBkg, opt) = set [$reservation];
entries(chkResvs, opt) = set [$reservation];
entries(chkCusts, opt) = set [$customer];
entries(newCust, opt) = set [$customer];
entries(addHotel, opt) = set [$hotel];
entries(remHotel, opt) = set [$hotel];
entries(addQuota, opt) = set [$hotel , $quota];
entries(remQuota, opt) = set [$hotel, $quota];

eType((custReq, opt), $hotel) = single;
eType((custReq, opt), $customer) = single;
eType((hotelReply, opt), $request) = single;
eType((hotelReply, altAvail), (hotel, altern)) = single;
eType((fixedBkg, opt), $reservation) = single;
eType((chkResvs, opt), $reservation) = setOf;
eType((chkCusts, opt), $customer) = setOf;
eType((newCust, opt), $customer) = single;
eType((addHotel, opt), $hotel) = single;
eType((remHotel, opt), $hotel) = single;
eType((addQuota, opt), $hotel) = single;
eType((addQuota, opt), $quota) = single;
eType((remQuota, opt), $hotel) = single;
eType((remQuota, opt), $quota) = single;

corrs(custReq, immOff) =
        set [($hotel, pre_booked_by], $quota), ($quota, is_for, $hotel),
        ($hotel, is_reserved_in, $reservation), ($reservation, reserves, $hotel),
        ($customer, holds, $reservation),
        ($reservation, is_reserved_for, $customer))];
corrs(custReq, inqFromH) =
        set [($hotel, pre_booked_by], $quota), ($quota, is_for, $hotel),
        ($hotel, is_requested_in, $request), ($request, requests, $hotel),
        ($customer, wants, $request),
        ($request, is_requested_by, $customer))];
corrs(hotelReply, availAsReqd) =
        set [($request, is_requested_by, $customer),
        ($customer, wants, $request),
        ($request, requests, (hotel, reqd)),
        ((hotel, reqd), is_requested_in, $request),

```
        ($reservation, is_reserved_for, $customer),
        ($customer, holds, $reservation),
        ((hotel, reqd), is_reserved_in, $reservation),
        ($reservation, reserves, (hotel, reqd))];
corrs(hotelReply, altAvail) =
        set [($request, is_requested_by, $customer),
        ($customer, wants, $request),
        ($request, requests, (hotel, reqd)),
        ((hotel, reqd), is_requested_in, $request),
        ($reservation, is_reserved_for, $customer),
        ($customer, holds, $reservation),
        ((hotel, altern), is_reserved_in, $reservation),
        ($reservation, reserves, (hotel, altern)),
        ((hotel, altern), pre_booked_by, $quota),
        ($quota, is_for, (hotel, altern))];
corrs(hotelReply, notAvail) =
        set [($request, is_requested_by, $customer),
        ($customer, wants, $request),
        ($request, requests, (hotel, reqd)),
        ((hotel, reqd), is_requested_in, $request)];
corrs(fixedBkg, opt) =
        set [($customer, holds, $reservation),
        ($reservation, is_reserved_for, $customer),
        ($reservation, reserves, $hotel), ($hotel, is_reserved_in, $reservation)];
corrs(chkResvs, opt) =
        set [($customer, holds, $reservation),
        ($reservation, is_reserved_for, $customer),
        ($reservation, reserves, $hotel), ($hotel, is_reserved_in, $reservation),
        ($hotel, pre_booked_by, $quota), ($quota, is_for, $hotel)];
corrs(chkCusts, opt) = emptySet;
corrs(newCust, opt) = emptySet;
corrs(addHotel, opt) = emptySet;
corrs(remHotel, opt) =
        set [($hotel, pre_booked_by, $quota), ($quota, is_for, $hotel)];
corrs(addQuota, opt) =
        set [($hotel, pre_booked_by, $quota), ($quota, is_for, $hotel)];
corrs(remQuota, opt) =
        set [($hotel, pre_booked_by, $quota), ($quota, is_for, $hotel)];

cType((custReq, opt), ($hotel, pre_booked_by, $quota)) = single;
cType((custReq, opt), ($quota, is_for, $hotel)) = setOf;
cType((custReq, immOff), ($hotel, is_reserved_in, $reservation)) = single;
cType((custReq, immOff), ($reservation, reserves, $hotel)) = single;
cType((custReq, immOff), ($customer, holds, $reservation)) = single;
```

cType((custReq, immOff), ($reservation, is_reserved_for, $customer)) = single;
cType((custReq, inqFromH), ($hotel, is_requested_in, $request)) = single;
cType((custReq, inqFromH), ($request, requests, $hotel)) = single;
cType((custReq, inqFromH), ($customer, wants, $request)) = single;
cType((custReq, inqFromH), ($request, is_requested_by, $customer)) = single;

– – For the remaining events, a shorter representation is shown here, which is
– – semantically equivalent to the simple schematic translation.
– – Also this translation could be obtained by a (more sophisticated) schema.
cType((hotelReply, opt), ($request, r, tg)) = single;
cType((hotelReply, opt), ($customer, r, tg)) = single;
cType((hotelReply, opt), ($reservation, r, tg)) = single;
cType((hotelReply, opt), ((hotel, role), r, tg)) = single;
cType((hotelReply, opt), ($quota, r, tg)) = setOf;
cType((fixedBkg, opt), ($customer, r, tg)) = single;
cType((fixedBkg, opt), ($reservation, r, tg)) = single;
cType((fixedBkg, opt), ($hotel, r, tg)) = single;
cType((chkResvs, opt), ($customer, r, tg)) = single;
cType((chkResvs, opt), ($reservation, r, tg)) = single;
cType((chkResvs, opt), ($hotel, r, tg)) = single;
cType((chkResvs, opt), ($quota, r, tg)) = setOf;
cType((remHotel, opt), ($hotel, r, tg)) = single;
cType((remHotel, opt), ($quota, r, tg)) = setOf;
cType((addQuota, opt), ($hotel, r, tg)) = single;
cType((addQuota, opt), ($quota, r, tg)) = setOf;
cType((remQuota, opt), ($hotel, r, tg)) = single;
cType((remQuota, opt), ($quota, r, tg)) = single;
endaxioms; }

C.2.3 Entity Life Histories

HA_ELH = { **strict**;
     enriches ELH_AUX;

     ELH: Entity → ERegExp Effect;

     axioms
     ELH(customer) =
          seq [atom (newCust, stdOpt, stdRole),
                 ** (alt [atom (custReq, inqFromH, stdRole),
                           atom (hotelReply, notAvail, stdRole),
                           atom (custReq, ImmOff, stdRole),
                           atom (hotelReply, availAsReqd, stdRole),
                           atom (hotelReply, altAvail, stdRole),

```
                              atom (fixedBkg, stdOpt, stdRole),
                              atom (chkResvs, stdOpt, stdRole) ] ),
                    atom (chkCusts, stdOpt, stdRole) ];
    ELH(reservation) =
          seq [   alt [    atom (custReq, ImmOff, stdRole),
                           atom (hotelReply, availAsReqd, stdRole),
                           atom (hotelReply, altAvail, stdRole) ],
                  eps,
                  alt [    atom (fixedBkg, stdOpt, stdRole),
                           atom (chkResvs, stdOpt, stdRole) ] ];
    ELH(request) =
          seq [   atom (custReq, inqFromH, stdRole),
                  eps,
                  alt [    atom (hotelReply, availAsReqd, stdRole),
                           atom (hotelReply, altAvail, stdRole),
                           atom (hotelReply, notAvail, stdRole) ] ];
    ELH(hotel) =
          seq [   atom (addHotel, stdOpt, stdRole),
                  ** ( alt [ atom (custReq, inqFromH, stdRole),
                             atom (hotelReply, notAvail, Reqd),
                             atom (custReq, immOff, stdRole),
                             atom (hotelReply, availAsReqd, Reqd),
                             atom (hotelReply, altAvail, Reqd),
                             atom (hotelReply, altAvail, Altern),
                             atom (fixedBkg, stdOpt, stdRole),
                             atom (chkResvs, stdOpt, stdRole),
                             atom (addQuota, stdOpt, stdRole),
                             atom (remQuota, stdOpt, stdRole) ] ),
                  atom (remHotel, stdOpt, stdRole) ];
    ELH(quota) =
          seq [   atom (addQuota, stdOpt, stdRole),
                  ** ( alt [ atom (custReq, immOff, stdRole),
                             atom (custReq, inqFromH, stdRole),
                             atom (hotelReply, availAsReqd, stdRole),
                             atom (hotelReply, altAvail, stdRole),
                             atom (chkResvs, stdOpt, stdRole) ] ),
                  alt [    atom (remQuota, stdOpt, stdRole),
                           atom (remHotel, stdOpt, stdRole) ] ];
    endaxioms; }
```

C.2.4 Operation Lists

```
HA_OPS = { strict;
    enriches OPS_AUX;
```

OPS: OptEvent × Target → List Opn;

axioms ∀ opt: Option **in**
OPS (%newCust, $customer) =
  [attSto(custNo), attSto(custName),
  attSto(custAddress), attSto(creditCardInfo)];
OPS ((custReq, inqFromH), $customer) =
  [attSto(dateLastReq), relMod(gain, wants, $request)];
OPS ((hotelReply, notAvail), $customer) = [relMod(lose, wants, $request)];
OPS ((custReq, immOff), $customer) =
  [attSto(dateLastReq), relMod(gain, holds, $reservation)];
OPS ((hotelReply, availAsReqd), $customer) =
  [relMod(lose, wants, $request), relMod(gain, holds, $reservation)];
OPS ((hotelReply, altAvail), $customer) =
  [relMod(lose, wants, $request), relMod(gain, holds, $reservation)];
OPS ((%fixedBkg, $customer) =
  [attSto(dateLastReq), relMod(lose, holds, $reservation)];
OPS (%chkResvs, $customer) = [relMod(lose, holds, $reservation)];
OPS (%chkCusts, $customer) = [];

OPS ((custReq, immOff), $reservation) =
  [attSto(refNo), attSto(period), attSto(numRooms), attSto(dateOffer),
  relMod(gain, reserves, $hotel),
  relMod(gain, is_reserved_for, $customer)];
OPS ((hotelReply, availAsReqd), $reservation) =
  [attSto(refNo), attSto(period), attSto(numRooms), attSto(dateOffer),
  relMod(gain, reserves, (hotel, reqd)),
  relMod(gain, is_reserved_for, $customer)];
OPS ((hotelReply, altAvail), $reservation) =
  [attSto(refNo), attSto(period), attSto(numRooms), attSto(dateOffer),
  relMod(gain, reserves, (hotel, altern)),
  relMod(gain, is_reserved_for, $customer)];
OPS (%fixedBkg, $reservation) =
  [relMod(lose, reserves, $hotel),
  relMod(lose, is_reserved_for, $customer)];
OPS (%chkResvs, $reservation) =
  [relMod(lose, reserves, $hotel),
  relMod(lose, is_reserved_for, $customer)];

OPS ((custReq, inqFromH), $request) =
  [attSto(refNo), attSto(period), attSto(numRooms), attSto(dateInq),
  relMod(gain, is_requested_by, $customer),
  relMod(gain, requests, $hotel)];

```
OPS ((hotelReply, opt) $request =        – – Variable opt covers three options
        [relMod(lose, is_requested_by, $customer),
        relMod(lose, requests, (hotel, reqd))];

OPS (%addhotel,  $hotel) =
        [attSto(hotelNo), attSto(hotelName), attSto(hotelAddress), attSto(price)];
OPS ((custReq, inqFromH), $hotel) = [relMod(gain, is_requested_in, $request)];
OPS ((hotelReply, notAvail), (hotel, reqd)) =
        [relMod(lose, is_requested_in, $request)];
OPS ((custReq, immOff), $hotel) = [relMod(gain, is_reserved_in, $reservation)];
OPS ((hotelReply, availAsReqd), (hotel, reqd)) =
        [relMod(lose, is_requested_in, $request),
        relMod(gain, is_reserved_in, $reservation)];
OPS ((hotelReply, altAvail), (hotel, reqd) =
        [relMod(lose, is_requested_in, $request)];
OPS ((hotelReply, altAvail), (hotel, altern) =
        [relMod(gain, is_reserved_in, $reservation)];
OPS (%fixedBkg, $hotel) = [relMod(lose, is_reserved_in, $reservation)];
OPS (%chkResvs, $hotel) = [relMod(lose, is_reserved_in, $reservation)];
OPS (%addQuota, $hotel) = [relMod(gain, pre_booked_by, $quota)];
OPS (%remQuota, $hotel) = [relMod(lose, pre_booked_by, $quota)];
OPS (%remHotel, $hotel) = [relMod(lose, pre_booked_by, $quota)];

OPS (%addQuota, $quota) =
        [attSto(hotelNo), attSto(availDate), attSto(numAvail),
        relMod(gain, is_for, $hotel)];
OPS ((custReq, immOff), $quota) = [attSto(numAvail)];
OPS ((custReq, inqFromH), $quota) = [];
OPS ((hotelReply, availAsReqd), $quota) = [attSto(numAvail)];
OPS ((hotelReply, altAvail), $quota) = [attSto(numAvail)];
OPS (%ChkResvs, $quota) = [];
OPS (%remQuota, $quota) = [relMod(lose, is_for, $hotel)];
OPS (%remHotel, $quota) = [relMod(lose, is_for, $hotel)];
endaxioms; }
```

Appendix D
Basic SPECTRUM Specifications

This appendix contains the library of basic SPECTRUM specifications which is used in this thesis at various places. The specifications given here extend the very small standard library of SPECTRUM [BFG+93].

D.1 Lists

For lists, we repeat here the specifications given in chapter 4 in an extended version, adding several useful functions which were omitted there.

```
LIST0 = { strict;        − − Simple specification for lists
        enriches Naturals;

        data List α = [] | cons( ! first: α, ! rest: List α);

        . ++ .:       List α × List α → List α;      − − List concatenation
        length:       List α → Nat;                  − − Length of list
        . !! .:       List α × Nat → α;              − − Selection of element by index
        last:         List α → α;                    − − Last element of list

        length, .++. total;

        axioms ∀ x: α, ∀ u, v: List α, j: Nat in
        [] ++ u = u;                                 cons(x, u) ++ v = cons(x, u++v);
        length([]) = 0;                              length(cons(x, u)) = 1 + length(u);
```

[] !! j = ⊥;   cons(x, u) !! 0 = x;   cons(x, u) !! (j+1) = u !! j;
last(u) = u !! (length(u));
endaxioms; }

LIST1 = { **strict total**; − − Extended specification of lists
       enriches LIST0;

       List :: (EQ)EQ;

       . elem .:   α :: EQ ⇒   α × List α → Bool;
       . subList .:   α :: EQ ⇒   List α × List α → Bool;

       axioms ∀ α:: EQ ⇒ x: α, ∀ u, v: List α **in**
       x elem u ⇔ (∃ v1, v2. u = v1++[x]++v2);
       u subList v ⇔ (∃ v1, v2. u = v1++v++v2);
       endaxioms; }

LIST = { − − Further extended specification of lists
         − − Partial adaptation of the Haskell library
         enriches LIST1;

       filter: List α × (α → Bool) → List α;
                        − − Filters a list according to a predicate
       map: List α × (α → α) → List α;
                        − − Transforms a list pointwise
       foldr1:   (α × α → α) × List α → α;
                        − − "Folds" binary operator over list
       all, ex: List α × (α → Bool) → Bool;
                        − − Extension of predicate to list
       noDuplicates: List α → Bool;
                        − − No duplicate elements in list?
       concat: List List α → List;
                        − − Concatenation of list of lists
       pairs: List α × List α → List (α × α);
                        − − List of all pairs out of two lists

       filter, map, all, ex, noDuplicates, concat, pairs **total**;

       axioms ∀ x: α, ∀ u, v: List α, p: (α → Bool), f: (α → α), g: (α × α → α) **in**
       filter([], p) = [];
       filter([x]++u, p) = **if** p(x) **then** [x]++filter(u, p) **else** filter(u, p) **endif**;

       map([], f) = [];
       map([x]++u, f) = [f(x)]++map(u, f);

foldr1(g, []) = ⊥;
foldr1(g, [x]++u) = **if** is_[](u) **then** [x] **else** g(x, foldr1(g, u));

all([], p) = true;   all([x]++u, p) = p(x) ∧ all(u, p);
ex([], p) = false;   ex([x]++u, p) = p(x) ∨ ex(u, p);

noDuplicates(u) = (∀ x. length(filter(u, λy. y = x)) ≤ 1);

concat([]) = [];
¬ is_[](u) ⇒ concat(u) = foldr1(.++., u);

pairs([],v) = [];
pairs([x]++u, v) = map(v, λy. (x, y)) ++ pairs(u, v);
endaxioms; }

D.2 Finite Sets

SET = { **strict total**;   – – Polymorphic finite sets over sorts with decidable equality
        enriches LIST;

sort Set α;   Set :: (EQ)EQ;

emptySet: Set α;
                             – – The empty set
addSet: α:: EQ ⇒   α × Set α → Set α;
                             – – Insertion of an element

Set α **generated by** emptySet, addSet;

remSet: α:: EQ ⇒   Set α × α → Set α;
                             – – Removal of an element
card: α:: EQ ⇒   Set α → Nat;
                             – – Cardinality
. ∈ .:   α:: EQ ⇒   α × Set α → Bool;
                             – – Membership test
. ⊆ .:   α:: EQ ⇒   Set α × Set α → Bool;
                             – – Subset relation
. ∪., . ∩ ., .\.: α:: EQ ⇒   Set α × Set α → Set α;
                             – – Union, intersection and difference

set: α:: EQ ⇒   List α → Set α;
                             – – Conversion list to set
– – Using the set function, set literals can be easily written like set [1, 2, 3]

allSet,exSet: α:: EQ ⇒   Set α × (α → Bool) → Bool;

                                              – – Tests set for a property
        filterSet: α:: EQ $\Rightarrow$ Set $\alpha \times (\alpha \rightarrow$ Bool) $\rightarrow$ Set α;
                                              – – Filters a set
        mapSet: α:: EQ $\Rightarrow$ Set $\alpha \times (\alpha \rightarrow \alpha) \rightarrow$ Set α;
                                              – – Transforms a set pointwise

axioms $\forall$ α:: EQ $\Rightarrow$ x, y: α, s, s1, s2: Set α, u: List α, p: $(\alpha \rightarrow$ Bool) **in**
addSet(x, addSet(x, s)) = addSet(x, s);
x $\neq$ y $\Rightarrow$ addSet(x, addSet(y, s)) = addSet(y, addSet(x, s));

remSet(x, emptySet) = emptySet;
remSet(x, addSet(y, s)) =
        if x = y **then** remSet(x, s) **else** addSet(y, remSet(x, s)) **endif**;

card([]) = 0;
card(addSet(x, s)) = 1 + card(remSet(x, s));

$\neg$ (x $\in$ emptySet);
x $\in$ addSet(y, s) = ((x = y) $\vee$ (x $\in$ s));

(s1 $\subseteq$ s2) $\Leftrightarrow \forall$ x. x $\in$ s1 $\Rightarrow$ x $\in$ s2;

(s1 = s2) $\Leftrightarrow$ (s1 $\subseteq$ s2 $\wedge$ s2 $\subseteq$ s1);

x $\in$ (s1 $\cup$ s2) $\Leftrightarrow$ (x $\in$ s1) $\vee$ (x $\in$ s2);
x $\in$ (s1 $\cap$ s2) $\Leftrightarrow$ (x $\in$ s1) $\wedge$ (x $\in$ s2);
x $\in$ (s1 $\setminus$ s2) $\Leftrightarrow$ (x $\in$ s1) $\wedge \neg$(x $\in$ s2);

x $\in$ (set u) $\Leftrightarrow$ x elem u;
allSet(s, p) = ($\forall$ x. x $\in$ s $\Rightarrow$ p(x));
exSet(s, p) = ($\exists$ x. x $\in$ s $\wedge$ p(x));
x $\in$ (filterSet(s, p)) $\Leftrightarrow$ (x elem u) $\wedge$ p(x);
y $\in$ (mapSet(s, f)) $\Leftrightarrow \exists$x: α. (x elem u) $\wedge$ (y = f(x));
endaxioms; }

D.3 Finite Maps

Finite maps are also known under various other names: aggregate (or grex
[BW82]), vector or environment. They realize a map from an index sort into an
information sort with a finite domain. For our purposes, we assume a decidable
equality for both the index and the information sorts.

MAP = { **strict**;   – – Polymorphic finite map over sorts with decidable equality
        enriches SET;

    sort Map α β;   Map :: (EQ, EQ)EQ;

    emptyMap: Map α β;
                                    – – The empty map
    addMap: α:: EQ, β:: EQ $\Rightarrow$ Map α β $\times$ α $\times$ $\beta$$\rightarrow$ Map α β;
                                      – – Insertion of an (index, value) pair

    Map α β **generated by** emptyMap, addMap;

    remMap: α:: EQ, β:: EQ $\Rightarrow$ Map α β $\times$ α $\rightarrow$ Map α β;
                                      – – Remove from map
    inMap: α:: EQ, β:: EQ $\Rightarrow$ Map α β $\times$ α $\rightarrow$ Bool;
                                      – – Test for appearance
    selMap: α:: EQ, β:: EQ $\Rightarrow$ Map α β $\times$ α $\rightarrow$ β;
                                      – – Map value selection
    domMap: α:: EQ, β:: EQ $\Rightarrow$ Map α β $\rightarrow$ Set α;
                                      – – Domain of map
    restrMap: α:: EQ, β:: EQ $\Rightarrow$ Map α β $\times$ Set α $\rightarrow$ Map α β;
                                      – – Domain restriction

  addMap, remMap, inMap, domMap, restrMap **total**;

  axioms $\forall$ α, β:: EQ $\Rightarrow$ x, y: α, a, b: β, m: Map α β, s: Set α **in**
  addMap(addMap(m, x, b), x, a) = addMap(m, x, a);
  x $\neq$ y $\Rightarrow$ addMap(addMap(m, y, b), x, a) = addMap(addMap(m, x, a), y, b);

  remMap(emptyMap, x) = emptyMap;
  remMap(addMap(m, y, b), x) =
      if x = y **then** remMap(m, x) **else** addMap(remMap(m, x), y, b) **endif**;

  $\neg$ inMap(emptyMap, x);
  inMap(addMap(m, y, b), x) = ((x = y) $\vee$ inMap(m, x));

  δ selMap(m, x) = inMap(m, x);
  selMap(addMap(m, y, b), x) = **if** x = y **then** b **else** selMap(m, x) **endif**;

  x $\in$ domMap(m) $\Leftrightarrow$ inMap(m, x);

  domMap(restrMap(m, s)) = domMap(m) $\cap$ s;
  inMap(m, x) $\wedge$ x $\in$ s $\Rightarrow$ selMap(restrMap(m, s), x) = selMap(m, x);
  endaxioms; }

Bibliography

[AG90]   Ashworth, C.; M. Goodland, SSADM: A practical approach. McGraw-Hill 1990.

[AR87]   Astesiano, E.; G. Reggio, SMoLCS-driven concurrent calculi. In: H. Ehrig et al. (eds.), TAPSOFT '87 Proceedings, Lecture Notes in Computer Science Vol. 249, Springer 1987.

[AS93]   Ashworth, C.; L. Slater, An introduction to SSADM Version 4. McGraw-Hill 1993.

[BBB+85] Bauer, F. L.; R. Berghammer, M. Broy, W. Dosch, F. Geiselbrechtinger, R. Gnatz, E. Hangel, W. Hesse, B. Krieg-Brückner, The Munich Project CIP, Vol. 1: The wide spectrum language CIP-L, Lecture Notes in Computer Science Vol. 183, Springer 1985.

[BD90]   Bjørner, D.; L. Druffel, Position statement: ICSE-12 Workshop on industrial experience using formal methods. In: 12th International Conference on Software Engineering, Proceedings, IEEE, 1990, pp. 264 ff.

[BFG+93] Broy, M.; C. Facchi, R. Grosu, R. Hettler, H. Hussmann, D. Nazareth, F. Regensburger, O. Slotosch, K. Stølen, The requirement and design specification language SPECTRUM, An informal introduction. Reports TUM I9311 and I9312, Technische Universität München, Munich 1993.

[BFG87]   Baats, W. E.; L. M. G. Feijs, J. H. A. Gelissen, A formal specification of INGRES. In: M. Wirsing, J. A. Bergstra (eds.): Algebraic methods: Theory, tools and applications. Lecture Notes in Computer Science Vol. 394, Springer 1987, pp. 207-247.

[BHS92]   Bittner, U.; W. Hesse, J. Schnath, Untersuchungen zum Methodeneinsatz in Software-Entwicklungsprojekten (in German). *Softwaretechnik-Trends* 12 (1992) 48-60.

[BMR93]   Borgida, A.; J. Mylopoulos, R. Reiter, "…And nothing else changes": The frame problem in procedure specifications. In: 15th International Conference on Software Engineering, Proceedings, IEEE, 1993, pp. 303-314.

[BRJ96]   Booch, G.; J. Rumbaugh, I. Jacobson, The unified modeling language for object-oriented development, Version 0.9, 1996. Most recent version available at http://www.rational.com.

[BW82]   Bauer, F.L.; H. Wössner, Algorithmic language and program development. Springer 1982.

[BW85]   Berry, D. M.; J. M. Wing, Specifying and prototyping: Some thoughts on why they are successful. In: H. Ehrig et al. (eds.). Proc. TAPSOFT 85 (CSE) Conference, Lecture Notes in Computer Science Vol. 186, Springer 1985, pp. 117-128.

[BW88]   Bird, R.; P. Wadler, Introduction to functional programming. Prentice-Hall 1988.

[CCT90]   CCTA (ed.), SSADM Version 4 Reference Manual, NCC Blackwell 1990.

[Che76]   Chen, P., The entity-relationship model – Toward a unified view of data. *ACM Trans. on Database Systems* 1 (1976) 9-36.

[CHL95]   Cornelius, F.; H. Hussmann, M. Löwe, The KORSO case study for Software Engineering with formal methods: A medical information system. In: M. Broy, S. Jähnichen (Ees.): KORSO: Methods, Languages, and Tools for the Construction of Correct Software, Springer Verlag (LNCS 1009), Berlin et al. 1995.

[Cut91]   Cutts, G., Structured systems analysis and design methodology. Blackwell ²1991.

[CY91]   Coad, P.; E. Yourdon, Object-oriented analysis. Prentice-Hall ²1991.

[Dat90]   Date, C. J., An introduction to database systems. Volume I. Addison-Wesley ^{5}1990.

[Dav90]   Davis, A. M., Software requirements – analysis & specification. Prentice-Hall 1990.

[DCC92]   Downs, E.; P. Clare, I. Coe, Structured systems analysis and design method Prentice-Hall ^{2}1992.

[DeM79]   DeMarco, T., Structured analysis and systems specification. Prentice-Hall 1979.

[DH92]   Duschl, R.; N. C. Hopkins, SSADM & GRAPES, Two complementary major European methodologies for information systems engineering. Springer 1992.

[Dij76]   Dijkstra, E. W., A discipline of programming. Prentice-Hall 1976.

[DL87]   DeMarco, T.; T. Lister, Peopleware. Dorset House 1987.

[Eva92]   Eva, M., SSADM Version 4: A user's guide. McGraw-Hill 1992.

[FD89]   France, R. B.; T. W. G. Docker, Formal specification using structured systems analysis. In: C. Ghezzi, J. A. McDermid (eds), Proc. ESEC '89, Lecture Notes in Computer Science Vol. 387, Springer 1989, pp. 293-310.

[FGJ+85]   Futatsugi, K.; J. A. Goguen, J. P. Jouannaud, J. Meseguer, Principles of OBJ2. Proc. 12th ACM Symposium on Principles of Programming Languages, New Orleans, ACM 1985, pp. 52-66.

[FJ92]   Feijs, L. M. G.; H. B. M. Jonkers, Formal specification and design. Cambridge University Press 1992.

[FKV91]   Fraser, M. D.; K. Kumar, V. K. Vaishnavi, Informal and formal requirements specification languages: Bridging the gap. *IEEE Trans. on Software Engineering* **17** (1991) 454-466.

[Fra92]   France, R. B., Semantically extended data flow diagrams: A formal specification tool. *IEEE Trans. on Software Engineering* **18** (1992) 329-346.

[Gau86]   Gaudel, M.-C., Towards structured algebraic specifications. In: ESPRIT 85, Status report of continuing work, North-Holland 1986, pp. 493-510.

[GBM86]   Greenspan, S.J.; A. Borgida, J. Mylopoulos, A requirements modelling language and its logic. *Information Systems* **11** (1986) 9-23.

[GH93]   Guttag, J. V.; J. J. Horning, Larch: Languages and tools for formal specification. Springer (Texts and Monographs in Computer Science) 1993.

[Gin92]   Ginbayashi, J., Analysis of business processes specified in Z against an E-R data model. Technical Monograph PRG-103, Oxford University Computing Laboratory, Oxford 1992.

[GIS89]   GISA (German Information Security Agency), IT Security Criteria: Criteria for the Evaluation of Trustworthiness of Information Technology (IT) Systems. 1st version, GISA (Bonn) 1989.

[Gog89]   Gogolla, M., Algebraization and integrity constraints for an extended Entity-Relationship Approach. In: J. Diaz, F. Orejas (eds.), Proc. TAPSOFT 89, Lecture Notes in Computer Science Vol. 351 and 352, Springer 1989.

[Gri81]   Gries, D., The science of programming, Springer 1981.

[Hal90]   Hall, A., Seven myths of formal methods, *IEEE Software* **9** (1990) 11-19.

[Har87]   Harel, D., Statecharts: a visual formalism for complex systems. *Science of Computer Programming* **8** (1987) 231-274.

[Het93]   Hettler, R., On the translation of E/R schemata to SPECTRUM (in German). Technical report TUM-I9333, Technische Universität München, 1993.

[Het94]   Hettler, R., A requirement specification for a lexical analyzer. Technical report TUM-I9409, Technische Universität München, 1994.

[HJW92]   Hudak, P.; S. Peyton Jones, P. Wadler (eds.), Report on the programming language Haskell, A non-strict purely functional language (Version 1.2). *ACM SIGPLAN Notices*, May 1992.

[HMM86]   Harper, R. W.; D. B. MacQueen, R. G. Milner, Standard ML. Report ECS-LFCS-86-2, University of Edinburgh, 1986.

[HÖ92]   Heym, M.; Österle, H., A semantic data model for methodology engineering. In: G. Forte, N. H. Madhavji, H. Müller (eds) , Proc. 5th Intl. Workshop on CASE, pp. 142-155, IEEE Computer Society Press 1992, pp. 142-155.

[Hus93]   Hussmann, H., Nondeterminism in algebraic specifications and programs. Birkhäuser (Progress in Theoretical Computer Science Vol. 8) 1993.

[Hus94]   Hussmann, H., Formal foundations for SSADM. Habilitation thesis, Technical University of Munich, June 1994.[1]

[Jac88]   Jackson, M., System development. Prentice-Hall 1982.

[Jon90]   Jones, C. B., Systematic software development using VDM, Prentice-Hall ^{2}1990.

[Jon93]   Jones, M. P., An introduction to Gofer, Draft version 2.20. Yale University, 1993.

[LPT94]   Larsen, P. G.; N. Plat, H. Toetenel, A formal semantics of data flow diagrams. *Formal Aspects of Computing* **3** (1994).

[Mey85]   Meyer, B., On formalism in specifications. *IEEE Software* **1** (1985) 6-26.

[MP84]   McMenamin, S.; J. Palmer, Essential systems analysis. Prentice-Hall 1984.

[Nau82]   Naur, P., Formalization in program development. *BIT* **22** (1982) 437-451.

[NW93]   Nickl, F.; M. Wirsing, A formal approach to requirements engineering. In: D. Bjørner et al. (eds.), Proc. International Symposium on Formal Methods in Programming and their Applications, Lecture Notes in Computer Science Vol. 735, Springer 1993, pp. 312-334.

[Par91]   Partsch, H., Requirements Engineering (Handbuch der Informatik 5.5), in German, Oldenbourg 1991.

[Pau87]   Paulson, L. C., Logic and Computation, Interactive proof with Cambridge LCF, Cambridge University Press 1987.

[PHP+94] Petersohn, C.; C. Huizing, J. Peleska, W.-P. de Roever, Formal semantics for Ward & Mellor's Transformation Schemas. In: D. Till (ed.), Proc. of the Sixth Refinement Workshop of the BCS FACS Group. Springer 1994.

---

[1]   Readers interested in the more detailed thesis from which this book was derived are invited to contact the author by email (hussmannh@acm.org).

[Pre87]   Pressman, R. S., Software eingineering - a practicioner's approach, MacGraw-Hill ²1987.

[PvKP91]   Plat, N.; J. van Katwijk, K. Pronk, A case for strctured analysis/ formal design. In: S. Prehn, W. J. Toetenel (eds.), VDM 91 Formal Software Development Methods, Lecture Notes in Computer Science Vol. 551, pp. 81-105.

[PW95]   Pepper, P.; M. Wirsing (eds.), KORSO: A methodology for the development of correct software. In: M. Broy, S. Jähnichen (Ees.): KORSO: Methods, Languages, and Tools for the Construction of Correct Software, Springer Verlag (LNCS 1009), Berlin et al. 1995.

[PWK93]   Polack, F.; M. Whiston, K. Mander, The SAZ project: Integrating SSADM and Z. In: F. C. P. Woodcock, P. G. Larsen (eds), FME ' 93, Lecture Notes in Computer Science Vol. 670, Springer 1993, pp. 541-557.

[RBP+91]   Rumbaugh, J.; M. Blaha, W. Premerlani, F. Eddy, W. Lorensen, Object-oriented modelling and design. Prentice-Hall 1991.

[Rei85]   Reisig, W., Petri nets - An introduction. Springer-Verlag (EATCS Monographs on Theoretical Computer Science Vol. 4) 1985.

[SAZ94]   Polack, F.; M. Whiston, K. C. Mander, The SAZ method, version 1.1, University of York, January 1994.

[SFD92]   Semmens, L. T.; R. B. France, T. W. G. Docker, Integrated structured analysis and formal specification techniques. *The Computer Journal* **35** (1992) 600-610.

[SM88]   Shlaer, S.; S. J. Mellor, Object oriented analysis - Modeling the world in data. Prentice-Hall/ Yourdon Press 1988.

[SM92]   Shlaer, S.; S. J. Mellor, Object Lifecycles - Modeling the world in states. Prentice-Hall/Yourdon Press 1992.

[SNM+93]   Slotosch, O.; F. Nickl, S. Merz, H. Hussmann, R. Hettler, Die funktionale Essenz von HDMS-A (in German). Technical Report TUM-I9335, Technische Universität München 1993.

[Spi92]   Spivey, J. M., The Z notation. Prentice-Hall 1989, 2nd ed. 1992.

[Sut88]   Sutcliffe, A., Jackson system development. Prentice-Hall 1988.

[TP89]   Tse, T. H.; L. Pong, Towards a formal foundation for DeMarco data flow diagrams. *The Computer Journal* **32** (1989) 1-12.

[Tse91]   Tse, T. H., A unifying framework for structured analysis and design models: An approach using initial algebra semantics and category theory. Cambridge University Press 1991.

[War86]   Ward, P., The transformation schema: An extension of the data flow diagram to represent control and timing. *IEEE Trans. on Software Engineering* **12** (1986) 198-210.

[Win90]   Wing, J. M., A specifier's intrduction to formal methods. *IEEE Computer* **23** (1990) 8-24.

[Woo88]   Woodman, M., Yourdon data flow diagrams: A tool for disciplined requirements analysis. *Information and Software Technology* **30** (1988) 515-533.

[You89]   Yourdon, E., Modern Structured Analysis, Prentice-Hall/ Yourdon Press 1989.

[ZJ93]   Zave, P.; M. Jackson, Conjunction as composition. *ACM Transactions on Software Engineering and Methodology* **2** (1993) 379-411.

Subject Index

Springer
and the
environment

At Springer we firmly believe that an
international science publisher has a
special obligation to the environment,
and our corporate policies consistently
reflect this conviction.
We also expect our business partners –
paper mills, printers, packaging
manufacturers, etc. – to commit
themselves to using materials and
production processes that do not harm
the environment. The paper in this
book is made from low- or no-chlorine
pulp and is acid free, in conformance
with international standards for paper
permanency.

 Springer

Lecture Notes in Computer Science

For information about Vols. 1–1247

please contact your bookseller or Springer-Verlag

Vol. 1285: X. Jao, J.-H. Kim, T. Furuhashi (Eds.), Simulated Evolution and Learning. Proceedings, 1996. VIII, 231 pages. 1997. (Subseries LNAI).

Vol. 1286: C. Zhang, D. Lukose (Eds.), Multi-Agent Systems. Proceedings, 1996. VII, 195 pages. 1997. (Subseries LNAI).

Vol. 1287: T. Kropf (Ed.), Formal Hardware Verification. XII, 367 pages. 1997.

Vol. 1288: M. Schneider, Spatial Data Types for Database Systems. XIII, 275 pages. 1997.

Vol. 1289: G. Gottlob, A. Leitsch, D. Mundici (Eds.), Computational Logic and Proof Theory. Proceedings, 1997. VIII, 348 pages. 1997.

Vol. 1290: E. Moggi, G. Rosolini (Eds.), Category Theory and Computer Science. Proceedings, 1997. VII, 313 pages. 1997.

Vol. 1291: D.G. Feitelson, L. Rudolph (Eds.), Job Scheduling Strategies for Parallel Processing. Proceedings, 1997. VII, 299 pages. 1997.

Vol. 1292: H. Glaser, P. Hartel, H. Kuchen (Eds.), Programming Languages: Implementations, Logigs, and Programs. Proceedings, 1997. XI, 425 pages. 1997.

Vol. 1293: C. Nicholas, D. Wood (Eds.), Principles of Document Processing. Proceedings, 1996. XI, 195 pages. 1997.

Vol. 1294: B.S. Kaliski Jr. (Ed.), Advances in Cryptology — CRYPTO '97. Proceedings, 1997. XII, 539 pages. 1997.

Vol. 1295: I. Prívara, P. Ružička (Eds.), Mathematical Foundations of Computer Science 1997. Proceedings, 1997. X, 519 pages. 1997.

Vol. 1296: G. Sommer, K. Daniilidis, J. Pauli (Eds.), Computer Analysis of Images and Patterns. Proceedings, 1997. XIII, 737 pages. 1997.

Vol. 1297: N. Lavrač, S. Džeroski (Eds.), Inductive Logic Programming. Proceedings, 1997. VIII, 309 pages. 1997. (Subseries LNAI).

Vol. 1298: M. Hanus, J. Heering, K. Meinke (Eds.), Algebraic and Logic Programming. Proceedings, 1997. X, 286 pages. 1997.

Vol. 1299: M.T. Pazienza (Ed.), Information Extraction. Proceedings, 1997. IX, 213 pages. 1997. (Subseries LNAI).

Vol. 1300: C. Lengauer, M. Griebl, S. Gorlatch (Eds.), Euro-Par'97 Parallel Processing. Proceedings, 1997. XXX, 1379 pages. 1997.

Vol. 1301: M. Jazayeri, H. Schauer (Eds.), Software Engineering - ESEC/FSE'97. Proceedings, 1997. XIII, 532 pages. 1997.

Vol. 1302: P. Van Hentenryck (Ed.), Static Analysis. Proceedings, 1997. X, 413 pages. 1997.

Vol. 1303: G. Brewka, C. Habel, B. Nebel (Eds.), KI-97: Advances in Artificial Intelligence. Proceedings, 1997. XI, 413 pages. 1997. (Subseries LNAI).

Vol. 1304: W. Luk, P.Y.K. Cheung, M. Glesner (Eds.), Field-Programmable Logic and Applications. Proceedings, 1997. XI, 503 pages. 1997.

Vol. 1305: D. Corne, J.L. Shapiro (Eds.), Evolutionary Computing. Proceedings, 1997. X, 313 pages. 1997.

Vol. 1307: R. Kompe, Prosody in Speech Understanding Systems. XIX, 357 pages. 1997. (Subseries LNAI).

Vol. 1308: A. Hameurlain, A M. Tjoa (Eds.), Database and Expert Systems Applications. Proceedings, 1997. XVII, 688 pages. 1997.

Vol. 1309: R. Steinmetz, L.C. Wolf (Eds.), Interactive Distributed Multimedia Systems and Telecommunication Services. Proceedings, 1997. XIII, 466 pages. 1997.

Vol. 1310: A. Del Bimbo (Ed.), Image Analysis and Processing. Proceedings, 1997. Volume I. XXII, 722 pages. 1997.

Vol. 1311: A. Del Bimbo (Ed.), Image Analysis and Processing. Proceedings, 1997. Volume II. XXII, 794 pages. 1997.

Vol. 1312: A. Geppert, M. Berndtsson (Eds.), Rules in Database Systems. Proceedings, 1997. VII, 214 pages. 1997.

Vol. 1313: J. Fitzgerald, C.B. Jones, P. Lucas (Eds.), FME '97: Industrial Applications and Strengthened Foundations of Formal Methods. Proceedings, 1997. XIII, 685 pages. 1997.

Vol. 1314: S. Muggleton (Ed.), Inductive Logic Programming. Proceedings, 1996. VIII, 397 pages. 1997. (Subseries LNAI).

Vol. 1315: G. Sommer, J.J. Koenderink (Eds.), Algebraic Frames for the Perception-Action Cycle. Proceedings, 1997. VIII, 395 pages. 1997.

Vol. 1316: M. Li, A. Maruoka (Eds.), Algorithmic Learning Theory. Proceedings, 1997. XI, 461 pages. 1997. (Subseries LNAI).

Vol. 1317: M. Leman (Ed.), Music, Gestalt, and Computing. IX, 524 pages. 1997. (Subseries LNAI).

Vol. 1318: R. Hirschfeld (Ed.), Financial Cryptography. Proceedings, 1997. XI, 409 pages. 1997.

Vol. 1319: E. Plaza, R. Benjamins (Eds.), Knowledge Acquisition, Modeling and Management. Proceedings, 1997. XI, 389 pages. 1997. (Subseries LNAI).

Vol. 1320: M. Mavronicolas, P. Tsigas (Eds.), Distributed Algorithms. Proceedings, 1997. X, 333 pages. 1997.

Vol. 1321: M. Lenzerini (Ed.), AI*IA 97: Advances in Artificial Intelligence. Proceedings, 1997. XII, 459 pages. 1997. (Subseries LNAI).

Vol. 1322: H. Hußmann, Formal Foundations for Software Engineering Methods. X, 286 pages. 1997.

Vol. 1323: E. Costa, A. Cardoso (Eds.), Progress in Artificial Intelligence. Proceedings, 1997. XIV, 393 pages. 1997. (Subseries LNAI).

Vol. 1324: C. Peters, C. Thanos (Ed.), Research and Advanced Technology for Digital Libraries. Proceedings, 1997. X, 423 pages. 1997.

Vol. 1325: Z.W. Ras, A. Skowron (Eds.), Foundations of Intelligent Systems. Proceedings, 1997. XI, 630 pages. 1997. (Subseries LNAI).

Vol. 1327: W. Gerstner, A. Germond, M. Hasler, J.-D. Nicoud (Eds.), Artificial Neural Networks — ICANN '97. Proceedings, 1997. XIX, 1274 pages. 1997.

Vol. 1329: S.C. Hirtle, A.U. Frank (Eds.), Spatial Information Theory. Proceedings, 1997. XIV, 511 pages. 1997.